'Shattering, cinematic and brave, Ez[...] biography of ballerina Nina Anisim[...] personal terms, a star of the cruellest art overcoming the cruellest political system. An astonishing book.'

'Christina Ezrahi vividly charts this brutal and uplifting story, bringing alive an extraordinary resourcefulness and determination to survive.'

'Christina Ezrahi has uncovered a remarkable, untold episode in Soviet ballet history, which she brings to life through her customary rigorous research, clarity of expression and elegance of prose. It is an account of how one artist is forced to draw on her dancer's discipline, determination and focus to survive circumstances of unimaginable physical challenge and emotional and psychological deprivation. Yet it is also the story of how, even in the most dehumanising of situations, art provided a lifeline, connecting her back to her former self, her dignity, to beauty and joy and, unexpectedly, onwards to a celebrated career in dance. Some of us will know the name Nina Anisimova as the choreographer of *Gayané* and a distinguished artist at the Kirov Ballet; none of us will have imagined that the two-year gap in her CV hides a story far more astonishing than any she would ever portray on the stage. This book is that story.'

'Deeply researched, clear-eyed about politics, and written with compassion, the book ends on an unexpected note of triumph.'

Dancing *for* Stalin

A true story of extraordinary courage
and survival in the Soviet gulag

CHRISTINA EZRAHI

Elliott&Thompson

First published 2021 by
Elliott and Thompson Limited
2 John Street
London WC1N 2ES
www.eandtbooks.com

This paperback edition published in 2023

ISBN: 978-1-78396-698-1

9 8 7 6 5 4 3 2 1

A catalogue record for this book is available from
the British Library.

Map on pages x–xi: JP Map Graphics Ltd

Picture credits for plate section:
Pages 1–3: © St Petersburg State Museum of Theatre and Music. Page 4:
(top) author's private collection; (bottom left) © Pushkin House; (bottom
right) © Mariinsky Theatre. Page 5: Karlag Memorial Museum for
Victims of Political Repression, Dolinka. Page 6: (top left) Pushkin House;
(top right) Mariinsky Theatre; (bottom) St Petersburg State Museum of
Theatre and Music. Pages 7 and 8: St Petersburg State Museum of Theatre
and Music.

Typesetting by Marie Doherty
Printed by CPI Group (UK) Ltd, Croydon,
CR0 4YY

MIX
Paper | Supporting
responsible forestry
FSC® C171272

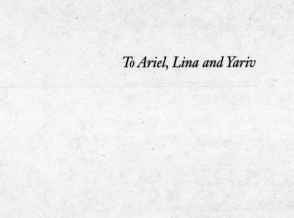

To Ariel, Lina and Yariv

'What do you feel when you are performing for your executioner?' 'Actually, the whole country was performing and dancing for Stalin.'[1]

Lazar Shereshevsky, poet, translator and former prisoner and camp performer (Beskudnikovsky corrective labour camp).

CONTENTS

Map of the USSR   x–xi
Introduction   xiii

1   The Arrest   1

2   Nina   15

3   Enemy of the People   33

4   The Confrontation   61

5   The Journey   85

6   The Kazakh Steppe   125

7   The Folly of it All   155

8   Dancing Behind Barbed Wire   185

9   The Return   229

10   The Great Patriotic War   263

11   *Gayané*   291

Epilogue   325
Acknowledgements   339
A Note on Proper Names and Translation   342
A Note on the Source Material   343
Notes   347
Selected Bibliography   377
Index   387
About the Author   400

Union of Soviet Socialist Republics, 1938–42

Territorial gains made by mid-1940

ARC

ATLANTIC
OCEAN

NORWAY

SWEDEN

FINLAND

Baltic Sea

Lithuanian SSR   Latvian SSR   Estonian SSR

Tallinn

Königsberg (Kaliningrad)

Riga

Leningrad (St Petersburg)

POLAND

Vilnius

Minsk

Byelorussian SSR

Moscow

UNION OF SOVIET SOC

Kiev

Molotov (Perm)

Russian SFSR

Moldavian SSR

Sverdlovsk (Ekaterinburg)

Chişinău

Ufa

Ukrainian SSR

Kuibyshev (Samara)

Volga

Omsk

Sevastapol

Stalingrad (Volgograd)

Akmolinsk (Astana/Nur-Sultan)

Black Sea

Dolinka   Karaganda

Georgian SSR

Tbilisi

TURKEY

Armenian SSR   Yerevan

Caspian Sea

Kazakh SSR

Azerbaijan SSR

Baku

SYRIA

Uzbek SSR

Alma-Ata (Almaty)

IRAQ

Tashkent

Frunze (Bishkek)

Turkmen SSR

Samarqand

Kirghiz SSR

Ashgabat

Dushanbe   Tajik SSR

IRAN

1000 km

AFGHANISTAN

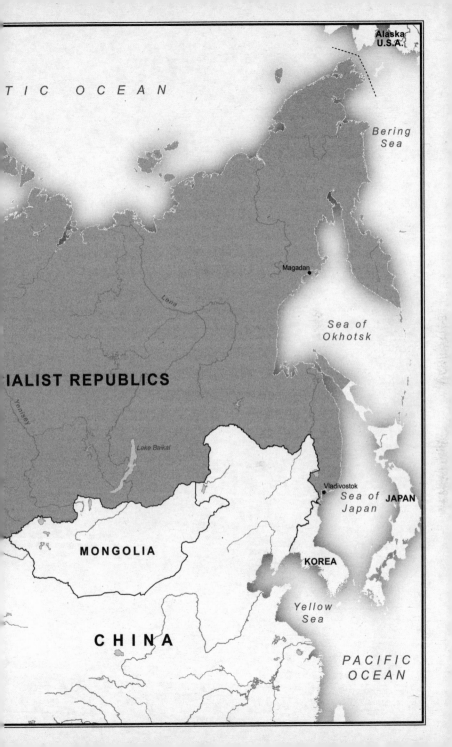

INTRODUCTION

I stumbled upon the Stalinist nightmares of Nina Anisimova by accident. One autumn morning, sitting at a large desk in the reading room of a St Petersburg archive, I stared uneasily at a document folder that should never have found its way into my hands. Outside, people wrapped up in coats and hats were rushing down Nevsky Prospekt and climbing on to crowded trolleybuses, the Admiralty's golden spire etched against the bright sky. Nearby, dance students were walking with turned-out steps towards the heavy wooden entrance doors of the world-famous Vaganova Academy of Russian Ballet.

While working my way through the private papers of a Stalin-era ballerina, I had ordered up a file from the archival depository because its title intrigued me – it contained an ominous reference to contact between Soviet artists and foreigners in the terrible year of 1938. The librarian had overlooked the clear instructions on the file's title page that the folder should not be handed out to researchers without special permission. A slim folder holding several sheets torn out of a school notebook was now lying open in front of me. On every sheet, written in neat Cyrillic cursive, were denunciations.

From July 1937 until November 1938, Joseph Stalin and his henchmen had directed one of the most murderous campaigns of a modern state against its own citizens, a campaign that is now known as the Great Terror. Day after day, the dictatorship's propaganda machine announced that spies, saboteurs and enemies of the people were hiding everywhere, in plain sight. Ordinary Russians listened in astonishment to the disclosure that even the highest levels of government and the military had been infiltrated. Arrests and mysterious disappearances of citizens from all walks of life plunged the entire Soviet empire into an abyss of fear and suspicion.

The denunciations that I was looking at had been written in 1938 by a young ballerina. Her reports incriminated around three dozen dancers, actors and conductors, including some of the most important names in Soviet cultural life. All these artists, according to the reports, had supposedly been in regular contact with foreigners from enemy nations such as Germany and Japan, an accusation that in Leningrad in 1938 could lead to arrest and a death sentence for espionage. It was unclear whether the ballerina had written them under duress or voluntarily; the longest reports in the file were about her own actions, implicating others in her attempt to justify her behaviour, and listing gifts she and others had received from foreigners several years previously. She was protesting her innocence, emphasising that she had since broken off all contact with her foreign acquaintances.

Such denunciations were common during the Great Terror, and a sad reality of Soviet life: by 1938 the NKVD, the Soviet secret police, had enlisted a spider's web of informers that linked it to virtually every communal flat and all Soviet institutions. Whether out of fear, malice or loyalty, informers fed a never-ending stream of incriminating information to the security services. The NKVD also routinely cornered people into denouncing others during their interrogations. The fact that a leading ballerina had written denunciations at the height of the Great Terror was therefore not surprising. But the fact that the reports had not been destroyed but had been preserved among the ballerina's private papers through the siege of Leningrad, the end of the Second World War and the collapse of the Soviet Union, and now found themselves in my unsuspecting hands seventy-five years later, was completely extraordinary.

The file contained one document in particular that sent a chill down my spine. Written neatly on two connected sheets, it was a list of thirty-four names which gave each person's age and professional affiliation. It consisted primarily of dancers, including the Kirov Ballet's entire upper echelon but also several actors and two famous conductors. The thirty-four artists had apparently all been guests at the home of an employee of the German consulate in Leningrad, the legal consultant Dr Evgeny Salomé.

As my eyes raced down the list, I felt transported back in time to a point in Russian history when individual destinies were like dots on a dice, shaken and cast by the NKVD in a game of life and death. The very existence of this list could have destroyed a generation of leading ballet dancers and conductors, potentially changing the course of Soviet cultural history. But while all the other reports bore no obvious signs of external influence, a stranger's hand had scribbled comments on this one – eleven names had been neatly ticked off, six others crossed out and a new one added in handwriting that was different from the ballerina's. I was aware that many of the artists whose names had been ticked had lived long and successful lives, but I did not recognise any of the names that had been crossed out, except for one: the Kirov Ballet's legendary character dancer Nina Anisimova.

The image of the crossed-out names burned itself into my mind. It marked the beginning of a quest to find out what had happened to the dancers of the Kirov Ballet during the Great Terror of 1937–8. As I dug deeper into archives in St Petersburg and Berlin, a surreal story started to emerge: of fabricated and genuine German spies, of innocent dancers and other artists who had been executed, their bodies dumped in mass graves, their memory erased. I began to focus my efforts on the mysterious fate of the list's most prominent name, Nina Anisimova, whose official biography appeared untarnished despite her name having been crossed out.[1]

Would I be able to unravel the secret story of Anisimova's life?

I

The Arrest

Nina Anisimova put on her low-heeled character dance shoes and straightened herself. She twisted and turned in front of the mirror in her changing room at Leningrad's Kirov Theatre, checking her costume and make-up. She was about to perform the part of the Basque woman Thérèse in Vasily Vainonen's ballet *The Flames of Paris*, a work written to glorify the French Revolution. Created six years earlier to celebrate the fifteenth anniversary of Russia's October Revolution of 1917, it had become one of Stalin's favourite ballets.[1]

Framed by the high arches of her eyebrows, Nina's expressive brown eyes burned with a fire appropriate for her tempestuous character. Her dark hair was kept in place by a white scarf knotted at the nape of her neck, its long ends trailing down her back. The bodice of her sleeveless dress softened into a blue volante, which was layered over a red skirt cut to give the illusion of a ragged hem. A rust-red shawl was thrown over her shoulders and tucked tightly into her belt. She tossed back her head, pumping her arms like a runner while pounding her heels in a rapid staccato rhythm. She stopped as abruptly as she had started, and checked her reflection in the mirror. Her costume had withstood the test and everything was still in place: she was ready to go on stage.[2]

The third act of *The Flames of Paris* was about to begin. Standing in the wings, Nina focused all her energy on transforming herself into Thérèse, a simple woman burning with hatred against France's *ancien régime*. After the October Revolution, Russia's own revolutionaries had attacked classical ballet as frivolous after-dinner entertainment conceived to dazzle the imperial family and tsarist elites. They had declared that, in order to survive in a state trying to build Communism, ballet would have to abandon fairy-tale princesses in favour of a social conscience. Nina's explosive performances as the revolutionary heroine Thérèse had played a central role in turning *The Flames of Paris* into a popular triumph of the nascent Soviet ballet.

Nina had worked hard to internalise the realistic acting method promoted by the Russian director Konstantin Stanislavsky. Her colleagues knew that sometimes Nina would get herself into such a state before her entrance that she would run on to the stage, shouting impulsively 'After me!', as if she were a revolutionary about to lead a popular uprising rather than a dancer performing in one of Russia's most venerable theatres.[3]

The conductor took his stand, and the rousing melody of 'La Marseillaise' began. The theatre's pre-revolutionary *trompe l'oeil* curtain with its gold-embroidered blue folds opened, revealing a Parisian square filled with workers, artisans, women, Jacobins and detachments of volunteers from France's regions, preparing to storm the Tuileries Palace. Suddenly trumpets started to play, accompanied by the insistent pounding of drums. Two Basque men jumped into the centre of the stage and were joined by a third, their bodies as tense as tightly strung bows. Facing each other, they exploded into an impulsive dance, throwing their bodies into virile poses, their feet pulsing intricate rhythmical patterns as if the stage itself were a drum. Linking arms, they spun around, precariously balancing off each other's weight before jumping up, their arms raised high into the sky and their fingers spread wide, a call to rebellion.

All of a sudden there was Nina as Thérèse, joining the dance of the men, the piercing staccato of which changed into a lilting but equally passionate melody. With tiny but rapid steps Nina seemed to float from one side of the stage to the other, her arms circling through the air as if she were drawing aside a curtain to look into a brighter future. Suddenly she leaned back as far as gravity would allow. Turning her face to the audience, she seemed electrified as she deftly began to move backwards, her heels pounding the stage. Later on the audience would be on the edges of their seats, ready to jump up as they watched her among the vanguard of the revolutionary masses storming the Tuileries. Holding high the tricolour flag, her frenzied eyes full of revolutionary fury, her face contorted as she was struck by a bullet. Sinking to the floor, she passed the tricolour flag to one of her comrades, dying a martyr to the revolution.[4]

~

It was 12 January 1938. Filing through the large swinging doors into the theatre's vestibule, some people were inadvertently slowing down their steps, as if reluctant to leave the brightly lit magic of the theatre for the dark outside. Dispersing through the winter night, many could feel a chill returning to their bones that had nothing to do with the low temperatures. Since the summer, the nights had been filled with terror: people were disappearing. The NKVD's dark cars, the Black Marias, or Black Ravens, were haunting the courtyards of Leningrad's sprawling apartment buildings until the early hours of the morning, collecting the newly arrested and delivering them to the city's overflowing prisons.

While ordinary citizens and the new Soviet elite were having trouble sleeping, the work never seemed to end inside a monumental building on Liteyny Prospekt, one of Leningrad's central avenues, at the corner of Shpalernaya Street and a stone's throw from the Neva River. Even years after the mass arrests of the Great Terror, many people dared to refer to the building only in a whisper: *Bolshoi Dom*, the Big House. Braver souls masked their terror by joking that the building was the highest in Leningrad because one could see Siberia from its cellars. Others would mutter a short verse to themselves:

> On Shpalernaya Street
> There stands a magical house:
> You enter this house as a child,
> But you leave it – an old man.[5]

The Leningrad NKVD had moved to its newly built headquarters in 1932, and the constructivist building loomed threateningly over the graceful, neoclassical buildings of imperial St Petersburg in its vicinity. Large blocks of dark granite formed an oppressive ground floor, its angularity emphasised by the square windows cut into the heavy stone. A plain portico framed the monumental doors leading into the building. On top of this massive base were seven further floors, a monotonous façade of narrow windows. The building was boxed in by a gigantic frame of dark stone that covered its windowless sides and flat roof, flanked on both sides by two towers of asymmetric heights. For the convenience of the NKVD agents, the Bolshoi Dom had been constructed next to the old tsarist prison on Shpalernaya Street, the infamous Shpalerka, officially, if euphemistically, known as the 'House of Preliminary Detention'.* Opened in 1875 as Russia's first prison for those under investigation, the Shpalerka's beige building with its red ground floor consisted of a large square surrounding a central courtyard.

On 31 July 1937, Stalin's Politburo began an operation that targeted the whole population, meticulously planning not only the elimination of real or imagined potential enemies but also setting specific targets for doing so. It commanded the arrest of 268,950 people, of whom 72,950 were to be shot and the rest sent to prisons or labour camps for eight to ten years.[6]

Initially, the massive operation was supposed to be completed within four months, in time for Stalin's new constitution and the elections to the Supreme Soviet that were scheduled for December 1937.[7] But ambitious local NKVD leaders saw the chance to demonstrate their loyalty and advance their careers and requested additional quotas; the deadline was extended again and again.

In Leningrad, Leonid Zakovsky was responsible for orchestrating the opening moves of this murderous campaign.

* At the time, the street was called Voinova Street.

A brutal opportunist, he liked to boast that he could have made Karl Marx confess that he was an agent of Bismarck.[8] During the summer of 1937, the NKVD's vast machine was working around the clock to compile arrest lists.

Zakovsky ensured that the terror quotas were exceeded – by the end of 1937, more than 19,000 people had been shot in Leningrad, almost five times the number demanded by the original order. Zakovsky was rewarded with a double promotion, but working for the NKVD was a dangerous profession and he did not have much time to enjoy his new status as head of the Moscow NKVD and deputy to the dwarfish NKVD chief Nikolai Yezhov, the grand organiser of the Great Terror: he was arrested by the NKVD in April 1938 and shot as a spy four months later.[9]

Zakovsky's successor as head of the Leningrad NKVD was Mikhail Litvin, a protégé of Yezhov who had only joined the NKVD in 1936. A balding man with thin wire-framed glasses, Litvin would pre-empt his own arrest by committing suicide before the year was over. But on 31 January 1938, barely ten days after his appointment as head of the Leningrad NKVD, he examined the new quotas for Leningrad and the surrounding region: 3,000 people were to be shot by 15 March 1938, while 1,000 others were to be sentenced to forced labour or prison.[10] More names had to be chosen.

CERTIFICATE

It has been established by the third department of the NKVD, that the inhabitant of the city Leningrad <u>Anisimova</u>, Nina Alexandrovna, born 1909 in Leningrad, Russian, citizen of the USSR, non-party member, ballet artist of the State Academic Theatre of Opera and Ballet named after S. M. Kirov, living on Kirov Prospekt, house 1/3, apt. 31, was a constant visitor of the German general consulate in Leningrad, being connected to the legal consultant of the German consulate in Leningrad – the established resident of German intelligence SALOME, on whose instructions she made acquaintances among Soviet citizens and she was recruited by SALOME for espionage on Soviet territory in favour of Germany.[11]

On the night of 2 February 1938 the winds were blowing across the Neva River, past the angel holding a cross atop the thin spire of the Peter and Paul Fortress. The Petrograd Side was the cradle of old St Petersburg, the site of the city's unlikely foundation on swampy land. NKVD Captain Kokhanenko reached Lidval House at No. 1/3, Kirovsky Prospekt, a sprawling Art Nouveau apartment block constructed in the late nineteenth century, when the district was turning into one of the city's most fashionable neighbourhoods. Unlike the standard layout of Russian apartment blocks with their maze-like backyards, the building's wings were arranged around a courtyard open to the street – but this was not the moment to admire the building's playful ornaments or the contrast between the decorative, undulating lines of the central block and the medieval motifs of the side wing.

It was long after dark, the most convenient time for arrests. The captain's target was likely to be at home in bed, drowsy with sleep. He would be protected from the attention of bystanders during her arrest and subsequent journey to prison.

Anyone still awake at that time would have frozen with dread as they heard the sound of an elevator, the creaking of floorboards, the ominous knock at the door. Led by the caretaker, the captain stopped in front of Flat 3.

Nina's family had been living in this building since 1909, the year of her birth, but the family's circumstances had changed drastically since the October Revolution. Before then, the Anisimovs had enjoyed the privileges that came with the successful military career of her father, Alexander Ivanovich Anisimov. Born in 1871 into a family belonging to the estate of hereditary 'honourable citizens' who enjoyed certain legal privileges, he graduated from the cavalry college attached to the Elizabeth Guards, joined the Imperial Army in 1892 and began to move up the ranks. At the turn of the century, the young captain fell for the charms of Maria Osipovna Alekseyeva, an artisan's daughter who performed as a singer and dancer on the city's variety stages. The couple soon had a daughter, Valentina, but, like many ambitious military men, Anisimov feared that marriage to a socially inferior performer would hinder his career and waited several years before marrying the mother of his child. In 1909 Nina was born, and Alexander Ivanovich continued to rise through the military ranks despite his marriage, reaching the respectable position of major general on the eve of the revolution.[12]

The Anisimovs lived a life of material comfort. Their household included several servants and a mademoiselle who oversaw the girls' education. The family owned a small estate in Peterhof, outside St Petersburg, and holidayed in the Crimea and the French Riviera.[13] But after the revolution the family was plunged into uncertainty and economic hardship. Anisimov voluntarily joined the Red Army, but was nonetheless briefly arrested by the Cheka* in 1918. As Petrograd descended into anarchy, he moved his family from their apartment in the city centre to Peterhof.[14] When they moved back to the Petrograd Side a few years later, they had to readjust to the cramped reality of a communal flat. Anisimov worked as a military instructor until his retirement in 1927 and died in 1934 of typhus.[15] Nina, her sixty-year-old mother Maria and her thirty-five-year-old sister Valentina continued to live among strangers thrown together by chance, involuntary witnesses to each other's joys and tragedies.

The shrill doorbell shattered the night-time silence. The caretaker led the captain through the flat to Nina's room and pointed at her:

'Last name?' asked the captain.

'Anisimova.'

'First name?'

'Nina.'

'Patronymic?'

'Alexandrovna.'

'Year of birth?'

'1909.'

The captain compared the dancer's answers to the information on the sheet in his hands. 'Let us enter your room. Here is the search warrant.'[16] Nina's mother and the caretaker were ordered to act as witnesses for the ensuing search of her room.

* The All-Russian Extraordinary Commission for Struggle Against Counter-Revolution and Sabotage, known by its acronym Cheka, was the predecessor of the NKVD and KGB.

As the captain rummaged through Nina's possessions, putting aside items to be confiscated as part of the investigation, the state tightened its iron fist around yet another individual. With the stroke of a pen, the NKVD had turned a twenty-nine-year-old dancer into a suspected enemy of the people.

In the early hours of 3 February 1938, Nina signed the first of many NKVD documents that would accumulate, page after page, in her NKVD investigation file. Intended to create an illusion of legal propriety, Nina's signature on the search warrant attested that the search had been conducted properly and that no items had disappeared, apart from those objects confiscated as part of the investigation, including her passport, letters and photographs. The caretaker and the captain dutifully added their signatures; the time had come to call for the car that would transport Nina to prison.[17]

The dancer's room was now closed and sealed by the NKVD. As Captain Kokhanenko led Nina out of the building and to the waiting Black Maria, mother and daughter had no way of knowing when, or if, they would see each other again.

∼

The car took Nina across the Neva and along the embankment, past the ornate gates of Peter the Great's Summer Garden, to the Shpalerka. She was told to get out of the car and wait while her police escort rang a bell. After a rattling of keys the heavy prison gates opened, then banged shut behind her. A long corridor loomed ahead, as in a surreal nightmare.[18] One side was a row of narrow closets running down its entire length, the sound of muffled voices emanating from some of them.

Nina was led to one of the closets and locked inside it. Prisoners could sit on the narrow plank fixed to the rear wall, underneath a small light that dangled from the ceiling in a metal net. A female prison warder entered and ordered her to undress and hold up her hands. The warder's coarse hands pulled back her ears, opened her mouth to see whether she was hiding anything in her cheeks or under her tongue, tipped back her head to check her nostrils, searched between her legs, and then focused on her pile of clothes. She cut off all the buttons, pulled out the belt and shoelaces and took away Nina's hairpins and the elasticated girdle that had been holding up her stockings, a standard procedure to prevent prisoners from committing suicide. Female prisoners who wondered how they were supposed to walk with stockings slipping down to their ankles were told to plait their seams together to hold them up. Nina was now allowed to dress herself.

The warder ordered Nina to follow her, and they walked down a corridor and stopped in front of a cell. As Nina took her first steps into the bare room the key turned in the lock behind her. On a typical night that winter, there would have been around twenty-five to thirty women in the large collection cell that held the new arrivals, all arrested that night.[19]

Later, the warder returned and told the women to line up in pairs, their hands folded behind their backs. They were led down long corridors, shuffling along institutional walls, the bottom half painted an unpleasant shade of green, the top half whitewashed. Marching up the open staircase, they felt the claustrophobic weight of a tightly woven metal lattice enclosing the open space above the banisters, installed to stop prisoners from jumping to their deaths. The warder led the women into a prison bathroom, ordered them to untie their hair so that they could be checked for lice, hand in their clothes for disinfection and wash themselves under the showers.

From the showers, the new arrivals were marched down a corridor to be distributed among the Shpalerka's 300 prison cells.[20] For the first time they breathed in the prison's distinctive stench, a suffocating mixture of sweat, fish, onions, damp, cheap tobacco smoke, excrement, urine and something else that was unidentifiable yet distinctive.[21] While the cells varied in size, they were all hopelessly overcrowded. From the corridor they looked like cages holding wild animals, despite the heavy black curtains that covered the floor-to-ceiling steel rods. The warder stopped in front of one of them and turned the key. As the door opened, the foul, stuffy air of the overcrowded cell enveloped Nina.[22]

During the Great Terror, a large cell of forty square metres would have been crammed with about seventy women from all walks of life – young students, old women, doctors, housewives, intellectuals, engineers, fanatic Bolsheviks and internal émigrés. The cells' large, barred windows overlooked the prison's courtyard, their lower halves boarded up with wooden planks. A lavatory of sorts and a large red-copper sink occupied one corner, shelves for dishes the other. Long tables were arranged around the edges of the cell while narrow benches stretched along its walls. Near the door, several boxes lay on top of a large pile of long wooden planks.[23]

Like most new arrivals, Nina had no idea why she had been arrested. She should have been getting ready for daily class and rehearsals at the Kirov Theatre – five days later, she was supposed to perform at a major concert showcasing her interpretations of national dances from Georgia, Dagestan, Uzbekistan, Azerbaijan, Armenia and the Crimea at the Leningrad Philharmonic. Nina and her stage partner, Sergei Koren, had been working on this production for months.

Nina had conquered Leningrad's highly knowledgeable and critical ballet audience not with the sparkling bravura or expressive lyricism of a classical ballerina, but with her artistic charisma and temperament, and her talent for Spanish, Russian, Eastern European and exotic national dances that were an intrinsic part of the city's classical ballet tradition. She was a striking woman, auburn-haired with unusually expressive, piercing eyes and a volcanic temperament. Her overflowing love of life and her art spilled over into the Kirov Theatre's turquoise-blue, white and gilded auditorium whenever the dancer burst from the wings on to the stage. It enveloped the spectators in their seats and made them feel more alive, whether the orchestra pit was playing the sun-filled, melodious rhythms of Tchaikovsky's Spanish Dance in *Swan Lake*, the exhilarating Polish Krakowiak from Glinka's opera *Ivan Susanin*, or the French Revolutionary melodies of *The Flames of Paris*. Her sudden arrest had clipped her wings on the eve of a new milestone in her career.

∽

A sharp command from the guard brought an end to Nina's first hours in prison. Pandemonium broke loose inside the cell as everybody jumped up and began to reorganise their quarters for the night. The prisoners pushed the tables to the side, and the wooden planks that had been piled in one of the corners were placed on top of boxes to create beds. Each inmate purposefully turned towards her assigned sleeping space, allocated strictly according to seniority by the *starosta*, the cell's senior prisoner, who was in charge of maintaining order. Those who had been in prison longest got the best spots, newcomers the worst. Within five minutes the cell was transformed. Prisoners called up for nightly interrogations would have to stumble awkwardly towards the door along the narrow gaps between the beds. Women lay down on the tables and on top of the plank-beds to sleep, while new arrivals crawled underneath the planks. The *starosta* showed Nina her spot, probably somewhere on the floor. There was often only enough space to lie on one's side. It was hard to breathe under the planks as the dust from the rotting wood above filled their nostrils.[24]

2

Nina

Nina's arrest had put an abrupt end to a life centred on movement. She had always loved to dance and act. As a little girl she had often accompanied her mother to her performances. Home alone, she would put on her mother's costumes, curiously observing her reflection as she danced in front of the mirror. Blissfully ignoring the fact that the garments were slipping off her shoulders and trailing on the floor, she would experiment with movements until the clothes became too creased to be used in her mother's next performance.[1] Not even the revolution had curbed her enthusiasm: Nina started her first dancing lessons in a private studio founded in 1917 by Baron Miklos in the former residence of Princess Ekaterina Yurievskaya, mistress and morganatic wife of Tsar Alexander II.[2]

Nina showed promise, but that alone was not always enough to secure a place at the Petrograd Choreographic Institute, formerly known as the Theatre School.* The revo-

* Russia's oldest ballet school underwent several name changes. At the time of its foundation in 1738 it was simply referred to as Dance

lution had opened the doors of Russia's oldest ballet school to children of the upper-middle and even the upper classes, whose families would previously have categorically forbidden them to train as performers. The imperial ballet had recruited its students primarily from families already employed by the imperial theatres as artists, ushers, tailors and so forth. But the revolution was making life difficult for 'former people', the Bolsheviks' derogatory term for Russia's former elites, namely the nobility, officers of the Imperial Army, high-ranking bureaucrats, the merchant class and the clergy. Barred from institutions of higher education as class enemies, children from Russia's most illustrious families were turning towards performing. In the chaos of post-revolutionary Petrograd, the Choreographic Institute distinguished itself as an oasis of pre-revolutionary culture, though it was not certain whether ballet as an art form would ultimately survive the Bolshevik Revolution. Ballet was identified with the old regime – the Romanov dynasty that had patronised it, and the ruling classes who had enjoyed it. The first commissar in charge of culture, Commissar* of Enlightenment Anatoly Lunacharsky, fought to keep alive the cultural institutions of imperial Russia, against the opposition of comrades who condemned Russian ballet as 'a specific creation of the landowner's regime, a caprice of the court' intrinsically alien to Communism and the proletariat.[3]

School. Today, it is called the Vaganova Academy of Russian Ballet. For the period discussed in this chapter, I will sometimes refer to the school as Theatre School and sometimes as Choreographic Institute, reflecting the custom of the time.

  * Soviet commissars served a function akin to ministers.

Despite ballet's uncertain future, winning a place at the school remained challenging. Applicants used whatever connections they had to gain points against competitors. Nina's parents enlisted the help of her aunt, who was married to a well-known actor at the Alexandrinsky Theatre. Evdokia Osipovna took her lanky niece to a performance by an acquaintance, the ballerina Olga Preobrazhenskaya, and led her to Preobrazhenskaya's changing room. Approaching fifty, Preobrazhenskaya was celebrated for her musicality and purity of form, but she was also a gifted teacher, and in charge of the senior girls at the school. The famous ballerina cast a glance at the girl with her expressive eyes, and passed her judgement: 'Well, what a little old lady, what a skinny thing. But maybe something will become of her.'[4] Before the beginning of the new academic year, the school's strict entrance commission had selected Nina for admission.

In the autumn of 1919, Nina became a student at the Choreographic Institute.[5] Each day, she travelled into town from the suburb Old Peterhof, returning after a long day filled with dance classes, rehearsals and regular academic classes.[6] Times were uncertain. Revolutionary Russia was enveloped in civil war. The anti-Bolshevik White Russian forces were mounting a last challenge to the Red Army. But whenever Nina pushed open the heavy doors of the school, she entered a universe that seemed to exist outside time and space.

Noisy conversations, running along the corridors and similar infringements on etiquette were strictly forbidden. Whenever an adult approached, the girls would sink into a deep curtsey and the boys would bow, greeting the grown-up in French. A graduate of the illustrious Smolny Institute for Noble Girls, inspectress Varvara Ivanovna Likhosherstova had been tyrannising the girls of the Theatre School for almost forty years. Dressed in black in winter and grey in summer, the tall, silver-haired woman could have been called beautiful. But whenever she became angry, her translucent blue eyes would fade until they were almost white and her dark pupils would penetrate her victim like nails. However, the revolution had softened even this tyrant. Varvara Ivanovna began to look warmly at her hungry charges, who were devoting themselves to St Petersburg's classical ballet tradition under almost impossible conditions.[7]

Ballet had occupied a special place in imperial St Petersburg. The tsars had brought ballet to Russia from France and Italy, but from the mid-eighteenth century it had grown deep roots in Russian soil and acquired its own distinct flavour by absorbing influences from Russia's rich folk-dance tradition. By the nineteenth century, St Petersburg had become the international capital of ballet. Under the guidance of the French ballet master and choreographer Marius Petipa, the Russian imperial ballet created the masterworks that still define our understanding of classical ballet: *Swan Lake*, *The Sleeping Beauty*, *Don Quixote*, *La Bayadère* and *The Nutcracker*. In imperial St Petersburg, ballet was associated with the city's high society, who went to the Mariinsky Theatre to see and to be seen. The term *balletoman* was coined to describe the fanatical admirers of the ballet, whose worship of ballerinas could take absurd extremes: it is said that a group of St Petersburg *balletomans* bought a pair of pointe shoes worn by the romantic ballerina Marie Taglioni and cooked and ate them for supper.

The school was now trying to pass on its imperial ballet tradition to the next generation of dancers against a revolutionary ideology that saw ballet as class-alien. Conditions were tough. During her academic lessons, Nina would look quizzically at the ink that had frozen in the bitterly cold classrooms of the unheated school, shuddering in her winter coat while trying to wriggle her numb toes in their felt boots. Always hungry* and cold, Nina and her classmates would enter one of the studios, their bodies adjusting to the sloped wooden floor built to prepare them for the raked stage of the former Mariinsky Theatre,† and wait for their teacher, the former soloist Zinaida Vasilyevna Frolova. A diminutive woman of advanced years, Frolova entered the studio wrapped in a cloak, a fur cap playfully pinned to a rust-coloured wig framing a pretty face with fine features. Her legs always maintained a perfectly turned-out first position, even while walking in impossibly high heels. Frolova had high hopes for Nina's future, envisioning her as a ballerina at the Mariinsky Theatre. Sometimes she asked Nina to show her fourth arabesque to the whole class, waxing lyrical about the suppleness of her spine and her classical line.[8]

In 1921, after shuttling between her family's home in Old Peterhof and the school in the centre of Petrograd for more than a year, Anisimova's father successfully petitioned that Nina

---

* During these hungry years, the legendary ballerina Anna Pavlova sent the students of her alma mater packages with cornflour porridge and cocoa from abroad.

† In 1920, the Mariinsky was renamed the State Academic Theatre of Opera and Ballet, GATOB. In 1935, it was renamed the Kirov Theatre of Opera and Ballet. Colloquially, after the revolution, it was often referred to as the former Mariinsky. For simplicity's sake I will refer to the theatre as the former Mariinsky for the years 1917–35, and as the Kirov for the period thereafter.

be admitted to the school's boarding school. Like apparitions from a time long gone, the forty boarders would walk in their prunella boots along the school's dark corridors, their long, cornflower-blue dresses gently swishing over the floor. Their shoulders were covered with white pelerines, their ends tucked into long black aprons, white ones on special occasions.[9] The girls slept in one dormitory, strictly separated from the boys who were quartered on a higher floor.[10]

Passers-by watched with curiosity whenever the girls filed out in pairs into Theatre Street* for their daily walk, promenading in institutional coats with puff sleeves, muffs hanging from their necks. On evenings when the children were participating in performances at the former Mariinsky Theatre, a wide, horse-drawn wagon would pull up in front of the school at around half past six in the evening. Street boys would run after the vehicle, merrily shouting at the girls in their long coats and blue felt hats: 'Ballet rats, ballet rats! Going to dance!' In winter the students were driven to the theatre in a low, wide sledge. Squashed up together, they would tumble into the snow whenever the sledge turned over, giggling hysterically and ignoring the angry looks of the ladies chaperoning them, to the delight of the street boys who would exclaim: 'The ballet rats have been thrown on the dump!'[11]

~

Nina was progressing at the school, but her body was changing. In her first years, her teacher had high hopes for her talented pupil. Now, all of a sudden, she had become a 'difficult case'.

---

* The street was renamed Rossi Street in 1923.

Towering over her classmates after a growth spurt, her body no longer seemed to belong to her. Gone were some of the physical abilities that she had taken for granted. By the time she came under the wing of Agrippina Vaganova, the school's foremost classical teacher in the girls' division, there was nothing exceptional about her physical gifts. On the contrary, her figure now had some peculiarities that made it more difficult for her to achieve a beautiful line in her movements. In class, feeling awkward about her height, her long legs and her angular body, Nina tried to make herself invisible by standing at the back of the studio, seeking cover behind the backs of her classmates. But nobody could hide from Vaganova's eyes, and especially nobody who intrigued her.

Nina had feared that Vaganova would take absolutely no interest in her because she could never be turned into a first-rate classical ballerina. She was wrong. Halfway through each class, Vaganova would without fail plant herself right in front of Nina and ask: 'Well, well, so show me what you are doing here?' She had noticed Nina's rare expressiveness and was already sensing that, with the right guidance, this slightly awkward girl could be transformed into something extraordinary. Nina would become Vaganova's favourite character dancer, but for now she was being pushed to adapt her body to the aesthetics of classical dance. Mastering the combinations in Vaganova's class would give Nina the key to expressing the full range of human emotions in dance: each step had to be executed not just technically perfectly, but with maximum expressivity. In Vaganova's class, Nina learned to infuse dance with the essence of her whole being and to give meaning to every movement.[12]

Vaganova did not confine herself to initiating Nina into the secrets of classical dance. Sometimes she would keep Nina back after class and go over character-dance movements with her. But Vaganova was not the only one who had taken Nina under her wing.

In the early 1900s, Alexander Shiryaev had created the first character-dance class for the school. At the time, there was no specialised training. Often, character dance was left to those who were technically too weak to perform classical parts. The character dances themselves also left much to be desired in terms of virtuosity and versatility. Dissatisfied, Shiryaev convinced another senior character dancer of the theatre, the Hungarian Alfred Bekefi, to go back to the sources. For two years, Bekefi and Shiryaev studied folk dances as they were performed by different national groups. Back in Petersburg, Shiryaev analysed the material he had collected and, mirroring a traditional ballet class, invented specific exercises at the barre and in the centre of the studio to prepare dancers for the more virtuoso demands of character dance. With Petipa's support, Shiryaev received permission to teach his character-dance class at the school in 1905, but the classes stopped when Shiryaev quit his teaching position three years later.[13] When Shiryaev came back to the school in 1918, the character-dance classes returned with him.

For the rest of her life, Nina would remember the day Shiryaev walked into one of Vaganova's classes and singled her out. From then on, Nina worked towards her new goal: to become the best character dancer she could be.

Short of stature, Shiryaev had a large head with a beaked nose, a deep, rumbling voice and almost ridiculously small feet which, in their flat, feminine slippers, transfixed Nina in class. Demonstrating increasingly difficult technical feats, Shiryaev's feet would acquire a life of their own, moving even at the highest velocity with such delicate agility that they 'seemed to be able to speak'.[14]

He began carefully to initiate Nina into the Mariinsky's classical character-dance repertoire: the *pas de mantille* from *Paquita*, the czardas and mazurka from *Coppélia*, the Indian dance from *La Bayadère*. But Shiryaev also composed new pieces, showcasing his charges' particular talents. His ability to predict a student's future artistic personality could be uncanny. For Nina he staged a Spanish duet, correctly sensing the important role that Spanish dances would play in Nina's future career.

A year before Nina's graduation, Vaganova prepared her for performing a classical variation from Arthur Saint-Léon's ballet *La Source* at the school's annual graduation presentation at the former Mariinsky Theatre. This was the first and last time that Nina danced in a serious classical piece, and years later she remembered how out of place she had felt dancing it.[15] But people outside the walls of the school were beginning to take notice of her as a character dancer. By the time she was in her last year, her character-dancing had become technically precise and stylistically exquisite. But it was her strong artistic personality that stood out. Critics praised her fire, passion and temperament and noted that there was nothing affected in her style. At her graduation performance Nina had a leading role, Nirilya in Petipa's ballet *Talisman*. The critic Yuri Brodersen wrote: 'The young artist dances with great élan and temperament. The fire of an enticing gaiety animates her face. Her gestures are broad and bold, powerfully and impetuously seizing the air.'

But there was an important dimension to Nina's dancing, even in this old-fashioned ballet about a young goddess and a maharaja in ancient India: Nina had matured into a distinct artistic personality who seemed instinctively in touch with the pulse of her own times. Earlier that year, another critic had written about Nina's performance in another Petipa ballet, *The Cavalry Halt*: 'Anisimova, who is graduating this year, convinced us once more that our academic stage is gaining in her an artist who is full of fire, temperament, precisely expressive, without affection, who is feeling the present. There is no doubt that in the new type of ballet, which without doubt will take root in our choreographic repertoire in the immediate future, there will be an especially urgent need precisely for character dancers like this.'[16]

Luckily for Nina, character dance was on the ascent, both artistically and ideologically. Ballet's detractors were continuing to attack classical dance as degenerate entertainment for the rich. The Bolshevik class-war rhetoric gave character dance the opportunity to step out of the shadow of classical dance: ballet was supposed to become more 'democratic', and character dance was by definition more democratic than classical dance because it was rooted in folk dance. By giving greater prominence to character dance, the ballet companies could demonstrate their willingness to 'democratise'.

Everybody seemed to expect that Nina would graduate smoothly into the company of the former Mariinsky. But the company's management could find no vacancy for her. Instead, Nina had to start her career at Leningrad's second opera

house, the Maly Theatre.* At the time, the repertoire for dancers at the Maly was very limited as the theatre did not yet
have its own independent ballet company. Instead, its ballet
ensemble serviced the theatre's opera and operetta performances. She started performing the czardas in operettas, urban
dances like the foxtrot and other jazzy numbers. But the Maly
had something else to offer: under its director, the conductor
Samuil Samosud, it had become the laboratory for new Soviet
opera. After her traditional training, Nina found herself at a
centre for artistic experimentation.

Nina would walk restlessly around Leningrad, trying to
make sense of everything she was experiencing. Watching the
innovative work around her, she realised that her work at the
Maly was not enough. She wanted to find her own artistic
voice. Like many in her generation, she was looking for truth
in art beyond the established forms she had been taught. But
for this she needed to experiment. The jumble of thoughts
and ideas in her head could be overwhelming, but the strict,
harmonious classicism of her native city came to her rescue,
calming her over-stimulated imagination. A few years later,
Nina would write: 'In these years, I sensed and for the first
time consciously grasped the lyrical and severe beauty of our
unusual city. Taking in the choppy waters of the cold-grey
Neva contained by the granite river-bed, much of the confusion in my thoughts about art came into focus and found its

* Dmitry Shostakovich's operas *The Nose* (1930) and *Lady Macbeth of
Mtsensk* (1934) both had their premiere at the Maly. Today, the theatre is
known as the Mikhailovsky Theatre.

form, much was resolved as I grasped the architectural clarity in the profile of its squares.'[17]

Seeking an outlet for her restless creative energies, Nina began to explore Leningrad's thriving variety stages.[18] Many ballet artists were looking for extra work, even though some theatres forbade them to do so. One reason was financial – the basic salary of a corps de ballet dancer was enough to provide food for only half a month – but many also enjoyed the freedom to experiment. Ballet dancers performed before movie showings at cinemas, at concert halls, outdoor perform-ance spaces, small theatres and even at gambling clubs and private restaurants.[19]

Nina danced in mixed programmes put together for work-ers, in cinema-divertissements, at Leningrad's popular Summer Garden and on the stage of the Philharmonic. Sometimes she performed character dances from the classic repertoire, but she also began to choreograph her own pieces and started to work with another young dancer and budding choreographer, Vasily Vainonen. It was probably around this time that Nina first met Vladimir 'Volodia' Dmitriev, an artist who had become a rising star among stage designers. Volodia was Vainonen's mentor, and he had also designed productions for the Maly. Both men would play a decisive role in Nina's career and life.

But Nina still felt unsatisfied – her own efforts were not enough to break the tedium of the Maly's repertoire. Fate came to her help. During a performance of Ernst Krenek's comic avant-garde opera *Der Sprung über den Schatten* around New Year 1927–8, a 600-kg disc suspended over the stage acciden-tally collapsed and almost killed Nina, who was carried off stage and hurried to hospital. Nina was convinced that the theatre management took pity on her because of this accident, transferring her to the former Mariinsky after her recovery. She had spent barely one season at the Maly.[20]

Nina arrived during tumultuous times. Towards the end of her first season, in May 1928, Soviet citizens were listening with bated breath to reports about the Shakhty trial of non-Bolshevik engineers and technicians on charges of conspiracy and sabotage. The regime was renewing its battle against non-Communist, bourgeois specialists. After the comparative calm and pragmatism of the New Economic Policy (NEP), class war was back, and not just in the economy and in industry. Communist militants were fighting against the old intelligentsia for absolute control of the arts, education and the sciences. Government authority over the theatres' repertoire was tightened, and the former Mariinsky's modernist ballet director Fedor Lopukhov came under attack and was removed from his position. Pressure to Sovietise the ballet repertoire increased.

Nina threw herself into the traditional character dances of the classical repertoire: the Ukrainian dance from *The Little Hump-backed Horse*, the Spanish Dance from *Swan Lake*, the Saracen dance from *Raymonda*. She still had a lot to learn, but she was already attracting attention. When the company's most senior male character dancer, Joseph Kschessinsky, chose her as his partner for the jubilee performance marking his sixtieth birthday, Nina modestly claimed that he had honoured her as the youngest character dancer in the company. But their czardas was equal to a coronation dance: Kschessinsky not only had great authority within the company, he was a member of an important ballet dynasty and the brother of the fabled ballerina Mathilda Kschessinskaya, mistress of the young Nicholas II, who was now living in French exile with her husband, Grand Duke Andrei Vladimirovich Romanov.[21]

Nina was still trying to define her artistic personality. She felt that, deep inside, a part of her creativity was still waiting to be awakened. Her unique gift finally revealed itself to her – and to the world – during the rehearsals for *The Flames of Paris*.* The part of Thérèse had not even been in the ballet's original libretto, but Nina kept adding layer upon layer of meaning during the rehearsals for the revolutionary mass scenes and the small Basque group dance she was supposed to perform until the character of Thérèse was born. It might have helped that the ballet's core creative team was an experimental one, open to improvisation: the choreographer was Vasily Vainonen, guided by the theatre director, Sergei Radlov, and stage designer Volodia Dmitriev.[22]

Directors from the dramatic theatre were supposed to help ballet and opera find a new, Soviet seriousness. Six months before the premiere of *The Flames of Paris* on 7 November 1932, the anniversary of the revolution, 'socialist realism' had been declared the mandatory method of artistic creation in all branches of the arts, but nobody knew what this was supposed to mean in practice; each art form embarked on the arduous process of interpreting it for itself. In the world of ballet, Radlov became the midwife to a new genre that would define Soviet ballet for decades to come: *drambalet*, narrative ballets constructed according to the laws of the dramatic theatre, often

---

* The ballet's premiere took place at the former Mariinsky on 7 November 1932 in honour of the fifteenth anniversary of the revolution.

on the basis of classic literature or contemporary plots reminiscent of Soviet propaganda movies.*

The critics had sensed correctly that Nina's creative core was deeply contemporary. She found herself as an artist when she got the chance to characterise a real person: Nina discovered that she could express the savage fervour of Thérèse's revolutionary heroism in dance. The 'old' character dances had added national flavour to ballets, or expressed a mood or temperament associated with a specific country. *The Flames of Paris* had shown Nina that character dance could also be dramatic. It could express the full range of human emotions and serve as a vehicle to build a character on stage.[23] With this new freedom, Nina's desire to choreograph larger pieces was awakened. Choreography was traditionally the domain of men, but, very subtly, Vaganova had set a precedent for female choreographers at the Kirov by adding her own choreography to her productions of the classics. Nina was ready to follow.

Nina staged her first larger independent work in 1935, a suite of Spanish dances performed by herself, two male dancers and a singer. The following two years proved exceptionally difficult for Russia's classical ballet, but intensively stimulating for Nina. In the rollercoaster of Soviet cultural politics,

---

* Later, the genre would ossify into pantomimic performances of little choreographic interest, but during its early days, the collaboration between innovative theatre directors and the former Mariinsky Ballet was truly innovative. Its crowning achievement would be Leonid Lavrovsky's staging of Sergei Prokofiev's *Romeo and Juliet*, who had worked on the ballet's libretto with Radlov and Adrian Piotrovsky.

she became the accidental beneficiary of an intensified clash between the creative intelligentsia's artistic aspirations and the regime's ideological demands.

To prove its right to exist in a Communist state, ballet had been exhorted year after year to contribute to the ideological education of the new Soviet man, but expressing Bolshevik propaganda in the courtly, elegant language of classical dance was easier said than done. The choreographer Fedor Lopukhov, the young star composer Dmitry Shostakovich and the librettist Adrian Piotrovsky seemed to have found a winning formula when their comedy ballet *The Bright Stream*, about life on a provincial Soviet collective farm, opened to great critical and public acclaim at the Maly Theatre in April 1935. Lopukhov's innovative yet classical choreography and Shostakovich's radiant music told a light-hearted story of love and jealousy between the inhabitants of the farm and a group of Muscovite ballet artists visiting to celebrate the farm's impressive production quotas.

Disaster struck shortly after the ballet's successful Moscow premiere at the Bolshoi in November 1935. A vicious series of unsigned *Pravda* editorials attacked different works of Soviet opera, ballet, film and the visual arts, marking the beginning of the notorious anti-formalism campaign against modernism that would paralyse Soviet artists. Artists were exhorted to resist the temptations of 'capitalist' Western art and to focus their energies on creating wholesome socialist realist art. Soviet art was supposed to be simple, inspired by folk art, life-affirming and optimistic, propagating an official version of Soviet existence that bore little resemblance to reality. Lopukhov was chastised for combining classical dance with false folk dances that had nothing to do with the folk art of Kuban, the Black Sea region settled by Cossacks where the ballet was set.[24] Instead of crafting credible, contemporary Soviet characters for the stage, the ballet's creators were accused of perpetuating pre-revolutionary conventions.

The *Pravda* attack pushed Leningrad's ballet world into desperate attempts to stomp out frivolity. Nina found herself in charge of staging a one-act ballet for the Leningrad Choreographic Institute's annual graduation performance at the Kirov in June 1936. Set in Spain, *Andalusian Wedding* was based on a work by the romantic Spanish writer Prosper Mérimée, author of *Carmen*, and told the story of a popular hero who, pursued by police, interrupts a wedding and is saved by the people.[25] Nina was supported by one of Leningrad's leading directors, Vladimir Solovyov.

After *Andalusian Wedding*, Nina was recognised as a new talent in choreography. Her star was ascending within the strict dance hierarchy of the former Mariinsky, renamed the Kirov Theatre in 1935 in honour of Leningrad's assassinated party boss Sergei Kirov. The official promotion of national dance literally propelled her centre stage. Back in 1933, inspired by her rousing portrayal of Thérèse in his ballet *The Flames of Paris*, Vasily Vainonen had staged a special concert number for Nina that showed her as a female partisan leader of a small detachment uniting people of different nationalities. After a successful premiere, Vainonen and Dmitriev decided to use it as the starting point for a new ballet libretto about the civil war: *Partisan Days*.[26]

In March 1936, just a few weeks after the attack on *The Bright Stream*, the Kirov took the plunge and agreed to stage

Partisan Days. It was to be the Kirov's first – and last – contemporary ballet based entirely on character dance. The moment seemed to belong to Nina and her partner, Sergei Koren. Dissatisfied by the Kirov's limited repertoire for character dancers, they had just started experimenting together beyond the walls of the theatre.[27] Now they could do so at the Kirov itself, the heart of Russian ballet culture. Nina and Koren were to be the stars of *Partisan Days*; Vainonen stubbornly resisted the pressure to include a role for a classical ballerina. Not a single pointe shoe could be spotted during the premiere on 10 May 1937. Nina was the ballet's central heroine, portraying a rebellious young Cossack woman who joins a group of partisans during the civil war that had followed the October Revolution. The theatre's classical ballerinas watched from the wings in disbelief, shuddering at the thought that they might be forced to hang up their own pointe shoes for good.

By an accident of fate, Nina had come to embody the Soviet aspiration of bringing culture to the masses and of forging a unique Soviet civilisation through art. She not only excelled in the fiery national dances that added spice and local colour to ballets, but her choreographic interpretations of dances from different Soviet regions were an ideal vehicle for demonstrating the 'brotherhood' that supposedly united the many nationalities that had been brought into the Soviet fold since the early days of the revolution, when Stalin had been Commissar of Nationalities. Despite formidable opposition from the traditional ballerinas, who were not willing to relinquish their monopoly on leading roles without a fight, and the usual theatrical backstabbing, Nina had held her course. But her arrest put an end to her ascent.

3

Enemy of the People

The black curtain covering the cell's steel-rod wall was pushed to the side:

'Somebody with the letter "A"?'

'Anisimova?'

'Full initials!'

'Nina Alexandrovna.'

'To the exit!'

It was Nina's third night in prison. Interrogations only took place at night, to catch the prisoners in their psychologically most vulnerable state. Whenever the guard approached the cell to collect a prisoner for interrogation, the inmates had to participate in a nerve-wracking charade. The guard would only give the first letter of the surname he was looking for. Woken from their troubled sleep, all prisoners whose last name started with the letter in question had to give their full name until the right prisoner was found. If the guard had approached the wrong cell, the identity of the prisoner he was looking for would remain secret. This was supposed to keep prisoners from communicating with their 'accomplices' in other cells and from inferring anything about their case from the identities of other prisoners.

Nina crawled out of her sleeping spot, put on her shoes and made her way to the cell's exit, climbing across the bodies on the floor. The lock turned with a clank. The guard briefly searched her. 'Hands behind your back! Move along!' Her stockings slipping down, Nina walked down the prison's semi-dark corridors. Wooden booths lined the walls at regular intervals. If a guard accompanying a prisoner realised that another guarded prisoner was approaching, he would push his charge into the booth and shut it tight until they had gone. If there was no booth in sight, the prisoner had to face the wall until the other prisoner had passed. Some guards rattled their keys to alert others to their presence; others simply waited when a figure emerged at the other end of the corridor.

Soon, she was no longer walking on the spittle-strewn stone floors of the prison's dimly lit corridors, but on a long runner covering the floor of a brightly lit, wide corridor. Nina was led into an office.[1]

For the *troikas*, the extrajudicial regional bodies created during the Great Terror's mass operations,* no proof of guilt other than a confession was needed to pass sentences, including death sentences. The *troikas* consisted of the head of the local

---

* In addition to the *troikas*, other bodies such as courts, military tribunals and the Military Collegium of the Supreme Court all participated in the Great Terror.

NKVD, the local procurator* and the secretary of the local party organisation. It was the NKVD's job to extract confessions. Some NKVD interrogators forged signatures under invented interrogation protocols without ever speaking to the prisoner in question. Others added false testimony to already signed protocols. Since the *troikas* passed verdicts *in absentia* in closed sessions, the accused would have no chance to protest. Not everybody used such comparatively humane methods. Prisoners were routinely tortured until they were willing to sign anything put in front of them.

Every night, the sound of wails travelled across the yard from the offices of the Bolshoi Dom into the cells of the Shpalerka. Sometimes, large trucks with running motors were parked inside the yard to drown out the noise, but the inmates continued to imagine what they could no longer hear.[2] Many prisoners were put on the 'conveyor', a marathon cross-examination whereby several interrogators took turns to question a prisoner non-stop for several days. Delirious with fatigue, the prisoner would often be forced to stand or sit in positions that became unbearable over time. Prisoners were beaten and kicked, but there was no limit to the interrogators' sadistic imagination.[3]

∽

Lieutenant Anatoly Kolodkin, head of the Germany/Hungary section of the Leningrad NKVD's counter-intelligence

---

* The Soviet procuracy was a government bureau supposed to ensure administrative legality. In theory, it was responsible for supervising the observance of the law, but in practice, it worked closely with bodies such as the NKVD to implement the policies of the Communist dictatorship.

department, had prepared everything for Nina's first interrogation.[4] He would share the job with M. Kolesnikov, an officer from his department. Kolodkin first asked Nina the standard catalogue of questions about social, political and professional background that every adult Soviet citizen had to fill out at their place of work or study. This was not a good starting point. Nina's social origins immediately marked her out as a potential enemy of the regime. Her father's successful military career in the Imperial Army could be pretext enough to send her straight off to the camps. NKVD interrogators approached their cases heavily steeped in class-consciousness, mindful of procurator Andrei Vyshinsky's warning against 'bourgeois weighing of punishments in relation to the gravity of what had been committed'.[5] To the Bolsheviks, it often mattered more who someone was than what they had done.

Kolodkin moved from the pitfalls of social origin to another minefield: human relations, the building blocks of conspiracy. He demanded the names of her relatives and closest friends. If need be, he could later frame any of them as her accomplices. Nina gave her mother and sister as her only relatives, describing herself as unmarried. When asked to name her friends, she listed six men, all in their twenties and thirties. Four were artists, one a movie director and one, Konstantin Derzhavin, a writer and theatre expert. Nina claimed that she didn't know their addresses, with one exception: the stage designer Volodia Dmitriev, who lived only a few houses down the road from her.

This was probably the last address she should have mentioned: two days after Nina's arrest, Volodia's wife Elizaveta Dolukhanova had been arrested, also on suspicion of espionage.* Any connection to their household had thus become dangerous, especially for Nina. In the early 1930s, shortly after Volodia and Elizaveta were married, he and Nina had embarked on a love affair. On a river cruise from Moscow, Volodia and Nina had travelled down the Rivers Oka, Volga and Kama in a party that included the choreographer Vasily Vainonen and Anna Kniper (Timiryova), the former lover of the civil war anti-Bolshevik General Kolchak who had been executed in 1920. The small group disembarked in Yelabuga and settled in a hayloft close to the forest. Smoking carelessly in the hay, Volodia looked out for imaginary bands of robbers while Nina danced around a bonfire. Together Nina, Volodia and Vasily began working on *The Flames of Paris*, the ballet that would make Nina famous. When they ran out of money, Nina charmed their way on to an overfilled boat that took them back to Moscow, and reality.[6] Their romance had ended, but they remained close friends and professional collaborators.

The NKVD pressed more names out of Nina. Even though her circle of friends was relatively small, she moved freely in the artistic circles of Leningrad and Moscow and knew almost everybody. Pushed, she listed Vasily Vainonen, the Kirov Ballet dancers Sergei Koren, Galina Ulanova, Tatiana Vecheslova, Natalia Dudinskaya and Vakhtang Chabukiani, and the directors of the Pushkin and Mikhailovsky Theatres, Sergei Radlov and Boris Khaikin, as acquaintances.

At this stage Nina had still been given no information as to why she had been arrested. After committing to paper the names of her family, friends and colleagues, the interrogator

* Dolukhanova was shot as a spy on 28 June 1938.

began to grill her on her relations with people working for foreign diplomatic missions in the USSR. Nina was asked to name every one of these whom she knew, to state when and where she had met them and who had introduced them. The interrogator was particularly interested in Nina's friendship with one man: Evgeny Salomé.[7]

～

Born in St Petersburg in 1885 into a highly respected German-Russian family, Evgeny Salomé had seen the world of his childhood go up in flames during the October Revolution. The Salomés traced their ancestry to Huguenots who had settled in the Baltics after fleeing from Avignon in the sixteenth century. Salomé's grandfather Gustav had attracted the attention of the imperial establishment when he became the youngest colonel in Russia's Imperial Army. Decorated for bravery at the Battle of Warsaw during the Polish uprising against Russian rule in 1830–1, Gustav would ultimately rise to the rank of general, catapulting his family to the highest level of the empire's military elite and into Russia's hereditary nobility.

Evgeny studied law at the Universities of Dorpat (Tartu) and Vienna before establishing himself as a lawyer in St Petersburg.[8] He was thirty-two when the Bolsheviks seized power. In 1918, during the uncertain period of the civil war, he acquired German citizenship but remained in Russia. A few years later, in 1922, he joined the newly reopened German consulate in Leningrad as in-house lawyer. Evgeny quickly gained the diplomats' trust. In addition to working on legal questions including detention issues, Evgeny was entrusted with communicating with the Russian authorities.[9]

About a year after joining the consulate, he married a woman fourteen years his junior. Like Evgeny, twenty-three-year-old Tatiana Isenberg belonged to a respected Russian-German family. Pictures of Tatiana as a young mother with her only son, Eugene, show a beautiful, serious woman with sad eyes. In the 1970s, she would sit at her desk in Boulder, Colorado, filling notebook after notebook with stories of families destroyed by the revolution and the Bolsheviks' secret police.[10] Real or imagined, her stories were rooted in her own experience. Her brother-in-law Vladimir Okhochinsky, an aristocrat, former officer, art historian and bibliophile, was forced into a never-ending cycle of arrest and punishment in 1920, perishing twenty years later in the camps of Magadan.[11] In 1933, Tatiana's older brother, also called Vladimir, was arrested in Leningrad. Beaten and tortured for eighty-three days, he resisted until the NKVD threatened to do the same to one of his sisters before his very eyes. Vladimir signed whatever the interrogator put in front of him. Informed that they would have twenty minutes to say goodbye before Vladimir was sent to Siberia, his mother and his sister Anna rushed to the prison. Waiting in the big meeting room behind a dividing wall with windows, his mother fainted when she saw Vladimir, his glasses broken, his teeth knocked out. Vladimir's bloodstained linen was laundered at Tatiana's and Evgeny's flat to spare their mother the sight of her son's blood.[12]

❧

Evgeny was a ballet fanatic. Fascinated by the dancers, it wasn't enough to watch them bathed in the magical light of the stage. Acquainted with the theatre's administrative director, Evgeny got himself invited to watch performances from the director's box situated right above the orchestra, as close to the action on stage as possible, and with direct access backstage.[13]

Nina met Evgeny Salomé around 1928 in the flat of a friend, a ballet dancer at the Maly Theatre. The Salomés liked to throw parties for dancers at their flat, but apparently took care to keep their different social circles strictly separate. The artists' evenings were for artists only; Nina told the NKVD that she did not remember ever meeting anybody but artists at the Salomés' flat. The Salomés were attentive hosts, usually providing food, spoiling their guests with foreign wines and liqueurs. The merry company would play billiards and dance the foxtrot until two or three in the morning. Salomé's generosity was not limited to these large evening gatherings: he gave Nina flowers for her birthday and spoiled her with little presents throughout the year. Despite this attentiveness, however, their friendship remained on a fairly superficial social level: Nina visited him only in the company of other artists.[14]

Inevitably, the NKVD asked Nina to name all the artists who had gone to Salomé's evening invitations. Salomé had liberally spread his attention across the entire ballet ensemble. According to Nina, some of the Kirov's most popular ballerinas and male principal dancers had attended, including Tatiana Vecheslova, Natalia Dudinskaya, Galina Ulanova, Olga Iordan, Vakhtang Chabukiani, Feya Balabina and Konstantin Sergeyev. They had been joined by many dancers from lower ranks in the ballet hierarchy. All in all, Salomé's circle of dancing acquaintances amounted to about thirty people.[15]

~

There have always been wealthy admirers of the arts who like to surround themselves with artists. But within the context of 1930s Leningrad, the Salomés were not the most natural candidates to fulfil this role – members of the local party elite were. Foreign diplomats also liked to mingle with Soviet artists, but the Salomés weren't diplomats. In fact, they were finding themselves in an increasingly precarious situation because of their ties to the German consulate. According to Hans von Herwarth, a German diplomat posted in Moscow from 1931 until 1939 and a future member of the resistance against Hitler, Soviet citizens were in principle allowed to associate with foreigners until about 1933. Although Herwarth found Moscow in the early 1930s fairly grey and oppressive, conscious of the people's prematurely aged faces and their old clothes, he was surprised to find Muscovites remarkably open to the few foreigners who made it to their city, especially to Germans. Initially, Herwarth was able to visit ordinary Russians in their flats and to experience firsthand the cramped living conditions of the communal flats and the extreme material shortages. Committed young Communists would ask him about life in Germany and openly debate the advantages and disadvantages of capitalism and Communism.[16]

Even if some Russians could mingle comparatively freely with foreigners in the early 1930s, they would still have attracted the attention of the secret police by doing so. The authorities were fundamentally suspicious of contact between Soviet citizens and foreigners, even though the boundaries of the permissible were constantly changing. In the 1920s, an observer would have counted at least fifty Russians – musicians, artists, intellectuals – at the large receptions regularly held at the German consulate in Leningrad, but around 1929 the authorities put a complete stop to such intermingling. Two years later, however, the German consul received word that he was again allowed to invite a select group of Soviet citizens.[17]

The secret police kept a close watch on Soviet citizens employed by foreign diplomatic missions. Herwarth knew that all the Russian ladies teaching Russian to diplomats had to report to the secret police. They also monitored the domestic staff of the German embassy in Moscow, two Volga German women whom the diplomats felt particularly close to because of their shared language. Hitler's rise to power in 1933 gave a different edge to the secret police's interest in Soviet citizens who had regular contact with German foreign missions, and Germans and Russians soon lost their appetite for socialising with each other. Before long, even the last safe havens of intermingling – the homes of German specialists married to Russian women – disappeared when most foreign specialists hired to speed up industrialisation decided to leave the Soviet Union. Even though Salomé's family had lived in Russia for centuries, he belonged to a special category because he had chosen German citizenship in 1918. He was thus technically a foreigner – but a 'foreigner' who was especially suspect to the authorities because he was a Russian-German whose family had belonged to the imperial establishment and who, after the revolution, had openly demonstrated his hostility to the Soviet regime by rejecting Soviet citizenship.[18]

～

Salomé was playing with fire. He must have been keenly aware of the omnipresent eyes and ears of the NKVD, but nothing could stop him where his dancers were concerned. Desperate to surround himself with artistic talent, he had assumed the role of a cosmopolitan man about town who had access to a world beyond the reach of the majority of Soviet artists – the world of foreign, scarce goods. Maybe Salomé feared that his adored Kirov dancers would not look twice at him if he relied on the power of his personality alone. Whatever his motivation, he wooed the dancers with small presents that held special value in an economy where everything was scarce.

Over the years, he had given Nina gifts including a string of pearls, perfume, compact powder, stockings, lipstick, chocolate, cigarettes, pyjamas won at a game of billiards and an elastic bandage. Many of the regulars at his evenings had received similar presents, including three of the most popular Kirov ballerinas: Tatiana Vecheslova, Natalia Dudinskaya and Galina Ulanova. Dudinskaya was even walking around with a foreign watch presented to her by Salomé.[19]

Salomé's generous behaviour in a land of scarcity was certainly out of the ordinary. As Aleksander Solzhenitsyn would lament: 'Oh, in how new a light does our past life appear when re-examined in the interrogator's office: abounding in dangers, like an African jungle. And we had considered it so simple!'[20] Asked by the interrogator about the reasons behind Salomé's generosity, Nina guessed that Salomé had wanted to attract as many people as possible, but added that she had attached no importance to his motivation in the past.[21] She did not realise that the NKVD was trying to frame Salomé as former local station chief of German intelligence, but perhaps she was beginning to question his motives now. Even if she wasn't, Nina must have wondered at some point how Salomé was procuring and paying for this ready supply of gifts.

After more than ten years at the German consulate, Salomé was the highest paid of five senior local employees there. In 1933, his monthly salary was 862 Reichsmark, the equivalent of about 399 roubles.[22] For the sake of comparison, the average salary of a worker was 125 roubles, while doctors received 150–275 roubles. Most importantly, however, Salomé would have received his salary regularly – which could not be said for Russian salaries – and in coveted Reichsmark.[23]

Paying for the presents was not necessarily the main problem. Today it would seem strange to give a ballerina stockings, powder and lipstick, but in 1930s Leningrad, like most other consumer items, they were hard to come by. Stalin's all-out drive to industrialise had left not much room for the production of regular consumer goods. Salomé probably bought his presents in one of Leningrad's state-run Torgsin stores, which sold scarce food items and goods to foreigners and Soviet citizens able to pay in gold, foreign currencies, jewellery or other valuables. The revenue raised by the Torgsin stores would emerge as a major source of finance for Stalin's rapid industrialisation plans.[24] Torgsin shops were supposed to showcase Soviet productivity, dangling an unattainable image of plenty in front of ordinary citizens pressing their faces against the window display. In 1933, an Australian visitor to Leningrad was 'diverted by the sight of a brightly lit shop with a crowd of people staring in the windows. It soon became apparent what had attracted them. The windows were filled with every sort of gastronomic luxury: Fortnum & Mason could scarcely rival them, and to the hungry crowd outside the food was as remote and unattainable as the Crown Jewels.'[25]

But even Torgsin had its limits. Herwarth remembers that

it was nigh impossible to go shopping in Moscow in the early 1930s. Like other foreign missions in Moscow, the German embassy was forced to order a lot of goods from abroad. Meat and fish were delivered weekly from Poland, Finland and Germany. Wine, beer and spirits were ordered from France, Italy or Germany. Twice a year, the embassy placed a big order for household items such as soap, hair water, shoelaces, cleaning material and toilet paper. Whenever the German diplomats were unable to find something they urgently needed, they would turn towards diplomats from other foreign missions for help.[26] Given these obstacles, Salomé must have been very determined to obtain a ready supply of foreign drinks and small luxuries.

Salomé had created a perfect scenario for the NKVD: a mysterious man of plenty associated with Germany, corrupting scores of young dancers with food, drink and presents until they were ready to betray their Soviet motherland. The scenario's weakness lay in the profession of Salomé's objects of interest: by virtue of their work alone, the dancers were nowhere near any information even remotely relevant for German intelligence. Moreover, given the climate of surveillance and suspicion, it would have been extraordinarily careless of German intelligence to recruit Salomé as its local station chief. Yet Salomé's behaviour begged the question: why was he going to such pains to get close to such a large number of dancers, why was he showering them with presents, and how was he managing to replenish his horn of plenty with foreign wines, liqueurs, stockings and lipstick?

Employed by a foreign power and drifting through a society that seemed to have no place for him, perhaps Salomé hoped to anchor himself as a patron of the Kirov Ballet. He certainly wanted to be loved by the dancers. There was something obsessive about his determination to get them to attend his evenings. Usually, he issued invitations through two male dancers, Andrei Mikhailov and Andrei Levanenok, who introduced him to others. But sometimes Salomé would drive to the flats of ballerinas to invite them personally.[27]

By 1933–4, however, domestic and international politics were casting a shadow over Salomé's invitations. Before Hitler's rise to power, Weimar Germany and the Soviet Union had been linked by a pragmatic partnership of outcasts. In 1922, Soviet and German negotiators had met secretly in the picturesque Italian town of Rapallo on the margins of an international debt conference held in Genoa. The two pariahs of international affairs had ended their isolation by establishing diplomatic ties, giving up all financial claims on each other. A secret pact on military and technical cooperation gave the Soviets access to German military expertise while offering the Germans an opportunity to circumvent the strict military limits imposed on them by the Treaty of Versailles. Between 1922 and 1934, German officers and weapons technicians travelled secretly to Russia to help the Soviets build their armaments industry and to train German and Soviet personnel in tank and aerial warfare.

This cooperation was abandoned after the Nazis came to power. The German fascists combined violent anti-Communism with a racial ideology and territorial ambitions that were decidedly anti-Soviet. Regarding Slavs as racially inferior to the Germans, and interpreting Bolshevism as a Jewish conspiracy, Hitler intended to conquer the lands east of

Germany's borders and colonise them after butchering, deporting or enslaving their populations.[28]

The rise of German fascism in 1933 might have been enough to scare off people from socialising with Salomé, an employee of the new arch-enemy, but the domestic situation inside the Soviet Union was also taking a turn for the worse. In December 1934, Leningrad's party boss Sergei Kirov was assassinated. Stalin used the assassination as a pretext to eliminate old oppositionists. In February and March 1935, Leningrad was purged of over 11,000 'former people' – former aristocrats, tsarist officials, officers, bureaucrats, clergy, landowners and capitalists who were identified with the old regime.[29]

In this poisonous atmosphere, Salomé became increasingly suspect. At the trial of the dancer Andrei Levanenok, arrested in October 1937 because of his friendship with Salomé, the Kirov dancer Evgeny Raguzin denounced his former colleague as a frivolous person fascinated by everything foreign. Raguzin claimed that he had warned Levanenok that there could be consequences to socialising with Salomé. If Raguzin is to be believed, Levanenok light-heartedly brushed his warning aside.[30]

Salomé might have managed to reassure Levanenok, but other dancers were beginning to distance themselves. Nina stopped visiting Salomé after the assassination of Kirov. Another promising young ballerina received a friendly warning from Agrippina Vaganova, the ballet company's artistic director, that she should not see Salomé because he was 'an element alien to us'.[31] They were not the only ones to stay away.

After all the trouble he had gone through, Salomé felt cheated. He complained to the Kirov Theatre's management that 'moral pressure' was being exerted on his friends to avoid him.[32] And with his brother-in-law Vladimir having been arrested the year before, the psychological strain was beginning to show.

Salomé started to look for a way out. Tatiana and their eleven-year-old son Eugene appear to have crossed the Finnish border first, settling in Helsinki. On 20 January 1936, Salomé reported sick to work. According to the records of the political archive of the German Foreign Office, he joined his family in Helsinki for health reasons. The terrors of daily life in Stalinist Russia were replaced by the everyday worries of immigrants struggling to make ends meet in a foreign country. In 1939, the couple separated. Salomé moved to Stockholm in 1945, dying alone in 1963.[33]

~

Nina's problem was apparently not only related to her connection to Salomé. Over the years, Nina and her fellow dancers attended officially sanctioned banquets held at the German consulate in Leningrad, where she met two German consuls, Rudolf Sommer and one of his predecessors, Karl Walther.* Invitations to these receptions were addressed to the management of the theatre. Nina had been singled out and introduced to the consuls because of her visible position within the company. Like many diplomats, Walther enjoyed Leningrad's rich cultural life. Nina would occasionally bump into the consul

---

* Karl Walther was the German consul in Leningrad from 1925 until 1928. He was succeeded by Erich Zechlin (1928–33) and Rudolf Sommer (1933–7).

in the auditorium of the Kirov Theatre, at the Leningrad Philharmonic or in the street. She would politely answer the German consul's questions, unaware that within a few years their short conversations would be interpreted as sinister exchanges between conspirators.[34]

In Leningrad, the restaurant of the Hotel Astoria served as a meeting place between foreigners and some select Soviet citizens. Designed by the architect Fyodor Lidval, who was also responsible for Nina's apartment building, the luxurious hotel on St Isaac's Square had opened in time for the Romanov tercentenary of 1913.[35] The hotel was conveniently located within walking distance of the Kirov Theatre – and opposite the German consulate. During the First World War, people claimed that there was a secret passage running underneath St Isaac's Square connecting the hotel – owned by Germans, who were considered spies – to the German consulate, whose employees were also all assumed to be spies.[36] Around 1931, during the devastating famine following forced collectivisation, the Soviet authorities reopened the Astoria as a fancy hotel with a restaurant and jazz band. Foreign diplomats and specialists rubbed shoulders with the Soviet elite. Nina dutifully reported during her first interrogation that a fellow Kirov dancer had introduced her to two Polish diplomats at the Astoria's restaurant.

On 28 October 1937, the NKVD issued an order 'to arrest all Soviet citizens who are connected to the staff of foreign diplomatic offices and who visit their businesses and private premises' and to 'place under constant surveillance all members of the German, Japanese, Polish and Italian embassies'. Even though far more people would be arrested as Polish or

Japanese spies than as German ones, in May 1937, on the eve of the Great Terror, Stalin had explicitly told Kliment Voroshilov, People's Commissar for Defence, and Nikolai Yezhov, People's Commissar for Internal Affairs and organiser of the Great Terror, that the German intelligence service was their number-one enemy.[37]

Solzhenitsyn writes that 'neither our education, nor our upbringing, nor our experience prepares us in the slightest for the greatest trial of our lives: being arrested for nothing and interrogated about nothing.'[38] There were many far-fetched reasons why people were arrested during the Great Terror and accused of a wide range of anti-Soviet activities. As far as accusations of espionage were concerned, the most indirect links to a foreign country could be fatal, especially if the country in question was Germany, Poland or Japan. Inside the many prisons scattered across the Soviet Union there were scores of people like Nina: doctors who had treated German consuls; a veterinarian who had treated consular dogs; an old man who was 'the brother of the woman who supplied the German consul's milk'; a man who had given the Polish consul a copy of the weather forecast pinned up in a public park.[39] In total, over 250,000 people were arrested for espionage during the Great Terror. Most of them would be shot. The majority were Soviet citizens belonging to national minorities who, it was feared, might potentially turn into fifth columnists in wartime because of their ethnic connection to countries such as Poland, Germany, Finland and Latvia.[40]

In the 1920s, the threat of capitalist encirclement from without and dangers emanating from the enemy within had been the central themes of Soviet propaganda.[41] In the late

1920s and early 1930s, the propaganda machine had focused on internal 'class enemies'.[42] Espionage only emerged as a major theme during the notorious Moscow show trials of 1936–8. By 1934, many party members had become deeply disturbed by the naked brutality of forced collectivisation and the economic costs of industrialisation. About 1.8 million peasants had been shot or deported as 'kulaks' in 1929–30. Another 5 to 7 million people died in the famine of 1932–3.[43] In the Politburo, dissent was stirring. Stalin's attack on the party leadership and oppositionists among the Old Bolsheviks culminated in the three Moscow show trials of 1936–8. But the purge was not limited to the top; it affected all levels of the party, leading to public self-flagellation for past 'mistakes' and fiery denunciations at the grass-roots level in factories, offices and lecture halls across the Soviet Union.

The espionage theme emerged in full force at the second show trial held in January 1937. The Old Bolshevik and former oppositionist Georgy Pyatakov, Comintern leader Karl Radek and other Old Bolsheviks were accused of terrorism and industrial sabotage, supposedly under the leadership of Trotsky, with the support of Germany and Japan. In his speech for the prosecution, Vyshinsky exclaimed that the group was 'not a political party. It is a gang of criminals, merely the agency of foreign intelligence services.'

The third and final show trial in March 1938 culminated in eighteen death sentences and three long Gulag terms. Almost 200 observers watched as three members of Lenin's Politburo,*

---

* Mikhail Bukharin, former leader of the 'Right Opposition' of economic moderates, Alexei Rykov, another leader of the Right Opposition

former secret police chief Genrikh Yagoda and other senior leaders (including four people's commissars) were convicted of belonging to a Trotskyite-rightist bloc, of wrecking and undermining Soviet military power and of colluding with the intelligence services of Germany, Great Britain, Japan and Poland in preparing an imperialist attack on the Soviet Union. Lenin's former comrades Bukharin, Krestinsky, Rykov and the fervent Bolshevik Christian Rakovsky confessed to having planned Lenin's assassination since 1918; the bloc was found guilty of assassinating Kirov and numerous others. Apart from a few exceptions, the defendants in all three trials were sentenced to death and executed.

It is hard to imagine that people at the time believed the defendants' fantastic confessions, but even some foreign observers attending the trials were duped into doing so. Walter Duranty, the *New York Times* long-standing Moscow bureau chief, was invited with a few other select foreign journalists and diplomats to witness the spectacle. He found it a shock, reporting: 'It is as if twenty years after Yorktown somebody in power at Washington found it necessary for the safety of the State to send to the scaffold Thomas Jefferson, Madison, John Adams, Hamilton, Jay and most of their associates. The charge against them would be that they conspired to hand over the United States to George III.'[44] But even though Duranty described the madness of the moment, both he and Joseph

---

and Lenin's successor as Chairman (akin to prime minister) of the Council of People's Commissars from 1924 until 1930 and Old Bolshevik Nikolai Krestinsky.

Davies, US ambassador to Moscow, pronounced the trials fair and the confessions real.

The 'unmasking' of spies at the highest level had an enormous psychological impact on the many Soviet citizens inclined to believe the official propaganda: if spies had even managed to infiltrate the top echelons of the party, they could be hiding behind every corner. The logical conclusion was that nobody could be trusted – especially as those who failed to report potentially suspicious actions would themselves become suspect because of their lack of vigilance.

The Kremlin's puppet masters were doing their best to get the masses behind the purges and to whip their emotions into a bloodthirsty frenzy. People outside the prison walls were living in an increasingly poisonous atmosphere. Loudspeakers fixed in strategic locations around town were an important feature of Soviet life, ensuring that official propaganda provided a constant background noise to daily existence. On boulevards, in parks, at markets, in clubs, reading rooms and canteens, loudspeakers transmitted radio broadcasts.[45] Diligent newspaper readers could learn from *Pravda* that 200,000 people had assembled 'spontaneously' on Red Square at minus twenty-seven degrees Celsius after the verdict of the second show trial had been announced, demanding the immediate execution of the condemned on banners held high above their heads.[46]

There was more to come. On 11 June 1937, Soviet citizens listened in shock to the announcement that the top of the army leadership, supposed to protect them against the fascist threat and Japanese expansionism, had been charged with treason. A day later they were told that the country's top military men had been tried and executed. Civil war hero

Marshal Tukhachevsky, Deputy Commissar of Defence and the Red Army's main strategist, and other high-ranking officers including the chief of the General Staff, the commander of the Special Far Eastern Army, who had just defeated the Japanese in a major incident, the commanders of the Kiev and Belorussian Military Districts and the commanders of the Black Sea and Pacific Fleets were accused of conspiring with Trotsky and the German High Command.[47]

Between 35,000 and 41,000 military men followed their leaders to the grave, depriving the Red Army of 60 per cent of its marshals, approximately 90 per cent of its highest army commanders, all of its admirals and about 90 per cent of its corps commanders.[48]

Spy mania had gripped the country. Common sense was suspended as fantastical ravings became a legitimate justification for deadly actions. In this climate, only a few weeks before NKVD order no. 00447 would start the Great Terror, a state security report claiming that police in the western borderlands had found dead crows wearing rings on their legs bearing the inscription 'Germania' naturally found its way on to the desk of the great leader himself. The report conjectured that German intelligence had dispatched the crows to study wind directions, to find out whether birds could be used for arson and bacteriological subversion.[49] In reality, the NKVD had stumbled upon a German research project studying crow migration.[50]

On 25 July, People's Commissar Yezhov signed an NKVD order commanding the immediate arrest of all German nationals who had worked or were working at military plants and enterprises with defence subdivisions and on the railroads. By September 1937, all German nationals employed at non-military enterprises were to be 'accounted for'. The operation against German nationals set the stage for a series of initiatives against other nationalities that were to become an important component of the Great Terror.[51]

~

Nina would not have been arrested if Stalin's seeming obsession with spies had limited its focus to possible opponents at the top, or even the party rank and file. But Stalin was expecting war. Convinced that one spy could change the outcome of a conflict, he intended to cast his nets as wide as possible: in a speech on the eve of the Great Terror he announced that if only 5 per cent of the alleged enemies turned out to be real enemies, he would be satisfied. Foreign diplomatic missions and all Soviet citizens who had contact with them were a special thorn in his side. His dislike of the missions was not entirely unfounded.

Japan, Poland and Germany were running intelligence operations out of their diplomatic missions on Soviet soil; the Soviet Union was doing the same abroad. Espionage activities were sometimes brazenly conducted in broad daylight under the cover of seemingly innocent activities: while pretending to be enjoying a picnic, 'diplomats' (intelligence specialists) from the Japanese consulate in Novosibirsk would monitor the Siberian railway. Lazing away whole days on riverbanks, they would carefully observe the freight cars passing by while others would survey nearby military bases and military factories. The diplomatic courier system – protecting communication between foreign missions and their capitals – also offered opportunities for intelligence-gathering: from 1936, Japanese couriers – often military intelligence officers – could be found at any given time on the Siberian railways. Overtly carrying diplomatic messages, they were evaluating the Soviet transport capacity and reconstructing an accurate railway schedule. They collected enough data to enable Japan to identify the best points for attack in the rail system and the bridges that should be destroyed in case of war. All this information was shared with Poland, which enjoyed close intelligence cooperation with Japan.[52]

Whereas Polish and Finnish intelligence on the Soviet Union was probably the best in the world in the 1920s and 1930s, German Soviet intelligence is perceived by some sources as being very weak in the first half of the 1930s, and almost non-existent between 1937 and 1939.[53] Nevertheless, German diplomatic missions were of course engaged in espionage, at least until 1937. From 1933 up to the end of 1937, Lieutenant-Commander Norbert von Baumbach, naval attaché at the German embassy in Moscow, was working closely with Rudolf Sommer in Leningrad to gather relevant information.

If Baumbach is to be believed, Sommer was the first to discover in 1933 that the Soviet Union had secretly begun to expand its submarine fleet. According to Baumbach, at the time nobody outside the Soviet Union knew about this. Over the next couple of years, Sommer carefully passed on information that allegedly enabled the German navy to get an almost 100 per cent accurate picture of Soviet warship construction, including advance intelligence about the launching of the cruiser *Kirov* on 30 November 1936.[54]

The diplomatic community was shocked when the Soviet government demanded in May 1937 that Germany, Japan and

Poland close some of their consulates. At first, the Soviets focused on the strategically important port locations of Odessa and Vladivostok, but by August they were demanding the closure of three additional German consulates. The verbal pressure from the Commissariat of Foreign Affairs was amplified by cruder methods on the ground. During the summer, the German consul in Novosibirsk, Maximilian Meyer-Heydenhagen, had to watch powerless as his entire domestic staff was arrested. Realising that the Soviet government was determined, in September Germany decided to close its consulates in Odessa and Vladivostok.[55]

Things were coming to a head. On 13 October 1937, Deputy People's Commissar for Foreign Affairs Vladimir Potemkin asked the German ambassador to Moscow, Count Schulenburg, to a meeting. At the commissariat, Potemkin read Schulenburg a long list of accusations against Sommer, based on statements extracted by the NKVD from both German and Soviet citizens. The first arrests of Salomé's dancing friends might have taken place against the backdrop of pressure to fabricate evidence. The accusations soon took on a fantastical character. Sommer was not only accused of military and industrial espionage, but also of having founded a National Socialist cell and of having planned the assassination of Leningrad's party boss Andrei Zhdanov, the destruction of factories and the poisoning of Leningrad's population. Potemkin demanded Sommer's departure and the closure of the German consulate in Leningrad.

The following day, Sommer was asked to report to the Foreign Office in Berlin.[56] He never returned to Leningrad. The German consulate in Leningrad was officially closed on

15 January 1938,[57] and by May 1938 there were no German consulates left on Soviet territory.[58] Baumbach would later claim that the Soviets never discovered Sommer's real espionage activities, forcing them to demand his recall and the closure of the consulate in Leningrad based on false accusations. According to Baumbach, even on the German side nobody had known about Sommer's activities apart from him.[59] Inevitably, the closure of the German consulate in Leningrad claimed its victims among the local staff. Sommer's driver was arrested, though it is not clear whether before or after the consul's departure. A maid, the consulate's house manager and its janitor were also all arrested and executed over the following months.[60]

❧

Inside the interrogator's office, Nina was tying herself in knots. She was being bombarded with questions: how many times and where had she met the German consuls Walther and Sommer? At Salomé's? Hadn't she stated that, apart from other artists, she had never met anyone but Salomé and his wife at their flat? Nina was accused of intentionally muddying the investigation and warned that any attempt to lead the investigation astray would prove futile. The interrogator ominously warned that it was time to give evidence about the anti-Soviet, counter-revolutionary activities she had undertaken together with Salomé and others. Nina protested that she had not had counter-revolutionary relations with anyone, but the interrogator hit back: 'You are not saying the truth, we know from reliable sources about your criminal work against Soviet power, we are essentially demanding truthful evidence.'

According to Solzhenitsyn, 'They used to say: "You are *not truthful* in your testimony, and *therefore* you will not be allowed to sleep!"' But the records do not indicate whether the interrogator's accusations were followed by any form of psychological or physical torture. The protocol of Nina's first interrogation concludes with Nina's testimonial: 'Once again, I attest that I have not engaged in counter-revolutionary activity', and the terse statement that the interrogation was broken off at the defendant's request.[61] Nina was taken back to her cell.

4

The Confrontation

Nina was pacing around her cell. It was late in the morning. Her colleagues at the Kirov would be in the middle of their daily class, preparing their bodies for the rehearsals that would fill the rest of their day. For Nina the hours had been dragging on since 6 a.m., the time of the guards' daily wake-up call. At 6.30 the inmates received 500 grams of dark bread, their daily ration, a matchbox with granulated sugar and fruit tea boiled in large red-copper teapots. Whiling away their time until lunch, the prisoners teamed up in pairs and walked behind each other, moving around the cell as if following the progress of time on a giant clock dial. Once a week the prisoners were taken down into the internal prison yard for a twenty-minute walk, circling around a male warder positioned in the centre of the yard.[1] The rest of the time, Nina, who was used to moving all day long, was limited to pacing back and forth in the overcrowded cell.

More than two months had passed since Nina's first interrogation. She had grown accustomed to the routines governing prison life. She knew that lunch would be brought to the cell at 1 p.m. It usually consisted of a fishy cabbage soup – twice a week the fish was replaced by meat – and either cold millet or barley gruel, accompanied by tea. At 7 p.m., gruel and tea would be brought to the cell for dinner. New arrivals often couldn't bring themselves to eat the food, listlessly chewing on the dark bread alone, but within a few days they learned to eat whatever was served.[2]

Nina had been fortunate in one respect. Her family had managed to establish where she was held. Her mother, or sister, had joined the long line of relatives waiting outside the prison to hand over money to a prison official in the hope that it would reach Nina. If they were lucky, the prison official would agree to pass on the money, but it could take several attempts until a prison acknowledged that the person was being held there.[3] This was often the only way to find out a prisoner's location. If a prison stopped accepting money, it usually meant that the prisoner was either seriously sick or dead or had been moved to another prison or labour camp.

Twice a month, prisoners who had a bit of money could order some basic supplies such as butter, lump sugar, onions, garlic and cigarettes. The cigarettes were handed to the prisoners only after they had been removed from their packet so that the packaging could not be used for writing, which was strictly forbidden. The days on which the prisoners received their orders were like holidays; those able to buy food usually shared their supplies with the less fortunate.

The significance of receiving money went far beyond its material value. Prisoners under investigation were forbidden to communicate with the outside world, but once a month they were allowed the cash. Many prisoners burst into tears when it arrived because it was the only sign of home they could hope for.[4] It meant your loved ones had not cast you off as a traitor but had done everything in their power to find out where you were held – no easy feat, since the NKVD did not volunteer this information.

Nina was brave – or reckless – enough to send a direct sign of life to her family. Someone agreed to act as a go-between, smuggling her tiny notes out of prison. Three of them have survived, measuring about six centimetres square. Prisoners were not allowed to possess any paper or writing implements; hiding a small pencil stub might have been possible, but not ink. But someone, most likely her mother or the go-between, had carefully cut unlined paper into small squares, writing Nina's full name, prisoner's ID number (8690) and that of her cell (No. 99 on one note; No. 42 on two others) on one side.* The paper was then smuggled into Nina's hands. On one of the notes, Nina only dared to give a sign of life by writing her last name. On the other two, written in pencil from cell No. 42, Nina dared to write more. On one, she wrote:

> I have received the things
> I kiss everyone
> healthy
> Nina
> Anisimova
> Send a dressing-gown, dress

* Nina did not write the address: the handwriting is different, most notably in the capital 'A' of her last name. Compared to the handwriting in letters written by her sister Valia and her mother, it resembles her mother's, especially in terms of direction and flow. The quality of the paper and its neatly cut edges suggest that the notes were not improvised but carefully planned.

On the other note Nina wrote: 'I kiss you, my dear ones, Mamochka, Valia, Kostia and Stepa',* followed by a short message vigorously crossed out, leaving only a few words barely legible: 'I await from Mummy', and signed with the words: 'I kiss you, Nina Anisimova.'[5]

Nina had proclaimed herself unmarried during her first interrogation, listing six men as her dearest friends without mentioning any romantic attachment. But her notes paint a very different picture. Konstantin 'Kostia' Derzhavin, the man she had neutrally listed second to last on her list, was much more to her than his place on her list indicated. Nina had carefully evaded the interrogator's demand to give his address, elusively claiming that she only knew that he lived somewhere on Vasilyevsky Island, but not where. The fact that Nina addressed her note to her mother, sister, dog and Kostia seems to indicate that she was not only in a romantic relationship with him, but that he was dear enough to her to be considered family. At the same time, her claim that she was unmarried suggests that their relationship had not been formalised. Reflecting Marxist ideas that traditional family structures would wither away in a socialist society, informal marriages were common and legal in Russia at the time. Many couples considered each other husband and wife without formally registering their relationships. By not revealing that Kostia was special to her, she was probably trying to shield him from the NKVD.

Nina was lucky; someone was looking out for her, enabling her to communicate with her loved ones. She probably wanted

---

* Valia is Nina's sister, Stepa is her dog.

a dressing gown because it could get very hot in the over-crowded cells, and opportunities to wash one's clothes were rudimentary. The accumulated heat inside the cells was unbear-able in summer, but even in winter the atmosphere could be tropical. Two heating engineers incarcerated at the Shpalerka during the Great Terror calculated that the body heat of their cellmates was equivalent to the heat of ten Dutch ovens. In summer, the women would strip down to their underwear and walk around the cell wearing nothing but their slips and bras; they would quickly throw on their dresses whenever they heard the guard scream: 'The head of the block – clothes on!'[6]

Once a week the prisoners were taken to the bathhouse to wash themselves and their underclothes. Back in the cell, the women would shake out their wet clothes, swinging them like flags to dry. Once a week, too, they were given a pair of scis-sors for a few hours to cut their nails. This proved impossible, as the scissors were huge, rusty and completely blunt, but the women devised a way to trim their nails with little pieces of brick, which were kept in the cell to clean the sink, or with glass splinters carefully hidden from the vigilant eyes of the warder. Once in a while they were given two or three needles with which to mend their clothes but had to make their own thread by pulling individual threads out of their jersey underwear. The 'official needles' always miraculously multiplied – their appearance gave prisoners the opportunity to surreptitiously pull out their own needles, which they usually kept hidden in a piece of soap or the lining of a coat.

The prisoners also had to look after their cell. Every morning, the cell's elder, or *starosta*, would assign two differ-ent women to wash the floor, scrape the tables clean, polish the copper sink and kettles until they shone, and to step out of the cell to bring in breakfast from the landing of the stairwell – a box with the bread rations, a bowl with sugar and several kettles with tea.[7]

~

As one day followed another, Nina continued to witness the NKVD's savage interrogation methods. Rape and brutal beatings were a daily reality throughout the Soviet prison and labour camp system. The pregnant poet Olga Berggolts, arrested in December 1938, was beaten badly during interrogation at the Shpalerka, losing her unborn child during the sixth month of pregnancy. Berggolts asked to be taken to a doctor, but her plea was ignored. After she was found unconscious in her solitary-confinement cell, swimming in blood, she was thrown on to a wooden cart and taken to hospital without guard – there was no longer a risk of her escaping. Berggolts made it to the hospital alive.[8] She would live to become the poetic voice of the siege of Leningrad.

Torture took many forms, but one of the most effective methods to break a prisoner's will was also one of the simplest and cleanest: sleep deprivation. Solzhenitsyn wrote that his interrogator broke him using nothing other than sleep deprivation, lies and threats. There are some heroic stories of prisoners withstanding the most brutal methods of physical torture, but it is virtually impossible not to succumb to extended sleep deprivation. Often, two or three days 'on the conveyor' (non-stop interrogation) would be enough to break a prisoner.[9]

Nina Afanasova – a doctor held at the Shpalerka around the same time as Nina Anisimova – remembered the devastating physical and psychological effects of the conveyor for the rest of her life. During her first interrogation, her investigator made her sit on her chair for many hours while he looked through some papers, asking her every once in a while whether she was ready to make a deposition. The following night, Afanasova was again interrogated. This time she had to stand to attention the entire time. She was not allowed to lean against the wall or to relieve her legs by alternating her weight-bearing leg. This was repeated many nights in a row. Afanasova stood for ten, twelve, twenty and finally forty-two hours. She was called a political prostitute, accused of all sorts of crimes including the murder of Kirov, abused with coarse swear words and threatened with torture and execution.

After standing for forty-two hours, Afanasova started to hallucinate. The walls of the office began to move, puppets in colourful dresses sitting on long shelves were sliding up the walls, flashing, disappearing before reappearing an instant later. Long arms and strands of a woman's hair emerged from the open doors of the cupboard holding the investigator's files, swaying and fluttering in the air as if moved by an eerie breeze. Looking at the investigator, Afanasova suddenly saw one of his feet become fat, sporting a bandage that hadn't been there before. When the investigator's renewed shouts finally got through to her, Afanasova agreed to write down a confession, dictated entirely by the investigator. Pleased with the result, the investigator poured Afanasova a cup of tea, served her some rusks and dismissed her with the words: 'Well, now go and sleep.'[10]

An overcrowded prison cell is in itself a form of torture as well, but the solidarity among the political prisoners was also a psychological lifeline that helped combat depression and mental breakdown. Inside Soviet prisons, during the various waves of intensified political repression, the cell could become a safe haven, at least as far as the interaction between political prisoners was concerned. Solzhenitsyn writes how, outside the cell, 'no one had addressed a human word to you. No one had looked at you with a human gaze. All they did was to peck at your brain and heart with iron beaks, and when you cried or groaned, they laughed.' Inside the cell, you were surrounded by human beings who shared your fate and considered you a fellow human being. Remembering his first cell in particular, Solzhenitsyn wrote: 'And those people, who shared with you the floor and air of that stone cubicle during those days when you rethought your entire life, will from time to time be recollected by you as members of your own family. Yes, in those days they were your only family.'[11]

Prisoners looked after cellmates who returned from interrogation more dead than alive. Nina Afanasova recalled how she returned to her cell in the early morning after her first interrogation. After one glance at her, her cellmates led her to a deep niche in one of the walls of their cell, marking a spot where there had once been a door. Sleeping during the day was strictly forbidden, but they told her to lie down immediately after breakfast was brought in, placing a bench in front of the niche. Several prisoners sat down on it to protect Afanasova from unwanted eyes, enabling her to get a few moments of rest. Prisoners would sometimes keep their morning tea, soaking rags in it to bandage the swollen, painful limbs of cellmates who had been tortured. The poet Nikolai Zabolotsky would remember: 'From time to time, prisoners who had already been interrogated would return to the cell; often, they were shoved into the cell in a state of complete exhaustion, and they would fall into our arms; others were almost carried in, and we would then look after those wretches for a long time, applying cold compresses and bringing them back to their senses with water.'[12]

Prisoners also worked together to communicate with other cells. Many political prisoners, worried that their loved ones had also been arrested, were eager to find out whether they were held in the same prison. Prisoners were strictly forbidden to communicate with other cells, but secretly established contact by knocking the prisoners' Morse code against their cell's wall, preferably masked by intentionally loud conversations. According to the writer Varlam Shalamov, the code had been devised by the Decembrists after their failed uprising against the autocracy in 1825. After that, it had been passed on from one generation of Russian revolutionaries to the next. A prisoner had to make a mental image of the Russian alphabet written down in five rows of six letters each. Each letter was communicated by a pair of knocks, the first marking the letter's row, the second its position in the row.[13] The female prisoners at the Shpalerka even found a way to communicate with the male cells across the yard; many of them had husbands incarcerated in the same prison. The conversations were conducted during dusk, in the fading daylight. A woman would stand on the boards used for sleeping that were still piled up against the back wall of the cell. From there, she could see the windows of the male cells. On her forehead she would draw with her hand horizontal lines to signify a letter's row, and vertical lines signifying the letter's position within the row.[14] But the prisoners had to be careful: there was always someone watching, even inside the cells. The NKVD recruited at least one informer – one stool pigeon – in every cell, who would try to influence prisoners, cajole them into cooperating with the investigation and report back on conversations.

∼

There was little to keep prisoners from withdrawing into the depressing space of their own private tragedies. But many were eager to break the monotony of the prison days, not just to fight boredom but also to recuperate some of their psychological resilience. Sliding into depression was dangerous; it decreased your ability to withstand the nightly interrogations. In some cells, the cell elder would try to organise cultural activities, or the prisoners would take their own initiative. Some elders designated a *kul'tstarosta*, 'cultural elder', a prisoner responsible for greeting new arrivals, and for organising *samodeiatel'nost'*, cultural activities.

Professional artists inevitably became the highlight of such endeavours. In all likelihood, Nina performed for her cellmates. Nina Afanasova shared her cell with Tatiana Oppengeim, a dancer with the Maly Theatre who had also been arrested because of her acquaintance with Salomé. Oppengeim's seemingly irrepressible temperament brought some joyful distraction to her cellmates. Her entire cell joined forces to transform any rags they could get their hands on into costumes for Tatiana and Tamara, another imprisoned dancer. Thus dressed up, the two danced to their cellmates' singing or to the sound of spoons beaten against bowls.[15]

In another cell, Viktorin Popov-Raisky (also known as Viktorin Raisky), before his arrest a leading tenor at the Kirov

Opera, quietly performed arias so as not to attract the attention of the guards.[16] Raisky became the elder of cell No. 9. Boris Sokolov, one of his cellmates, would remember him as a tall, good-looking man who courageously pulled himself together; his authority among the prisoners was absolute. During interrogation he was so severely tortured that prison guards had to drag him back into the cell, but Raisky held his ground. One time, his interrogator tried to force him into signing a confession by telling him that his colleague, the opera soloist Lev Vitels, had signed a paper incriminating him before being executed; soon thereafter, Raisky spotted Vitels alive among a group of prisoners who were being led to the bath.[17]

On the day of his arrest, Raisky was due to sing the title role in Tchaikovsky's *Eugene Onegin* at the Kirov,[18] but, like any other Soviet institution during the Great Terror, the Kirov had to cope with the sudden disappearance of its employees. The show had to go on, even if the lead singer had vanished. October 1937 – the month of Raisky's arrest – had been a particularly difficult month for the Kirov in this respect: at least fifteen of its employees disappeared without a trace.[19] All were shot, fourteen of them as spies. From the launch of the mass operations in July 1937 until their end in November 1938, twenty-five employees of the Kirov Theatre were arrested and executed. These numbers do not include those who, like Nina, were arrested and subsequently sent to the camps, exiled or released.*

---

* The death toll goes up to twenty-eight people if one includes the year 1936.

71

The NKVD targeted the Kirov at all levels of the theatre's hierarchy; employees arrested between September 1936 and November 1938 and subsequently executed included the theatre's general director, the head of its personnel department, the head of its artistic production department, the head of safety devices, a senior technician, the head of the theatre's radio relay centre, thirteen artists (four singers, three dancers, six musicians), the person in charge of stage props, a carpenter, two firemen, a set-shifter, a prompter, a porter for the government box, a cashier, a building supervisor and the telephone operator of the fire guard. Statistically, the most dangerous position at the Kirov was the highest: three consecutive directors were arrested, even though two of them had moved on to a different job by the time of their arrest.

The overwhelming majority of executed Kirov employees had been declared guilty of espionage, or of a combination of counter-revolutionary crimes that included espionage. Fourteen were also convicted of belonging to a counter-revolutionary group. This was typical of the Great Terror. Emulating the example of the Moscow show trials, local NKVD chiefs tried to 'unmask' as many counter-revolutionary organisations with links to foreign intelligence organisations as possible.[20] Eleven Kirov employees were shot as members of a theatrical Japanese espionage-sabotage-terrorist group, even though most had even less of a connection to Japan than Nina had to Germany. The NKVD spun a far-fetched tale, claiming that the group of artists from different theatres had spied on behalf of Japan, planned a terrorist attack against Leningrad's party chief Andrei Zhdanov and intended to vandalise the theatres they were working at with arson.[21] According to one source, they were accused of preparing acts of sabotage at the Kirov and Pushkin Theatres to coincide with the twentieth anniversary of the October Revolution.[22]

Alexandra Liubarskaya, an employee at a children's book publisher, was arrested in September 1937 and accused, along with several of her colleagues, of belonging to a Trotskyite spy ring working for Japanese intelligence. She would later remember bitterly:

> They needed spies. It didn't matter for what country. It didn't matter who they were – a watchman of a market garden on the outskirts of the city, or a scholar, or a man of letters, or an editor of books for children. Anyone would do . . . I saw in prison scores of Japanese, Finnish, Polish, 'Latvian' spies, active in our town. That in itself was stunningly implausible. Unless they are sending spies in crowds? . . . One time, when I was being led to interrogation, there was no empty office. I was taken to some kind of chief and sat down in the far corner of his office. The chief was worried about something and didn't even pay attention to me. He was extremely unsatisfied with the work of the investigators standing near him. 'Remember,' he pronounced strictly, 'by the end of the week I need on my desk: 8 Finnish testimonies, 12 German, 7 Latvian, 9 Japanese. From whom – that doesn't matter.'[23]

The reality of political arrests, even before the Great Terror, prompted Moscow's Bolshoi Theatre to keep a file with lists of employees who had been arrested. In 1933–4, eighteen service

personnel and twenty members of the theatre's artistic staff
were arrested. Between 15 September 1937 and 15 March 1938,
forty-seven employees were apprehended, including eighteen
singers and musicians. The theatre administration noted down
possible reasons for the arrest of some, for example having
relatives living in the Chinese town of Harbin. It also compiled
various untitled lists of employees who were at risk of detention
because of 'compromising material' in their biographies; some
of these names reappear on the arrest lists. The most common
'compromising factor' on a list of sixty orchestra musicians was
relatives living abroad. Also mentioned were family origins,
imprisoned relatives, earlier imprisonment, correspondence
with relatives overseas, exclusion from the Communist Party,
former foreign citizenship or a long stay in a foreign country.
On a list of thirty-nine 'endangered dancers', aristocratic origin
was the most common compromising factor.[24]

～

Nina's life was hanging by a thread. Through her acquaintance
with Salomé, the NKVD apparently had enough to connect
her to Nazi Germany. On 29 March 1938, she was again called
up for interrogation.* In this environment, the chances of Nina
surviving were approaching zero.

This time, Nina was not alone; a fellow prisoner, a man
with a long beard who looked vaguely familiar, was also in the
room. His fingernails were disturbingly long, his complexion

---

* I have not seen pages 15–18 of Nina Anisimova's NKVD file,
the pages between her first interrogation and the confrontation
with Levanenok. It is possible that they contained the protocol of
additional interrogation/s.

was the familiar greenish prison grey.[25] Recognition dawned on Nina:

'Do you know the citizen sitting in front of you?'

'Yes, I know him. The citizen sitting in front of me is Levanenok Andrei Anisimovich. A dancer of the Kirov Theatre.'[26]

Levanenok was two years older than her; they had studied at the ballet school at the same time. Levanenok had graduated in 1925, only one year before Nina. They had been colleagues at the Kirov until 26 October 1937, the day Levanenok suddenly disappeared.

Confrontations were a standard method to cajole uncooperative prisoners into confession. Prisoners would be presented with an acquaintance, close friend or relative who had already been forced into confessing and implicating others. The 'cooperative' party had often been badly tortured, threatened or tempted with promises that cooperation would lead to a more lenient sentence. We will never know what exactly Nina saw when she sat opposite Levanenok, but confrontations often shook prisoners to the core, not just because of the sense of betrayal – each prisoner knew only too well what their opposite had been through. There is a story of a Comintern worker who returned to her cell from interrogation, incensed that a close comrade had allegedly betrayed her; the investigator had shown her his testimony in his own handwriting. Before long, she returned from a further interrogation in tears: 'How could I? How could I? Today I had a confrontation with him and I saw not a man, but live raw meat.'[27]

Sitting opposite each other, Nina and Levanenok confirmed that they had been acquainted since childhood, that they had never argued and that neither of them had a private score to settle with the other. Then their versions of the past began to take drastically different turns. The only record of what happened in that room is the protocol written by the investigator – and Nina's fearless protest against the lies it contained. Nina and Levanenok were asked to put their signature next to every statement of theirs to confirm that the protocol had recorded their words correctly. Levanenok signed without protest. But not Nina. In order to establish close links between the two defendants, the protocol claimed that Nina had said: 'We are childhood friends and even danced for a while together on stage', but Nina added defiantly in her neat cursive: 'I don't consider Levanenok a friend.' On the next page, the protocol recorded Levanenok's statement that he had been to Nina's flat, and Nina's confirmation of this fact, but she added at the bottom of the page that this meant nothing: 'I am once more communicating that Levanenok was never my friend.'

Nina probably guessed that inside an NKVD investigator's office, nothing good could come of protestations of friendship by someone who had merely been a colleague. After building a connection between the two dancers that supposedly went beyond the merely professional, the investigator came to the point: he asked Levanenok to confirm his testimony of 26 March about Nina's counter-revolutionary activities against Soviet power.

Nina protested; Levanenok did as told:

I declare that I know that Anisimova is acutely hostile against Soviet power, she has been systematically expressing her hostile attitude towards the leadership of the

VKP (b)* and the Soviet government among the circle of people close to her. She has expressed her opinion that Soviet power will not hold its ground, that instead of the Soviet government a bourgeois government will have to be put in place. Anisimova said that in the impending war between Germany and the USSR, victory will belong to Germany as the technically more advanced country. Anisimova has expressed all kinds of slanderous fabrications directed at the leadership of the VKP (b) and the Soviet government.

The investigator turned to Nina:

'Defendant Anisimova, do you confirm Levanenok's testimony?'

Nina was appalled: 'No, I don't confirm it. This is a brazen lie.'

Prompted to explain how he knew about Anisimova's hostility towards Soviet power and her counter-revolutionary propaganda, Levanenok continued:

We often visited the flat of Salomé E. A. together, an employee of the German general consulate in Leningrad, attending drunken evenings at his place, where usually, as a rule, counter-revolutionary conversations were conducted in which Anisimova took an active part. And in addition to this, in those conversations between us that had political character, I shared her counter-revolutionary

* All-Union Communist Party (Bolsheviks).

mood and opinions completely and to the extent that we got closer and as a result of this, she didn't feel shy in her expressions.

The NKVD was pitting Nina and her former colleague against each other in a struggle for life or death, but Nina refused to be pushed into the role of gladiator. Maybe she had an extraordinary sense of truth that prevailed even under such circumstances; maybe she couldn't rein in her fierce temperament even in this environment. No matter how outraged she might have been by her former colleague's willingness brazenly to slander her in her presence, Nina had spent enough time in prison to be able to guess how Levanenok had ended up in this position. Nina braced herself:

> I categorically deny this. I really was repeatedly at Salomé's with Levanenok. But there were never any drunken evenings there, even though all evenings as a rule included drinks ... And I categorically declare that at these evenings at Salomé's, there was not only no counter-revolutionary talk from my side, but no such conversations were conducted even by Salomé himself. I also never heard any counter-revolutionary talk from Levanenok.

Trying to defend herself against slander, Nina was also protesting her opponent's innocence. It seems almost too fantastical to be true, but given Nina's comments in the margins of the protocol and the future progression of her case, there is no reason to doubt the accuracy of the protocol in this respect. The

investigator ignored Nina's objections, prompting Levanenok
to proceed with his speech about their counter-revolutionary,
terrorist work. One wonders how Levanenok must have felt
when he heard Nina insisting on his innocence, but he had
clearly reached the point of no return. Levanenok repeated his
'testimony' from 26 March 1938: he stated that they had not
undertaken any 'practical steps', unless one counted expound-
ing terrorist ideas among people close to them. But he claimed
that they had approved of Kirov's assassination, which had led
both of them to the conclusion that terrorism was the most
effective way to plunge the Communist Party into turmoil
and to weaken the internal and external position of the USSR.
They had agreed carefully to spread these opinions among
Soviet citizens and had carried out this plan in practice. The
investigator turned to Nina:

'Defendant Anisimova, are you also going to deny this part
of Levanenok's testimony?'

Nina remained steadfast: 'Yes, I deny it. Because it is not
the truth. It's a lie.'

The investigator then prompted Levanenok to talk about
Roman Iakovlevich Galebsky, a White émigré and former officer of the Imperial Army and an acquaintance of Anisimova's
father. Anisimova had supposedly confided to Levanenok that
Galebsky had lived in their flat for some time after his return
to Leningrad in 1929, and that even though he had been sentenced in 1933, he had managed to hide from the investigation
the true motivation for his return to the USSR. Responding
to the investigator's flippant question whether she was also
going to deny this part of Levanenok's testimony, Nina stated
that she had never talked to Levanenok about Galebsky, but

that he had maybe seen him at her flat, although Galebsky had never lived there.

At the end of the confrontation, both prisoners were asked to sign a declaration at the bottom of the protocol confirming that they had read it and that it accurately recorded their words. Nina signed the declaration, but only after neatly adding her protestations. Maybe Levanenok had decided to cooperate in a desperate attempt to avoid being executed as a spy by pushing the investigation in the direction of a much lesser crime – anti-Soviet agitation. If this was his calculation, it would tragically misfire.

~

So many stories ended tragically at this time. Two days after Nina's arrest, Elizaveta – Veta – Dolukhanova, the wife of Nina's old friend Volodia Dmitriev, was arrested at the couple's flat, situated across the street from Nina's building. Admired both for her extraordinary beauty and intelligence, Veta had become a fixture of Leningrad's literary life since moving from her native Georgia to Petrograd in the 1920s. According to contemporary rumours, her popularity attracted the attention of the NKVD, which wanted to recruit the witty salon hostess as a permanent informer. It is believed that Veta was ultimately arrested because she had repeatedly refused. According to official records, she was shot as a spy on 28 June 1938, but the literary scholar and political activist Marietta Chudakova maintains that Veta did not live to the date of her execution, dying under torture during the course of the investigation.[28]

What thoughts must have gone through the minds of family and friends, who were witnessing these disappearances at close quarters? One of the Dmitrievs' neighbours, Lyubov Shaporina, founder of Leningrad's Puppet Theatre and wife of the composer Yuri Shaporin, wrote a dangerously open diary at the time, recording her thoughts so candidly that, if found, the diary alone would have sufficed to land a bullet in her head. Shaporina and the Dmitrievs had many acquaintances in common; Shaporina appears to have known Nina. In the diary, Shaporina describes the scene of Veta's arrest as witnessed by her daughters, mentioning Nina's arrest in the same entry:

> They came at 7 in the morning, they locked them in, they conducted a search. They called the NKVD: 'There is nothing to take here.' Veta, saying goodbye to Tanechka (4 years), said: 'When I return you will already be big.' My daughters (Mara and Galia) were taking a walk in the yard, they saw how Veta was put into the Black Raven. They came back in tears. Anisimova (the ballerina) was arrested. I feel nauseous from the accumulation of crimes in the whole country. The Morlocks* grab their victims, the victims disappear, very many without trace . . .[29]

At the start of the Great Terror, Shaporina recorded her increasing sense of doom: 'And now I have all the time the impression that I'm walking in the middle of Bryullov's painting *The Last Day of Pompeii*. From all sides, there are columns falling one after the other, but there is no end in sight, women are running with terror in the eyes. Infinite weariness.' In

* A humanoid species in H. G. Wells' science fiction novella *The Time Machine*.

October 1937, as more and more people kept disappearing,
she wrote:

> I feel nauseous when I hear calm accounts: so-and-so was
> shot, someone else was shot, shot, shot – the word hangs
> in the air, resonates through the air. People pronounce
> this word completely calmly, as if they were saying: 'He
> went to the theatre.' I think the real meaning of the word
> doesn't penetrate our consciousness, we are only hear-
> ing the sound. Internally, we are not seeing those people
> who are dying under bullets. They are naming Kadatsky,
> Vitels – the singer, he just sang at a competition. Natalia
> Sats – the director of Moscow's Children's Theatre. And
> many others ... I am one of the 'lucky ones', but this
> position – on the abyss of a dark region – is nauseating.
> Deathly nauseating. You are walking around a graveyard
> with freshly dug graves. Who will fall into them, maybe
> you yourself? And this is already so ordinary that it is not
> frightening. The puppets are my sanctuary. A fairy tale. A
> living fairy tale. Lord, have mercy on the living and give
> repose to the dead.[30]

A few days later, Shaporina woke at around 3 a.m. Maybe Nina
and Veta had also woken up, listening to the sounds of the
Terror in the silence of the night:

> There were no trolleybuses, it was completely quiet
> on the street, from time to time, a car drove past.
> Suddenly, there was a burst of fire. After about ten min-
> utes, there was another one. The bursts of shooting with

intermissions of ten, fifteen, twenty minutes continued
until the beginning of the sixth hour. Trolleybuses drove
by, there were beginning to be sounds . . . And our consciousness has become so blunt, that the impression slips
like on a varnished surface. To listen a whole night long
to the execution of some living people, who are probably
innocent – and not go mad. To fall asleep after this, to
go on living as if nothing had happened. What horror.[31]

Writing in her diary on 11 March 1938, as the third show
trial was unfolding, Shaporina described the atmosphere:
'Everybody in Moscow is in such a panic that I really felt sick.
As the peasant women say, my heart choked. An advocate,
Irina's aunt, said that every night around two, three members
of the Bar are arrested . . . but to live in the middle of this is
unbearable. As if you are walking near a slaughterhouse and the
air is saturated with the smell of blood and carrion.'[32]

∾

Nina had resisted the pressure of the investigators. But her
body had paid a price. Two weeks after Nina's confrontation
with Levanenok, on 13 April 1938, Shaporina recorded in her
diary: 'Anisimova's mother brought money to her daughter, a
parcel. They didn't accept the money: "Your daughter is in hospital, come back next time, if she comes out of hospital we will
give it to her." No matter how much the unhappy woman went
around pleading, she didn't find out anything. A stone wall.'[33]

5

The Journey

Nina's mother feared for her daughter's life. But ever since the day of Nina's arrest, she was not alone in her worries – Konstantin 'Kostia' Derzhavin had been by her side. Kostia had been in love with Nina for the past two years, but their lives had run on parallel tracks long before that. Nina had been eight and Kostia fourteen years old when the October Revolution broke out. Ironically, the total chaos that followed had enabled each of them to pursue their love for the theatre.

Kostia was the only child of Nikolai Sevastianovich Derzhavin, a well-known though somewhat contentious Slavist, and his wife Maria Ivanovna, a hereditary noblewoman. Nikolai Sevastianovich was a prominent member of Leningrad's intelligentsia. He had demonstrated his allegiance to the Bolshevik regime in the early years of the revolution. A stocky, middle-aged man with drooping cheeks and thoughtful, bespectacled eyes, he resembled a melancholic walrus. He had earned respect as a capable head of various university departments and institutes, but mean tongues whispered that he was a conformist and careerist. Some even insinuated that, in 1931, he had been elected an academician of the influential Soviet Academy of Sciences without the customary probation period purely because of his unwavering support for the Soviet Union's leading linguist, Nikolai Marr.[1]

Kostia shared his father's love for languages and literature, but his inclinations were much more artistic. In June 1918, fifteen-year-old Kostia enrolled in Vsevolod Meyerhold's newly founded Instructor's Courses in the Training in the Craft of Stage Productions, Kurmastsep.[2] Within a year, he would become one of Meyerhold's favourite students and his trusted secretary. The iconoclastic avant-garde director Meyerhold was one of the few cultural heavyweights who had immediately thrown their weight behind the October Revolution. While the cultural establishment and the intelligentsia were mostly refusing to collaborate with the Bolsheviks, some avant-garde artists saw the revolution as a train speeding towards the future and were pushing to get on it.[3] Meyerhold soon institutionalised his position as a key figure in revolutionary theatre as deputy head of the Petrograd Theatre Department (TEO) of Narkompros, the Bolshevik commissariat in charge of education and culture.

Established under the auspices of TEO, the Instructor's Courses were supposed to attract new forces 'from the democratic masses' to the theatre, and to train them as directors, stage designers and instructors for the country's burgeoning new drama groups.[4] In the middle of civil war, Kostia threw himself into the exciting world of Petrograd's revolutionary theatre with all the enthusiasm of his young years. His native city was turning from a bustling imperial capital into a silent ghost town. By June 1918, Petrograd's population had shrunk from 2.5 million to 1.5 million. People were fleeing or dying of hunger and disease. By 1920, there would be only 750,000 people left in the city.[5] But cold and hunger could not kill Kostia's thirst for the stage. And he was not alone. In the midst of chaos and death, Russia began to act. Amateur and professional drama clubs, studios, workshops and schools multiplied like mushrooms after a rainy day.

The October Revolution catapulted young Kostia to the front line of the avant-garde's utopian project to reform humanity and rebuild the world through radical cultural transformation. Kostia and his fellow students were supposed to form a theatrical vanguard that would guide Russia's acting mania into revolutionary channels, but Meyerhold was basically just adapting his radical artistic ideas to the Bolsheviks' ideological requirements. Kostia and his cohort – which included Volodia Dmitriev – would become important collaborators in Meyerhold's search for a revolutionary people's theatre supposed to attract new, non-bourgeois audiences. Just as a star scientist would attract talented assistants to work with him, their laboratory was devoted to the ultimately impossibly task of creating a stable compound out of avant-garde art and Bolshevism.

In 1919, Meyerhold was replaced at Kurmastsep by a former student, twenty-seven-year-old Sergei Radlov. That same year, Kostia started to act as double of the circus acrobat 'Serge' (Alexander Alexandrov) at Radlov's newly founded, experimental People's Comedy Theatre, constantly practising his circus tricks with the acrobat.[6] Homeless adolescents, working-class families, soldiers, sailors and janitors would carelessly spit sunflower seeds on the asphalt floor, roaring with laughter as they watched Serge in the play *The Adoptee* escape up a rope from acrobat-policemen trying to seize him and the secret papers he was supposed to deliver to a group of revolutionaries. Radlov proudly claimed that not a single old-school intellectual had been to his theatre or knew his plays, which Petrograd's homeless teenagers knew by heart.

For most of 1919, Petrograd had been threatened by approaching White armies, but by spring 1920 the city and its surrounding territory were firmly under Bolshevik control. Eager to boost the former capital's standing, Petrograd's party boss Grigory Zinoviev funded artists to stage revolutionary mass spectacles, the most dramatic product of the avant-garde's alliance with Bolshevism, intended to outshine all other festivals being staged across Russia. The party was taking up the artists' fantasy of transforming humanity by letting art spill out into the streets.

Oscillating between inspiration and madness, Petrograd's artists had become intoxicated by the revolutionary city's symbolism, enthusing that life and art were about to merge into a revolutionary whole. Petrograd would become the hero of its own drama, and the harbinger of a new civilisation. Creatively, these were the most exciting years in Kostia's life. By the third anniversary of the October Revolution, he had reached the pinnacle of his directorial career. On 7 November 1920, the seventeen-year-old stood inside a command booth erected next to the Alexander Column on the vast square in front of the Winter Palace. Kostia was one of five co-directors about to conduct the crowning achievement of the avant-garde's theatrical experiments. Ready to press electronic switches and to shout commands through a telephone as if they were generals commanding their battalions, they were about to choreograph 10,000 soldiers, sailors, actors and extras, as well as the cruiser *Aurora*, in a mass spectacle reimagining the storming of the Winter Palace of 1917, accompanied by an orchestra of 500 musicians.

The actual storming of the Winter Palace had been a much less grandiose affair. Bolshevik troops had simply entered it and arrested the remainder of the Provisional Government. Over the next couple of days, rumours of the tsar's legendary wine cellar had quickly made the rounds. The Bolsheviks had tried unsuccessfully to control the drunken vandalising by pumping the wine out on to the street, but the crowds simply threw themselves on the ground to lap up the wine from the gutter.[7] The extravagant re-enactment of 7 November was supposed to replace people's disjointed memories of the Bolshevik coup in October 1917 with a heroic myth of revolutionary creation.

Also inside the command booth was the avant-garde artist Yuri Annenkov, who had designed the production's sets and costumes. Only that morning, two enormous stages connected by a steep bridge had been erected under torrential rain in front of the arch of the General Staff Building, but Annenkov feared they would collapse once thousands of actors attempted to climb on to them.[8] Despite the awful weather, approximately 100,000 people had streamed into the square and were standing behind rope fences with their back to the Winter Palace, looking expectantly at the two massive stages reaching up to the third floor of the General Staff Building. Abstract factories marked the stage on the left as the 'red platform', while a stylised throne room on the 'white platform' stood for the 'reactionary forces' of the Provisional Government.

At 10 p.m., a cannon boomed through the night. The pageant had started. To the accompaniment of the 'Marseillaise' and waltzes, a motley crowd of bankers, merchants, crippled soldiers and ladies surrounded Alexander Kerensky, head of the Provisional Government, and a group of high officials, who were bobbing their heads in meaningless agreement. Meanwhile, on the red platform, Vladimir Lenin and his comrades were gradually rousing a passive crowd of workers, transforming them into Red Guards to the stirring sounds of revolutionary songs. The two sides clashed on the bridge connecting the red and white platforms. Cars carrying the Provisional Government raced across the square towards the palace, pursued by lorries packed with Red Guards armed with machine guns.

The moment had come for the cruiser *Aurora* to re-enact her historic part. Up in the command booth, a button was pressed: a salvo from the *Aurora* pierced through the night, but then came a second shot, and a third. The directors jabbed their fingers on the button, but the salvo continued – the electric connection to the cruiser had gone down. As gunshots mixed with the never-ending cannonade, a man in the crowd of spectators mumbled sarcastically that there hadn't been that many shots in October 1917. Pushing his way through the enormous audience on a bike, an assistant finally managed to signal to the cruiser to stop shooting. For their creative re-enactment of world history, Kostia and his co-directors received a tobacco ration of 100 cigarettes and two kilos of frozen apples.[9]

∼

Improbable as it may sound, the world of ballet and that of Petrograd's revolutionary theatrical avant-garde were closely intertwined. Perhaps many of Kostia's fellow students felt an intrinsic affinity for ballet because they had internalised

Meyerhold's credo that actors needed to be trained through movement. Maybe they were simply young men, receptive to the dancers' graceful beauty.

Kostia had been attracted to the world of ballet from his early days in Kurmastsep. By the time Nina was finishing her second year at the school, Kostia had added ballet lessons to his intensive efforts to master circus acrobatics. To please his parents, he was studying literature and Romance languages at Petrograd University, but his ambitions continued to revolve around the stage. With his Kurmastsep colleague Vladimir 'Volodia' Dmitriev, he was working on two productions: Pushkin's plays *The Stone Guest* and *Scenes from Times of Chivalry*. But his thoughts were turning towards uncharted waters. In June 1921, Kostia wrote to Meyerhold in Moscow: 'My thinking is nevertheless shifting the centre of gravity of my work towards directing ballets . . . There are no choreographers at the moment, and there is no ideological culture among the masses of the ballet workers. There is a fertile field for work for me here.'[10]

❧

Nina and Kostia met for the first time in June 1936 at the premiere of Nina's first ballet, *Andalusian Wedding*. They certainly had plenty to talk about. Apart from many common acquaintances, their professional interests had followed parallel paths for the past couple of years. As Nina worked on *The Flames of Paris*, Kostia was putting the finishing touches to his first major publication, a history of the theatre of the French Revolution. While Nina was becoming increasingly interested in Spain, Kostia was publishing a book on Cervantes and

Don Quixote.* When they met, Kostia was the head of the literary section at the former Alexandrinsky Theatre,† now known as the Pushkin Theatre.[11] Their worlds were merging: Nina's first major success in a Soviet ballet, Thérèse in *The Flames of Paris*, had been supervised by Kostia's former mentor Sergei Radlov, and Kostia was already acquainted with Vladimir Solovyov, the director of *Andalusian Wedding*.

Kostia began to court Nina by inviting her to a performance of the ballet *Esmeralda* at the Kirov. He had obtained some of the best seats in the house for his new romantic interest, in the third row of the stalls. To treat a Kirov dancer to prime seats at the Kirov might seem curious, but Kostia's choice appealed to Nina. Before long, she agreed to meet him in Feodosia on the Crimean Black Sea Coast. While Kostia was trying to make out whether the tall figure slowly coming into focus on the pier was indeed his Nina, Nina was watching the approaching steamboat on which he was arriving, and it seemed the most marvellous steamboat she had ever seen. On another trip they went to Batumi, on the Georgian Black Sea Coast, admiring a silver fox which had appeared out of nowhere, basking in the warm sun next to the dark-blue sea.[12]

By the time of Nina's arrest, the couple had been in love for several years. Like many of their contemporaries, however, they

---

* Before *Andalusian Wedding*, Nina had flexed her choreographic muscle with an evening at the Leningrad Philharmonic titled 'Spanish Suite' (1935).

† Kostia held this position from 1933 until 1936.

had not rushed into officially registering their relationship. They had been living their own independent lives, both professionally and privately – Nina with her mother and sister on the Petrograd Side, Kostia with his parents on Vasilyevsky Island. Maybe the decision not to live together had been driven by practical considerations: given the chronic housing shortage, it was difficult for young couples to get their own space. Neither might have been keen formally to move in with the other's family. It is therefore impossible to be sure of the depth of Nina's attachment to Kostia at the time of her arrest. Possibly, Volodia Dmitriev and Kostia were not the only former – or current – lovers on that list of male friends. Was Nina really shielding Kostia by naming him second to last, or had he not yet managed to defeat potential competitors for her affection?

There are some circumstantial facts that raise questions: during the search of her room, the NKVD confiscated a bank savings book in the name of Mikhail Konstantinovich Kalatozov, a film director, for the sum of 1,533 roubles and thirteen kopeks. It included a power of attorney, which allowed Anisimova to draw money from the account. To the NKVD investigator, Nina listed Kalatozov last, right after Kostia. Maybe the two men named last were the significant ones in her life at the time of her arrest.

But there is no doubt that, for Kostia, Nina was the love of his life. Only unwavering commitment would have propelled him to act as he did following her arrest, focusing all his determination on convincing the NKVD that Nina was innocent.

On 7 February 1938, five days after Nina's arrest, Kostia was sitting opposite Saul Gantman, head of a section of the Leningrad NKVD. Gantman had no inclination to help Kostia.

Instead, he seemed to take pleasure in conveying to Kostia that Nina's fate was completely up to the whims of the secret police. He revelled in his sense of omnipotence: 'We don't intend to release Anisimova, but once we have investigated her case, maybe we will release her, maybe we will impose some sort of punishment on her, but neither one nor the other will depend on the degree of her guilt.'[13]

Kostia refused to give up. He was stubborn, he was meticulous, and he did not care about his own safety. Ignoring Gantman's warning that nothing could be done to influence the progress of the investigation because it was irrelevant whether or not Nina was guilty, he decided to try other channels. He did what he did best, and set forth his arguments in writing. Kostia wrote to Leonid Zakovsky, already the head of the Moscow NKVD at the time, but until January 1938 the head of the Leningrad NKVD. He wrote to Boris Pozern, procurator of Leningrad province and, as such, a member of the province's three-person special *troika*. He even wrote to Andrei Vyshinsky, procurator of the USSR. Kostia developed a series of arguments to prove the impossibility of charging Nina with any article of the Criminal Code in general, and with any of the counter-revolutionary crimes listed in article 58 in particular.

He continued to push Nina's case in person, using his and his father's contacts where possible. On 22 February, Kostia met Assistant Procurator Izraelit of the special department of the Procuracy for Leningrad province. Comrade Izraelit shiftily declared that Nina's case was a difficult one because it had multiple layers and side-stories. A month later, on 27 March, two days before Nina's confrontation with Levanenok, Kostia met with Naum Rozovsky, the senior military procurator of the Red Army.[14]

Kostia was playing with fire: his unflinching support for an enemy of the people showed that he trusted his own judgement more than the authorities. The chances of improving her lot were remote, while the risk of getting himself arrested increased with every meeting. One woman lobbying on behalf of her husband later described how she was called to the NKVD at midnight to receive a dressing-down: 'I order you to stop running about like a lunatic trying to get your husband released! I order you to stop bothering us! That's all! Get out!'[15] Kostia was not even Nina's legal husband. His determination to leave no stone unturned to get Nina released at a time when fear compelled many to distance themselves from arrested loved ones was extraordinary.

～

The wheels of the NKVD continued to turn. The indictment of Nina's case, dated 17 April 1938, summarised the NKVD's 'findings', detailing her interactions with Salomé and her supposed counter-revolutionary conversations and activities between 1928 and 1934: Nina had consorted with Salomé, the 'resident' of German intelligence in Leningrad; they had visited each other in their flats; Salomé had introduced Nina to the German consuls Walther and Sommer; Salomé had given her presents. Counter-revolutionary conversations were a central feature of the gatherings at Salomé's; Nina had taken active part in them, spreading defamatory fabrications about the leadership of the CPSU in general and Stalin in particular; within a close circle of acquaintants, Nina had spoken favourably of

a Soviet defeat and the establishment of a bourgeois government, approved of Kirov's assassination and expressed support
for terrorism as the most effective way to sow confusion within
the ranks of the Party and to weaken the internal and external
situation of the Soviet Union. With Andrei Levanenok, she
had carefully spread these ideas among Soviet citizens; she
had also known about the counter-revolutionary work of the
former White officer R. Galebsky, who had emigrated from
Russia in the wake of the revolution but returned in 1929 and
been sentenced in 1933.

According to the indictment, Nina had admitted only
her connection to employees of the German consulate. On
all other counts, she had been 'unmasked' by Levanenok during his own interrogation and during their confrontation.
Although Nina had been arrested on suspicion of espionage,
the investigation had shifted to anti-Soviet agitation and to
belonging to a counter-revolutionary organisation. In the end,
Nina was charged only with conducting counter-revolutionary
and terrorist propaganda (par. 58-10), but not with belonging to a counter-revolutionary organisation. On the same day,
Kolesnikov informed Nina that the investigation was now
closed. Her case was about to be passed on to the Special
Council of the USSR NKVD for judgment, but it looked
unlikely that she would be shot as a spy. Incredibly, perhaps,
Kostia's gamble was paying off.

On 27 May, Comrade Shmulevich, military procurator
of the Leningrad Military District, examined Nina's file and
found that the investigation had not established concrete facts
of espionage. Shmulevich concluded that Nina was socially
dangerous because of her connections to Salomé and because

she had conducted counter-revolutionary agitation. Her case was passed to the Special Council.[16]

～

Levanenok had not been that lucky. On 21 May 1938, at 2.40 p.m., he was led before a closed session of the war tribunal of the Leningrad Military District to stand trial for espionage on behalf of Nazi Germany. Comrade Marchenko, the chairman of the tribunal, read out the indictment, accusing the thirty-year-old dancer of having passed sensitive military information to the Germans. Levanenok had reached the point of no return: 'I understand the accusation. I do not confess guilty of espionage because I did not engage in espionage. I am only guilty of having known Salomé.'

The tribunal ignored his declaration that his confession had been extracted by force and reiterated the outlandish scenario fabricated by the NKVD, stating that Levanenok had used performance tours as a cover for collecting military intelligence. They took no notice of the ballet dancer's desperate cry that he didn't even understand what they were talking about: 'I don't know what the term "military preparedness" means . . . I was forced to sign this protocol.'

Levanenok not only tried to plead for his own life, but to qualify the testimony about others that had been extracted from him: 'Dudinskaya, Mikhailov and Kuznetsova were guests at Salomé's, but I cannot say anything about their acquaintance and meetings with Sommer, because I don't know about this.' Levanenok had clung to the possibility of protesting in court, but he was stripped of such hope brutally swiftly. At 4.30, the tribunal proclaimed Levanenok guilty of espionage and sentenced him to the highest punishment. He was executed by shooting on 25 July 1938.*[17]

Given the NKVD's obsession with unmasking large conspiracies, it is miraculous that Levanenok's case wasn't blown up into a large spy ring of Kirov dancers. And considering Nina's association with him, it is equally miraculous that she did not share his fate.

~

Levanenok's corpse was thrown into a mass grave. Nina was still alive, waiting day after day for her verdict as spring turned into summer. The summer of 1938 was unusually hot in Leningrad, and it became almost unbearable in her cell.[18] Eventually (the exact date is unknown) she was called up to present herself 'with belongings'. The time had come to leave the House of Preliminary Detention on Shpalernaya Street. She wasn't taken far – just across the Neva lay Leningrad's women's prison on Arsenalnaya 9, a five-storey red-brick building built in the 1880s at the same time, and by the same architect, as the adjacent Kresty prison on Arsenalnaya 7. Separated from the riverbank only by the street and another

* Thanks to the work of the Centre 'Vozvrashchennye imena', Andrei Levanenok was rehabilitated sixty-four years later, on 21 November 2002: it was officially acknowledged that Levanenok had been innocent because the case against him had been fabricated. His father Anisim and his mother Efrosinia died in June and May 1942 during the siege of Leningrad. His only brother Aleksey, a Red Army soldier, also died in 1943. His sister appears to be the only one who survived the Terror and Second World War (name search in electronic database, *Kniga pamiati 'Blokada'*, http://visz. nlr.ru/blockade; Levanenok's sister is the only member of his immediate family who does not appear in the database, accessed 29 December 2020).

forbidding red-brick wall, the grey cupola of the church inside the Kresty's administrative building was widely visible, even though its cross had been taken down after the revolution. The poet Anna Akhmatova's poetic immortalisation of the Great Terror starts in a line outside the Kresty, where her son was imprisoned:

> In the fearful years of the Yezhov terror I spent seventeen months in prison queues in Leningrad. One day somebody 'identified' me. Beside me, in the queue, there was a woman with blue lips. She had, of course, never heard of me; but she suddenly came out of that trance so common to us all and whispered in my ear (everybody spoke in whispers there): 'Can you describe this?' And I said: 'Yes, I can.' And then something like the shadow of a smile crossed what had once been her face.[19]

Once again, heavy prison gates closed after Nina. She was led through a gloomy courtyard, flanked by dark buildings surrounded by an equally dark fence six to seven metres high topped by barbed wire. Watchtowers with armed sentries were located in the corners of the yard. Nina was initially taken to the investigation wing. A female prisoner would later remember entering a cell in this wing in November 1938:

> I enter through a narrow, heavy door bound with iron. Before me is a small cell a metre and a half wide, about four metres long, approximately three metres high. Dirty-yellow plastered walls, a cement floor, a dark-green door with a peephole for the warder and a wooden hatch

for the distribution of dinner. A small window with bars and a screen right under the ceiling. Along the walls two narrow bunks with shields. In the left-hand corner in the back a lavatory pan not screened off by anything. Next to it a water tap with a small sink. Under the window a bedside table, a stool and a small cupboard for dishes and provisions, all in the same dark-green. When I entered, there were five people in the cell.[20]

Days at the women's prison were similar to days at the Shpalerka, but at least the prisoners' walks took place in a yard about twice the size.[21]

∾

Although he feared he was running into nothing but brick walls, Kostia was never far behind the investigation. On 9 June he managed to meet Shmulevich, who emphasised that the investigation had not established any facts of espionage but maintained that Nina had caused harm simply by virtue of her connection to Salomé. For this alone, Shmulevich thought that Nina should be punished with eight years in a camp. Luckily, the Special Council proved more lenient: on 4 August 1938, Nina was branded a socially dangerous element and sentenced to five years in a corrective labour camp.[22]

Strictly speaking, this wasn't a proper 'sentence'. The NKVD's Special Council was an administrative organ serving as a convenient tool of extrajudicial administrative repression, bypassing the courts of the regular legal system. Its origins lay in tsarist Russia: in the 1880s, a Special Council had been created under the auspices of the Ministry of Interior that had the power to send people into exile for one to five years. The Soviet secret police expanded the imperial practice of extrajudicial administrative punishment to an unimaginable scale. During the Great Terror, the NKVD's Special Council supported the work of the extrajudicial *troikas*. While the *troikas* could hand out any punishment, including death sentences, the Special Council had the more limited ability to deport and exile, and to imprison people deemed dangerous to society in a camp for up to eight years.* Not bound by any legal norms, it could focus exclusively on speed – sometimes it decided over 1,000 cases in a single session, conveniently in the absence of the accused, who lacked the right to any form of legal defence.[23] In the camps, the inmates joked: 'There is no court for nothing – for that there is an OSO [Special Council].'[24]

≈

On 9 September, more than a month later, Nina was finally informed of her sentence.

11 September

My dear Mamochka, Kostia and Valia.

I now have the right to write to you and to receive letters from you every day . . . I received my sentence on 9 September I have the right to appeal to the Moscow Special Council. I am healthy I feel strong and I beg you,

* After the re-organisation of the Soviet secret police into the NKVD in 1934, the Special Council was formed with the right to condemn people to up to five years of imprisonment or exile. As of April 1937, this was extended to eight years.

my loved ones dear ones not to worry about me. Thank you for all your troubles and efforts on my behalf. Every minute, I think about all of you and live in the hope to see you soon. I kiss you strongly.

I really ask Kostia to look after my beloved Mamochka and to not let her fall apart. Otherwise I will feel very miserable. Collect all my sheet music and theatrical costumes from work and my partner so that nothing is lost. Put soap in the package. I hope we will see each other soon!

I kiss you strongly Mamochka, Valia and Kostia.

Your Nina Anisimova

My address: Arsenalnaya 9 prison No. 3[25]

Nina was alive, and not ready to give up. She was planning to appeal to the Moscow Special Council as soon as she reached the camp.* For the past seven months, Nina had been reduced to a case number, a piece of human grain to be ground by the NKVD's machinery. At least she was now able to communicate with her family; if she was lucky, she might even see them before starting her long journey. In the 'fixed-period block' (*srochnyi korpus*), the wing reserved for those who had received their sentences, prisoners were allowed to see visitors while waiting to be put on a transport. Nina wrote to her family that there were two more visiting days that month, 16 and

---

* In her first letter, written on 11 September, she mentions that she has the right to appeal. In her second letter, written on 19 September to Kostia, she writes that she will appeal once she has arrived in the camp.

26 September. Nothing in her fluid, neat handwriting gave away the turmoil of emotions she must have felt.

Across the Neva, the leaves in the Summer Garden were beginning to change colour. The Kirov Ballet was preparing for its new theatrical season. Walking to the theatre under the northern autumn sky along Leningrad's canals, Nina's colleagues could delight in the crisp reflection of the city's façades in the water. Nina did not know where she would be sent or whether she would ever come back. There was not much time to take charge of the fragments of her former life. For Nina, this not only meant preparing for a future that lay beyond her imagination; it also meant fighting to preserve something to come back to. The thought of her sealed-off room filled her with anxiety. Her property had not been confiscated, but would a power of attorney be enough to enable her family to unlock her room, and to hold on to it in a city notoriously short of living space?* There were many people eager to move into the empty rooms of those who had disappeared. Some were even denouncing their neighbours in the crowded communal flats because they coveted their living space.

About to embark on a journey into the Soviet Union's parallel universe of labour camps, Nina had no idea whether she would be able to communicate with her family once she had arrived at her final destination. Her thoughts were predominantly with her loved ones, but also with her former self: Nina, the dancer and budding choreographer. Underneath her stormy temperament lay an iron strength that had enabled

---

* Nina's worry about the future of her room is a recurring theme in her initial letters.

her to emerge from the Shpalerka humiliated but not broken. Preparing for the geographic separation from her former life, her costumes and sheet music became physical placeholders of her artistic essence: they embodied her hope that one day she would return to her home, and to her theatre. Waiting to be put on a prisoners' transport, Nina continued to think like an artist. Limiting her first letter to the essentials, Nina had instructed Kostia to collect all her sheet music and theatrical costumes so that they would not be lost. After seven months in prison, her dancing career still took precedence over the indignities of daily life as a prisoner.

～

A few days later, the warder opened the door to her cell. Nina was led down the long prison corridors into a room bisected by a wooden structure topped by ceiling-high wire meshing. Within this were rudimentary cubicles separated from each other by a narrow plank. Each cubicle had its own meshed window. Behind one of them, Nina could make out Kostia's face.[26]

When she finally saw Kostia, Nina allowed herself to let go, at least to the extent that this was possible in a crowded prison meeting room. It was a brief meeting, but for the first time since her arrest Nina felt that she was not alone. Later she wrote to Kostia: 'After I saw you, I really calmed down, many thanks that you came. It's so nice to know that you are worrying about me and that Mamochka and Valia are not alone.'[27]

Yet the relief was only temporary. Nina was struggling with herself: on the one hand, she yearned to draw strength from the knowledge that Kostia would continue to love and miss her – and to push her case and take care of her mother and sister. But could she expect him to dedicate five years of his life to an enemy of the people locked up in a remote camp? Nina poured out her doubts on paper, pushing aside any fears that the censor would read her innermost thoughts. Her second letter from prison was to Kostia. Nina's writing was much smaller than usual, covering a checked notebook page in neat lines closely packed together: 'Sometimes I think that all of this is a great burden for you, and wonder whether you will be able to endure all of this. Know that I will never resent you if your life will somehow turn out differently. Five years is a long time and there is no point for you to ruin your life because of me.'[28]

But, having calmed her conscience, Nina immediately pleaded that he wouldn't take up her offer: 'If you really love me and if you will wait, then know that everything good and happy that will be in my future life, I will give to you and that I will never forget you and your concern about me. Forgive me that I am writing all this to you, don't be offended. When a person has a great sorrow, he looks at everything in a deeper and stricter way.' Nina, as impulsive and impatient as she was spirited and creative, felt that the horrors of the past seven months had changed her irrevocably: 'I have become many years older than I am. I have learned to control my impulses, to wait and I have understood genuine human relations. And I have understood that there are fake and real friends. No matter how bitter this is, this is the way it is. What is there to say about them, I will cross them once and for all out of my heart!'[29] In Stalinist Russia, standard workplace clashes of ambition and personality could easily turn into vicious vendettas that could end in arrest and death. Unsavoury characters within every Soviet institution relished the opportunity to further their careers under the cloak of patriotic duty, 'unmasking' their competitors as enemies of the people. Perhaps Nina's colleagues had done the same to her.

But Nina's new-found seriousness had not obliterated her old vivacity. Just as she was thinking bitterly about her former colleagues and the Kirov's theatrical intrigues, she heard the warder at the door: 'They opened the door now and brought a letter from you, now this is a great joy, I almost started dancing. You are such a dear, it's only a pity that the letter is so short. To the camp write long letters, how you are living, how Mamochka and Valia are doing.' Whenever Nina's playfulness gained the upper hand, thoughts about her other big love, her dog Stepa, were not far off. 'Stepa has probably grown a lot and become a big walker. Kiss him strongly, strongly on the nose – and look after him until my return home ... I often think about how you go for walks with Stepa and what he looks like now. Whether he's still so funny and splay-footed. Write whether he's been to the dacha and how he behaved himself.'[30]

Nina could not indulge in daydreams for long. She was worried about the material burden of her imprisonment on her family. She could no longer support her sixty-year-old widowed mother, who only received a small pension for her father's Red Army service. Her thirty-five-year-old sister Valia had her own worries: her husband Mikhail Kontorovich, a military engineer, had also been arrested and sent to the camps. At least at the time of Nina's arrest, Valia had been without a permanent job.*

---

* In the two questionnaires recording personal details included in Nina's NKVD file, Nina does not give a profession or place of employment for Valia.

Nina already understood that her chances of survival would increase if her family managed to send food and clothes to the camp, but for this they would need money. She had sent her mother a list of everything she would need, but this was partially contingent on being able to get into her room. Nina was counting on Kostia to get the NKVD to remove the seal: 'I am very worried how Mummy and Valia will arrange themselves with the room, I fully rely on you, because I don't understand anything about this question and cannot help. Don't desert them and visit them more often.' Once her room was open, her mother would be able to send her some things and maybe sell others for cash, if Kostia could manage to convince her.[31]

Nina's readiness to rely on Kostia supports the theory that she had concealed the true nature of their relationship during the investigation. His commitment to her was astonishing: the Soviet state had preached for years that a person's loyalty was first to the state, and then to family. During the Great Terror, fear or expedience convinced many to turn away from family or lovers, publicly renouncing their ties to the condemned. But not Kostia.

There was a lot to organise, but Nina could not limit her mind to practicalities alone. Coming to the end of her letter, she pushed her new persona – Nina the Convict – into the background, reverting to the professional kinship between Kostia the Writer and Nina the Dancer/Choreographer: 'Write what book you are planning to write ... I believe and hope that I will again work and dance. I have a lot of strength now and I am convinced that I will soon return to my work and that I will manage to stage a good, big ballet in the future, and if my legs won't get ruined, also dance.' Thinking of her profession brought back memories of her artistic comrades-in-arms. Nina refused to accept that she was now an outcast whom people might shrink from. Defiant, she wrote to Kostia: 'Regards to the boys, and to everyone who hasn't forgotten me.' The thought of leaving focused her thoughts on her loved ones, and on her artistic placeholders in Leningrad, her costumes: 'I kiss you all. To meeting each other soon. Write whether Mummy needs a power of attorney for my salary. And take my costumes from the workshop and work.'[32]

∾

Nina had barely finished the letter when the warder told her to pack her things. The time had come to move to the fixed-period block.* By some accounts, the building housing this wing was less gloomy: its windows were larger, and although they were still disfigured by the obligatory prison bars, they were at least not covered by screens. From some of the cells, one could catch a glimpse of children playing ball games in the yard opposite.[33]

> My dear, beloved Mamulya, Kostia and Valia,
>
> I've been transferred to the fixed term b. I think that any day I will leave for the camp, where to, I don't know. I would really like to see you all before my departure, but I'm afraid that I won't manage because I didn't know the exact schedule of the meeting days and only found it

---

* Nina's second letter is dated 19 September. Her third letter is not dated but it is likely that she wrote it on 19 September as well since it includes 20 September in her list of visiting days.

out now. The days are the 20th, 25th, 26th and 29th. If I already won't be here on the 25th, let Mamochka find out in the meeting room in the *propusk** office where I've been sent to.[34]

Getting the NKVD to unseal her room took absolute priority. She might be put on a transport any day now. Nina had sent a power of attorney to her mother, but was leaving another in case the first one had been lost. She instructed her mother to pick up the power of attorney on the meeting day on 25 September in the *propusk* office and to go to the NKVD's housing office, next to the Bolshoi Dom, to hand in an application to have Nina's room unsealed. Once the room had been opened, her mother should sell whatever was necessary.

Since Nina had no idea where she was going, it was difficult to anticipate what she would need. For the time being, she asked her mother to send her galoshes, warm stockings, gaiters, black shoes, two dresses (a grey one and a lightweight black one), a skirt, a cardigan, her nightshirt and underwear. She knew it would be foolish to take too much on her journey – not just because of the physical burden, but also because things might get stolen. As it was, she already had two large bundles to carry. If her family managed to visit her one more time, they could bring her the most urgent items (and five roubles) and send anything else to the camp.

---

* A *propusk* is an official document, a pass that grants the permission to live in a place or the right to enter a certain institution such as a place of work or study.

Although she was worried about her mother's health, Nina was determined to sound brave and full of hope: 'I feel well, calm and confident.' Now that her departure was imminent, any valiant thoughts of releasing Kostia from any obligation evaporated: 'I hope that my dear and only husband will not abandon me and you and that we will see each other again and be happy.'[35] Nina's emphasis on Kostia's status as her husband rings with a special gravity. Probably responding to her last letter, Kostia must have vowed his commitment to her as she was about to be put on a prisoners' transport; he had made it clear that he intended to act as Nina's husband, not just privately but before the eyes of the world.

Nina was trying to brace herself for the future, but found it impossible to disconnect from the core of her former identity. Trying to forget the past in order to cope with the present, she nonetheless drew strength from the hope that she would one day return to her former life. Such psychological acrobatics were inevitably confusing. In a reflex action, she added ballet shoes to the urgent items to be sent to the labour camp upon her arrival, but then talked in the same breath about the need to forget her former life:

And now I am going to a new difficult life. Everything that was – my career, my theatre, my home all this was left behind, I'm not allowing myself to remember it. I have enough strength to endure this difficult ordeal, I am still young and will be able to return everything to myself, to vindicate myself and to work again for my beloved art. The only thing important to me is to know that you love me, that you are all alive healthy and that all is well with you. Strongly kiss my boys: I am wishing them a happy life. I ask Mamochka to look after her health, even if only for my sake. I ask Valia not to argue with Mummy and not to leave her. In everything I rely on Kostia, he will help you. I am kissing Kostia strongly strongly, thank you for everything that is good. Look after Stepa until my arrival, if only he doesn't forget me. I'm really worried how things are with the room but I can't help with anything . . . I kiss you, your cheerful Nina.[36]

No matter how brave and upbeat Nina tried to sound, she was writing with the awareness that these might be her last words to her loved ones. Fears about her future were exacerbated by the NKVD's policy to keep prisoners completely in the dark about everything. Filling the page with her neat writing while carefully trying not to put too much pressure on her pencil, she was oscillating between hope, practicalities and thoughts that sounded like a personal testimony. But as it turned out, she still had a little bit of time left in Leningrad. Kostia appears to have visited Nina once more, but for some reason she did not see her mother. Just before being put on a transport, Nina wrote three separate letters to her mother, her sister and Kostia. On the page addressed to her mother and sister, Kostia added his own appeal to Nina's mother: 'I turn to you in Nina's name, I hope you will answer me. Ninochka was really miserable about you, about the fact that she had to leave not having seen her Mummy.'[37] Had Nina given precedence to seeing Kostia? Was there some tension between Kostia and Nina's mother? Was her mother too unwell, scared, overwhelmed or angry to say farewell to her daughter?

Nina's own words give away little, save the fact that her mother had failed to come on the last visiting day:

My dear Mamochka!

I am leaving and will not be able to see you at the meeting. It is very bitter and painful for me that I didn't see you on the 8th. How are you, my own Mamochka, please don't worry and don't cry. When it will be possible, come to me and everything will be good ... Look after your health, I really ask you not to worry about me, I have a lot of strength, I will work and I will of course be able to vindicate myself. I still intend to dance and to stage ballets. I will return sensible and very tidy. I am placing all concern for you on Valia and my husband. I think that you want to see me again, I also very strongly want to be with you – so look after your health, I am begging you once more.[38]

After all these months of sitting idly in prison, Nina seemed to look forward to being put to work. Astonishingly, given that she had experienced the NKVD's methods first-hand and that she must have heard stories about the camps, she believed that working in an NKVD labour camp would be a step up from her current life in prison. She was not alone in this. The idea of contributing to society and the construction of socialism through work was a central theme of the Soviet self, and many prisoners hoped that after the terrible 'mistake' of their conviction they would be able to prove that they were honest Soviet citizens through their work.[39] Absurd or naïve as this may sound, there is a compelling logic to Nina's hope that she could prove her worth through work and reintegrate into society by demonstrating her usefulness. Her generation had been told to dedicate their lives to constructing a new, socialist civilisation. Like any successful artist, Nina was a hard worker. Her accomplishments had been considered an important milestone in moving her art form closer to the needs of the society she was living in, but her arrest had reduced her overnight to an 'enemy of the people'.

Nina was also trying to lighten the difficult moment of departure by infusing her parting words with gallows humour, writing facetiously that 'corrective labour' would hopefully not only vindicate her as a citizen but also tame her wilful and chaotic nature. She promised her mother to return 'improved' from the Gulag. Nina kept up the playful tone – and the emphasis on self-improvement – in the letter to her sister:

My dear Valia!

I am entrusting you Mummy, Stepa and our whole house. How is your work, what are you doing and what shape has your whole life taken. I really ask you to write more often to the camp about Mummy and yourself. I have learned to embroider well. (I never thought that I would have a calling for this.) You would even envy my kerchiefs. I'm not yet able to knit, but I think I will learn it soon. I in general plan to learn everything that I see that is good. I would like to become an engineer but I fear I don't have enough of a brain. More than anything I hope to see you all soon. Kiss Stepa on his black nose, let him wait for his mistress. I really ask you to send me any type of material for embroidery and good needles, mouline [embroidery thread]. A little bit of crepe de Chine would be good. Well, whatever you will send will be good. Look after yourself, stop worrying and live calmly. I kiss you strongly, strongly Nina.[40]

In her parting letter to Kostia, however, a note of deep-felt seriousness crept in. In her letters she usually addressed him by his name. Now she started differently:

Dear husband!

I am leaving and I'm very happy that I will finally be able to work. I'm only really sorry about one thing, that I will not see you, my dear, again. I am waiting for letters from you but no and no. And if I get one it's so short that it's frankly offensive. After all, as long as I am here you could write me letters every day and I would feel more cheerful. Well, never mind, I have already got used to patience and will wait with great impatience for news and a meeting with you there at the destination. Look after Stepa and take care of him, after all, he was left completely alone and he is not guilty of anything. I am very much relying on you and believe that your feelings for me are genuine and that you will take care of everything. I kiss you strongly, strongly, remember everything good that we had (if I offended you in anything please forgive me) and I believe in our future good happy life. I kiss you again. Thank you for everything, for Stepa

you have already done a lot I only understood this now.
See you soon

Your wife Nina.[41]

∽

Prisoners about to be put on a transport were often first assembled in their prison's collection cell. Once there, waiting times varied. The actor Georgy Zhzhenov and about forty other prisoners were held in the collection cell of the Kresty for about fifteen hours:

> The prison authorities tried to make the last hours of our stay at the Kresty especially memorable. We were kept standing for about fifteen hours, pressed so tightly against each other that it was not only impossible to turn, but to lift up a hand ... Throughout the entire time, we were not once led out ... People were bathed in sweat ... There was not enough oxygen ... Whoever couldn't hold it urinated under himself. The stench became unbearable! ... And despite this, the prison authorities gave orders to feed us *balanda* [prison soup] ... And people ate. They ate despite the stuffiness and stench – they ate because they wanted to eat and because they didn't know when and where food would be given the next time.[42]

The Russian intelligentsia had a time-tested strategy to protect their sanity in situations like this:

> Behind my back, they were conversing under their breath. I listened, trying to make out what they were talking

115

about . . . Unbelievable! They recited poetry! 'I sent you a black rose in a goblet of Ay,* golden like the sky . . .' In the middle of a crowd of people hanging on each other half-faint from stuffiness and stench, the poems about the Beautiful Lady could be heard!† People who had been flattened like livestock in a pen, who had just been branded, humiliated and trampled upon, were hearing Blok's mournful and beautiful words about beauty, about love, about Petersburg . . . about eternity.[43]

For some, the sound of the verses transported them temporarily into a different world.

From the collection cell, prisoners were taken down to the prison yard and driven either straight to the station or to the transit prison on Konstantinogradsky Street. Obsessed with secrecy, the NKVD tried to disguise the vehicles transporting prisoners around town by painting words such as 'bread' on their sides. The drive from the Kresty prison to the train station was not very long but could be tortuous. A woman transported with a group of wives of enemies of the people would later recall: 'One night, they woke us up very roughly and ordered us to prepare for departure . . . they literally

---

* Champagne. Ay is a major champagne production centre in France.

† Alexander Blok (1880–1921), one of Russia's most important symbolist poets, wrote his poetry cycle *Verses about a Beautiful Lady* between 1900 and 1902, after having fallen in love with his future wife Lyubov Mendeleyeva, daughter of the chemist Dmitry Mendeleyev. Lyubov Blok would play an important role in Petrograd/Leningrad's ballet world in the 1920s and 1930s as dance scholar and critic, assisting Agrippina Vaganova during the writing of her seminal textbook of classical ballet, *Fundamentals of Classical Dance* (1934).

shoved us in until it was impossibly crowded ... We drove
a little, several women fainted because of the stuffiness, we
started to scream and knock. They stopped the vehicle. The
guards pulled out those who had fainted and laid them straight
on the road. The fresh air revived them.'[44]

On the tracks – but usually far away from the regular railway platforms to avoid detection – trigger-happy
guards kept counting their charges, ordering them to sit
or kneel on the ground to make escape more difficult.[45] A
female prisoner bound for Karlag from the transit prison on
Konstantinogradsky Street in January 1940 remembered:

> Late at night, they led us out of the cell, searched us,
> handed out a dry ration – bread and salted fish – and handed
> us over to the guard. A 'Black Raven' brought us to the
> station. It stopped far from the building of the Moscow
> station, somewhere on the tracks. We were taken down
> from the vehicles and ordered to sit on the earth. We
> sat on our things. We were recounted and after about
> twenty minutes got up and moved. We soon came up to
> a 'Stolypin' wagon standing by itself on the tracks.[46]

Most prisoners were transported either in Stolypin wagons
– named after the early-twentieth-century reformist Russian
prime minister Pyotr Stolypin, who supposedly introduced
them – or in cattle wagons. The Stolypin wagons looked
almost like ordinary train carriages from the outside, but special protection features revealed their purpose to inquisitive
eyes: barbed wire was wound around them, they had external
wooden platforms for guards, electric lights at the top and

bottom and small windows protected by iron bars. From the inside, they resembled regular third-class carriages which had been customised to transport prisoners: the compartments were divided by steel netting instead of walls and an iron fence separated the compartments from the corridor, enabling the guards to watch the prisoners around the clock.

The red cattle wagons, on the other hand, were often fitted with a small stove in the centre – earning them the nickname *teplushka* (heated wagon) – and two or three sets of planks on either end to form wide, primitive bunks. Both types of wagon would have been hopelessly overcrowded during the Great Terror: the compartments of the Stolypin wagons were intended for four to six people, but often up to twenty-five were crammed in. Unable to get up or lie down, the prisoners would only be able to stretch out their aching limbs at most twice a day, when the guards led them to the toilet at the end of the carriage.

Fifty to a hundred prisoners could be crammed into the more primitive cattle wagons. If no planks had been fitted, they would have to crouch on the floor. If a set of wooden planks had been installed to form two or three levels of bunk-like platforms on either end, the prisoners could not sit up without banging their heads. Those on the top bunk could touch the wagon's ceiling while lying down, but were considered privileged because there was more air. Within the context of the abysmal conditions on the prisoner transports, the cattle wagons offered two distinct advantages: there was in principle more room to move about, and the hole cut into the floor liberated the prisoners from the guards' whims if they had to relieve themselves.[47]

Those travelling in the Stolypin wagons were at the complete mercy of the guards, who would leer through the toilet spyhole. Diarrhoea was widespread on the transports, but the guards could not always be bothered to lead the prisoners to the toilet. Between stops, 'prisoners who could not hold themselves would whimperingly foul their pants and often also the prisoners next to them.' In the cattle wagons, the prisoners could in theory relieve themselves whenever necessary, provided the hole in the wagon's floor wasn't blocked. In winter a frozen tower of human excrement sometimes formed above the blocked hole. Trapped in a wagon where the hole had been frozen over, a prisoner remembered how they 'pissed through a crack between the floor and the door and shat into a piece of cloth, making a small, neat parcel and hoping that somewhere they would stop the train and open the door so that we could throw it out'.[48]

The biggest problem, however, was the lack of food and water. Sometimes the prisoners were given hot food; usually they received a dry ration consisting of bread and salted fish, but they were given very little water.[49] The situation varied across different transports. A woman travelling in a cattle wagon from Leningrad to Potma in early 1939 recalled a bucket of water placed inside the wagon, another travelling inside a Stolypin wagon from Leningrad to Karaganda in early 1940 remembered being given boiling water three times per day.[50]

Prisoners were sent on the transports without any utensils for eating and drinking. One female prisoner remembered being happy to share the drinking cup of a woman infected with typhoid; another recalled sharing a rusty can with sixteen other women. Once again, the prisoners were completely dependent on the goodwill of the guards. There were also

practical limitations beyond the guards' control. The transports did not take water reserves with them, so any drinking
water had to be sourced by the guards when they stopped near
stations. They would hurriedly carry buckets of water to the
wagons, spilling part of it on the way. The prisoners could not
even enjoy the relief of drinking when they were given water:
whoever reached the front of the line would feel the impatience of those waiting behind. Often, prisoners choked out of
haste or because their dehydrated mouths and throats couldn't
take in the water, irritating the other prisoners and the guards
because of the delay they caused.

The lack of water had catastrophic consequences for
hygiene. The prisoners could not clean themselves for weeks
– the trains moved slowly, stopping frequently for many hours
on side tracks. Prisoners could dip a rag in water and try to
wipe off the soot and dirt, but some considered this a foolish
luxury given their thirst. There was also no way to clean the
wagons during the transport. The prisoners were plagued by
lice and there was no medical care; scurvy, scabies and colds
were common and spread quickly. Most arrived at their destination sick and weakened; the elderly and infirm often died en
route. Sometimes the dead bodies were moved into a separate
wagon; at other times they were only removed when the train
reached a larger station.[51]

~

After a few days, Nina's train reached the city of Sverdlovsk,
formerly known as Ekaterinburg*, about 1,800 kilometres

* Ekaterinburg was renamed Sverdlovsk after the Bolshevik leader
Yakov Sverdlovsk in 1924, reverting to its old name in 1991.

south-east of Leningrad. Twenty years earlier, members of the
local Cheka had taken Nicholas II, his wife Alexandra, their
thirteen-year-old son Alexei, their four daughters (aged seventeen to twenty-two), the family physician and three servants
down to the basement of the Ekaterinburg house that had been
their prison. A firing squad of eleven executed them all by pis-
tol fire without formal charges or trial. Some of the daughters,
protected from the bullets by jewels concealed in the bodices
of their dresses, were bayoneted to death. Sulphuric acid was
poured over the bodies; they were burned beyond recognition
and buried off a dirt road in a village north of Ekaterinburg.[52]

By the time Nina's train arrived there, Sverdlovsk, east
of the Ural Mountains, had become a regular stop for trains
transporting prisoners to the NKVD's labour camps. Transit
stations allowed the Gulag administration in Moscow to regu-
late the distribution of prisoners among the myriad camps,
organising new transports to different destinations and mixing
up the prisoners again, putting a stop to friendships and other
forms of solidarity. In the transit prisons the prisoners could
clean themselves, while their clothes were subjected to a usually
futile course of disinfection.[53]

Nina's train stopped far from the station's building. The
prisoners were loaded into Black Ravens and driven to the
transit prison, a three-storey stone building on the outskirts
of town. Nina and her fellow prisoners were taken to the bath
and then to their cells. A female prisoner passing through
Sverdlovsk prison on her way from Leningrad to Karaganda
in January 1940 described her cell as a room of about eighty
square metres with four large, barred windows half closed
with screens:

Iron beds with planks without mattresses are standing in many rows. There are many people and the public is of the most diverse kind. Here, side by side to the politicals are criminals from the criminal world. The uninterrupted, loud humming of voices is standing in the cell, obscene swearing can be heard, petty brawls are taking place. From the cell, one can freely go out unto a small corridor and to a lavatory with a wash-basin. In that same corridor, the distribution of food is taking place. They don't feed richly – bread, boiling water and twice a day watery *balanda*.[54]

❧

As soon as she had a chance, Nina wrote to her family, carefully limiting the size of her letters to the tiny squares on the small piece of paper:

27 September

My dear Mamochka, Kostia and Valyusha!

I am in transit in the Sverdlovsk prison where I will probably stay for a few days and then I will travel further. I am feeling well, I am healthy and all things are in order. As soon as I arrive at the camp I will immediately try to write to you.[55]

Nina's letter has an upbeat tone, hiding the hardships of her journey. Like all political prisoners, she was at the complete mercy of the criminal prisoners, who casually robbed the 'politicals' while fraternising with the guards. Criminals with a violent record and repeat offenders often organised brutal operations against the political prisoners on the transport with impunity, a foretaste of the camp hierarchy. The guards turned a blind eye while also stealing from the politicals in their own way. They often withheld bread rations in order to barter them at the next train station for meat, fish, milk or tobacco. Sometimes they withheld the prisoners' rations in order to 'exchange' them against any valuables the prisoners might still own. They drank themselves close to oblivion, loosening whatever restraints there still might have been against sexually harassing or raping their charges.[56]

The food situation on the trains was even worse than in prison. Not sure whether she would have a chance to write again before she arrived at her destination, she asked her family to send a food package as soon as they heard from her, and to include, if possible, some chocolate. Astonishingly, Nina still had the spirit to worry about her costumes – or maybe she drew strength from the ability to think about something so outlandish: 'Preserve all my theatrical costumes, all of this I will still need.' Nina felt closer to her family just by writing to them:

Most importantly, look after yourselves, and don't forget that a small piece of news from you is a big joy for me. I hope that Kostia continues to take care of Stepa and doesn't abandon him. I kiss you all strongly, strongly, I think of you all the time and miss you! . . . Dear Kostia and Valia, I ask you to look after my Mamochka. Write to me what is happening with my room and how you are living, I'm not losing the hope to see all of you soon.[57]

Putting pen to paper momentarily allowed her to block out the barbarity of her surroundings, the coarse noise, stench and damp discomfort assaulting all her senses. Feeling calmer, she added as an afterthought in tiny script on top of the first page of her letter: 'Send the picquet blanket and something pretty.'

～

The train continued east, along the tracks of the Trans-Siberian Railway. It stopped again in Kurgan, halfway between Sverdlovsk and Omsk. Named after a large burial mound – a *kurgan* – in its vicinity, the town had served the tsars as a frontier post defending Russian settlements from attacks by nomads from the south, and as a remote place of exile for unwelcome elements. Nine days after writing to her family from Sverdlovsk, Nina was desperate to use the brief break in her journey to send another sign of life. On a piece of cigarette paper she wrote: 'Dear Mamochka, I am on transit in the city Kurgan. I'm alive, healthy and feel OK.' Nina knew by now that she was heading to Kazakhstan, south of Kurgan: 'When I arrive in Karaganda I will try to write immediately. I'm worried whether you have opened my room . . .'. Nina took another cigarette paper and made an envelope out of it. Most likely she slipped the improvised letter through one of the cracks in the wagon's side as it was leaving the station; across Russia, compassionate strangers picked up such letters and sent them on. Nina's note was posted two weeks after she wrote it, on 21 October, without postage; her family in Leningrad would dutifully pay forty kopeks for it.[58]

6

The Kazakh Steppe

The train stopped in the middle of the steppe. On one side of the tracks, the flat grassland stretched uninterrupted into the distant horizon. On the other side, a small mountain range rose in the distance. Between the tracks and the low mountains, a settlement of flat-roofed bungalows built of bleached bricks broke the monotony of the endless plain. Its name, Karabas, derived from the Kazakh word *karabash*, 'black head', inspired by the blue-black stone that had been extracted from the nearby mountains long before the Gulag claimed this strip of land. The camp rose from the steppe a little further away. Wooden watchtowers and three rows of barbed wire formed a deadly barrier four metres high around the camp and its long, flat barracks.[1]

෴

The steppe eagles were flying over land that had seen devastating changes. For thousands of years, nomads and their herds had moved across the vast territory that would become Kazakhstan. The nomadic tribes had evolved a territorial-based system of clan allegiances based on the location of summer and winter pastures. But this decentralised arrangement made the region vulnerable: between 1763 and 1895, the Russian empire conquered Central Asian territories.[2] Russian settlers received land, and a policy of forced settlement put nomadism, the heart of Kazakh life, under threat.

After the October Revolution of 1917, secular Kazakh nationalists set up an independent national government, loosely aligned with Admiral Kolchak's White forces. But even after the Red Army gained nominal control of Turkestan in the summer of 1920, local resistance to the Bolshevik take-over continued. Partisan groups, collectively called *basmachi* (brigands), continued to fight. It took two more years until the heart of the resistance was broken. Following the establishment of the Soviet Union in 1922 and the division of Turkestan into five Union republics, the Kazakh Soviet Socialist Republic became the second-largest after Russia in terms of size.[3]

Under the Bolsheviks, de-nomadisation of Central Asia became an ideological mantra: the sanctity of ancient familial and tribal bonds and the nomadic way of life had to be destroyed. The assault on ancient practices that had been moulded by geographic necessity – aridity and heavy winds make the steppe unsuitable for agriculture – would have catastrophic consequences.

The first Five Year Plan in 1928 evoked a utopian vision of a new world constructed by heroic workers pushing industrialisation at breakneck speed, catapulting Russia into modernity. Stalin believed that mechanised collective farms would dramatically increase agricultural output, feeding and financing industrialisation in the process. But the peasant revolution of 1917 had created a smallholding population of 25 million households that did not share the Bolsheviks' dream of abolishing private property. Collectivisation could only be accomplished by extreme force and mass de-kulakisation,* pursued from autumn 1929 onwards with complete disregard for the human cost.

Instead of increasing agricultural output, forced collectivisation plunged the Soviet Union into disaster and famine. Of all the regions within the Union, none was hit worse in terms of deaths per capita than the Kazakh republic: 35 to 40 per cent of Kazakhs died from starvation or disease. About half a million Kazakhs resettled outside the region, 200,000 of them beyond Soviet territory. A report in August 1932 stated that the number of livestock in the Kazakh republic – which had been the Union's main meat supplier – had gone down from 40 million in 1929 to 6 million.[4]

While the Kazakhs and their livestock were dying, Moscow pushed relentlessly for the implementation of another policy linked to Stalin's fanatical vision of speedy industrialisation: the transformation of the Soviet penal system into a system of slave labour. By autumn 1929, mass collectivisation and de-kulakisation had led to a dramatic increase in prisoners and 'special' (forced) settlers – alleged kulaks who had been deported from their homes. In June 1929, the Politburo had already decided to imprison anyone sentenced to more than

---

* Stalinist propaganda claimed that more prosperous villagers, *kulaks*, were at the heart of the resistance to collectivisation and needed to be 'de-kulakised' – eliminated as a class by shooting or deportation. In reality, the term was used for any peasant accused of opposing collectivisation or Soviet power.

three years outside the existing prison system in secret police-run camps, which were meant to support themselves financially. If the previous camps had been intended to isolate and somehow 're-educate' undesirable elements, these new 'corrective' labour camps were supposed to re-forge them into compliant Soviet citizens through hard physical work. Kazakhstan was rich in 'empty' space, making it an ideal dumping ground for undesirable elements ranging from Leon Trotsky, deported to Alma-Ata in January 1928, to peasants, political prisoners and entire nations.*

Crucially, the camps were supposed to support rapid industrialisation through the exploitation of the rich natural resources found on the peripheries of the Soviet empire, often in remote, inhospitable regions where nobody wanted to settle. The coal, gas, oil and wood so urgently needed could be found in Siberia, Kazakhstan and the far north. Large gold deposits were hiding under the permafrost and tundra in the north-eastern region of Kolyma – gold that was needed to import foreign machinery and to finance industrialisation. Within a few years, massive camps could be found in all these locations. It is estimated that between 1929 and 1953, 18 million people passed through the camps, while another 6 million were forced into exile. From 1934 onwards, a special NKVD division in Moscow would manage the vast network

---

* Stalin would deport entire nations to Kazakhstan, accusing them of espionage or of collaborating with enemy powers, especially during the Second World War: Koreans were deported from the Soviet Far East to Kazakhstan in 1937, Volga Germans in 1941, and the small Caucasian nations of Karachai, Chechens and Ingush in 1943 and 1944. In the long term, the large population of ex-prisoners and special (forced) settlers would transform Kazakhstan into a multi-ethnic state.

of corrective labour camps spreading across the Soviet Union. Its acronym would become synonymous with the camp system as a whole: Gulag stands for *Glavnoe upravlenie lagerei*, 'Main Camp Administration'.[5]

One of the largest, most enduring camps of the Gulag was in Kazakhstan's Karaganda region, home to the Soviet Union's third-largest coal reserves; in 1930–1, developing them into the Soviet Union's third major coal basin had become a priority. But this required enormous manpower: mines, factories and railroads had to be constructed, a city to house hundreds of thousands employed in the new industries built and the arid lands of the steppe transformed into fertile fields and pastures to feed the hungry miners and factory workers.

To achieve all of this, the order was given to establish an enormous labour camp in the region.[6] The first prisoner transports arrived in 1930 and Karagandinsky corrective labour camp (Karlag) was officially founded in 1931.

At the same time, thousands of free workers were sent to Karaganda to develop the coal basin. The workers had arrived to build socialism in a place completely unprepared to house or feed them. Moscow was pushing free workers, deported peasants and prisoners simultaneously into a remote, underdeveloped region ravaged by famine. The wife of a high-ranking official in the Kazakhstan NKVD described Karaganda in 1931 as:

a way station under a pile of snow ... There were only temporary shanties, built by deported kulaks. There was nothing in the shop, the shelves were empty. The saleswoman says: 'I don't work, I don't sell, there is nothing. They forgot bread, that's what it looks like.' ... she told me: 'They sent special trains of de-kulakised people here, but they are all dying because there is nothing to eat.* Do you see the shanty over there? The father and mother died, three small children were left. The youngest boy, two years old, also soon died. The oldest boy took a knife and started to cut off pieces, and to eat, and to give some to his sister, and so they ate him.'[7]

About 5,000 Kazakh families and their herds were spread over the territory allocated to Karlag, predominantly nomads to be collectivised and forced into settlement. Many nomads offered fierce armed resistance, but to no avail; they found themselves prisoners of the camp built on their ancestral lands or drafted into collective farms.[8] Around 1,000 'European households' – Ukrainians, Russians and Germans, many of whom had moved to the region in 1906–10 – were also living in several settlements. Once emptied of its inhabitants, the largest of them, Dolinka, would be transformed into the seat of the camp administration and a camp division.

Swallowing up about 34,000 square kilometres, Karlag soon covered a territory slightly larger than Belgium.[9] One of the largest camps of the Gulag both in terms of expanse and prisoner numbers, Karlag was 'a state within the state'. The camp's administration answered directly to Moscow, leaving the local authorities with absolutely no authority over it. Karlag had its own power structures, enforced by an army

---

* During collectivisation, 189,000 people were deported from central regions of Russia to Kazakhstan. Of this number, 150,000 were sent to the central and northern regions of Akmolinsk, Karaganda, Pavlodar and Kokshetau.

of armed guards; operated its own transport and postal system; and worked according to its own state production plan.[10] On 1 October 1938, just before Nina's arrival, there were reportedly 40,109 prisoners there.[11] Like all camps, Karlag was supposed to contribute to the Soviet economy, but slave labour turned out to be economically utterly ineffective. Even the strongest prisoners struggled to survive the savage cruelty, practical inefficiencies and gross material inadequacies of a system that could not dress or feed its prisoners.

~

Nervous activity spread through the train: the transport had left Leningrad at the end of September and now it was the end of October. It sometimes took hours until the guards would fling open the doors, roughly commanding the prisoners to get off with their belongings. Weakened by the excruciating weeks in cramped conditions, the prisoners had to be careful not to injure themselves as they jumped down a metre and a half to reach the ground; there was no platform on which to disembark in the steppe.

One of the guards climbed into the wagon for a final inspection; another shouted at the prisoners to start walking. Under the watchful eyes of the soldiers, the prisoners marched in a column through the undulating steppe grasses towards the camp. The transport stopped in front of several sergeants in khaki pea coats at the camp's closed gates, which were flanked by two wooden watchtowers, high enough for the guards to oversee the terrain but low enough to make them disconcertingly close to the prisoners. After many months of claustrophobic confinement in prison and on the train, many prisoners felt relieved, even happy at the sight of the camp.[12] They had to be checked before the gates were opened: each convict was called up by their last name and was expected to respond by shouting out their first names and patronymics, the paragraph of their conviction, and the length of term. The whole process could take many hours.[13]

Nina had arrived in Karabas, a large transit camp for prisoners bound further north or east, and the gateway to Karlag. Barbed-wire fences divided the camp into different zones: a general zone subdivided into a male and a female zone and a separate quarantine zone. The exhausted arrivals bound for Karlag were supposed to spend two to four weeks in Karabas's quarantine zone before being moved to the camp's general zone, where they waited to be distributed among Karlag's various divisions.[14] Inside the zone, prisoners in rags scanned the new arrivals for acquaintances – or easy prey. For the hardened criminal prisoners, the transit and distribution camp was a rich hunting ground; their gangs often tried to stay there for as long as possible, in anticipation of fleecing newly arrived, inexperienced political prisoners whose clothes or valuables hadn't yet been stolen.[15]

Nina was searched for forbidden objects and sent to the primitive bathhouse. All items of clothing were supposed to be disinfected while the prisoners were washing themselves, but clothes were often returned not only singed, but with even more lice. As she undressed, Nina could hear the shrill protest of female voices and loud, male laughter: the overseers of the bath were all men. Some women were protesting that the men should leave; others shrugged their shoulders, resigned to the constant humiliation ruling their daily lives.

Stinking, naked bodies were pushing against each other in the foul-smelling, slippery, humid space. Each woman received a small metal token, to be handed in at the water boiler for half a wooden tub of hot water. Trying not to drop her microscopically small piece of soap, Nina could hear some women arguing about whether one of them had received more than her allotted share of hot water. A man pushed through the bustle of the naked women to fill the water tubs, slapping any backside within his reach amid the angry curses of the women. After the bath, male prisoners shaved the women's pubic hair.[16]

The barracks in the quarantine division were of the *zemlianka* type: huts built out of clay into the earth. Covered by a roof that reached down to the ground, the *zemlianka*'s living space was located below ground like a cellar. After entering a small vestibule, Nina stepped into a large room with a clay oven and wooden planks coarsely carpentered together to serve as beds. There was no proper flooring, only dried clay covered with dirt.[17] As night fell, two miserable oil lamps dangling from the ceiling were lit, barely illuminating the aisle across the room. Like thousands before her, Nina spent her first night in the overcrowded barracks listening to the restless tossing of alien bodies on wooden boards and the loud coughing, swearing and arguing of strangers.[18] After the noise had died down, the new arrivals could hear the eerie rattling and howling of the chained guard dogs pacing back and forth.[19]

~

Nina felt intensely lonely. Her new life was so removed from her family in every sense of the word that she was consumed by the fear that her loved ones would forget about her existence.

Being forgotten is another way of dying. During the last four weeks, Nina had travelled 4,000 kilometres under dehumanising conditions. Each jolt of the train, each insult and humiliation seemed intended violently to shake any recollection of her former life out of her soul.

The right to correspond and to receive packages was a privilege that could be taken away any moment. Most of those arrested and sentenced during the Great Terror for counterrevolutionary crimes were forbidden to correspond with their relatives, some for several years. From August 1939, prisoners convicted of such crimes were in principle allowed to write a letter every three months, but the frequency varied. Correspondence rights differed between the different categories of prisoners. As a socially dangerous element, Nina was technically considered a criminal prisoner; she therefore had the right to send and receive mail:[20]

> My dear Mamochka, Kostia, Valia and Stepa.
>
> I am in Karabas. I think that within days, I will be at my destination. I arrived safely, I am alive, healthy and feel well. I ask you, my dear ones, not to worry about me. My dream is to receive news from you as soon as possible, and to find out that all of you are healthy and that everything is well with you. I really missed you and I worry about Mummy's health.[21]

Emaciated, Nina desperately needed calories to build her strength back up. She asked her mother and Kostia to send a kilo of speck, a kilo of lard, oils, sugar, sweets, a box of cocoa, sweet rusks, biscuits, cheese and ham, as well as cigarettes and light tobacco. She needed vitamins from compote and dried fruit, she wanted pasta, condensed milk, some tinned meat, soap, paper, envelopes, stamps, a spoon, a knife, a mug, a sauce-pan to keep the lard in. Writing about food made her even more hungry; it made her think of butter mixed with honey as a delicious, satisfying concoction her family might be able to send her. And lemons – hardly anyone survived the transports without suffering from one of the common illnesses caused by extreme malnutrition and lack of hygiene.[22] Nina had not lost her sweet tooth, prompting her to add to her survival list a request for something delicious, maybe chocolate.

Nina didn't only need food. It was the end of November and the winters on Kazakhstan's steppe were brutal. Untamed Siberian winds and snowstorms swept freely over the land, encountering no natural resistance in the form of groves, forests or significant mountain ranges. She asked for various items of clothing, but particularly her felt boots and fur jacket, her brown skirt, woollen stockings or gaiters, a warm scarf and mittens.[23]

Her list was long – all of this would cost money, and food supplies were generally scarce. Nina felt bad: 'Of course send things to me depending on how much money you have. I write many things, but you send what you can. At the post office, ask how much the package weighs, it seems you are allowed 16 kilograms.' Nina continued to worry about the financial burden of her situation on her family. She urged Kostia that her sister Valia should wear whatever she needed from her old things and sell everything else: 'everything that is not needed, for example my evening dresses, you should sell and it's better to send me packages. I know that you will not agree to this, and that you will work like an ox, but that is stupid, because I don't need these things now, and if I will be home, then all of this is acquirable. So it is better to liquidate what isn't needed.'[24]

There was also the technical problem of storing her provisions and belongings: the prisoner barracks had no closets or chest of drawers. Nina asked for the goods to be sent in a crate, and everything else in a suitcase. Protecting her things against criminals, however, would be a matter of luck.

She finished her first letter to her family with a heartfelt plea: 'Don't forget your Nina. I kiss you strongly, strongly, my beloved family, I think of you and I really miss you. I beg you not to forget me.'*

Nina sometimes found it hard to believe that her old life had ever existed. She felt as if she had been swallowed by a remote, alien universe. Starting her first letter from the camp to Kostia, she sounded distinctly dejected:

> I am writing to you, my beloved, whom I miss very, very
> much. How are you living, Kostia, what are you doing
> and are you thinking even a little bit about me. I really
> miss you, Mummy and Valia, I would very much like to
> see Stepa and my dear boys. But you are so far from me
> that at times it seems to me that all this is a dream and
> that all of you never existed . . . I will write you exactly
> twice per month, but you write to me as often as possible
> and you can even send telegrams.[25]

* In her first letter from the camp, Nina implores her family twice not to forget her.

Nina was scared and lonely, but her artistic soul still craved whatever beauty it could find: 'In the evenings, my eyes are feasting on the sunset, here in the steppe there are very beautiful colours and at night there are prominent and large stars.'[26]

Writing to Kostia grounded Nina in her familiar self. Conversing with him on paper, the hope returned that, one day, she would go back to her former life and the stage. She asked Kostia to pass on a message to her trusted dancing partner, the Kirov Ballet's character soloist Sergei Koren, seemingly oblivious to the fact that she was now considered an enemy of the people whom most of her colleagues would prefer not to remember.

❧

Other than at roll calls and mealtimes, Nina was left to her own devices. At Karabas, prisoners were either waiting to be put back on the transport or moved to one of Karlag's subdivisions to start their term of hard labour. Initially, many prisoners felt a strange sense of liberation after the overcrowded prison cells and the suffocating claustrophobia of the transport: they were allowed to walk freely around the zone without the constant, coarse supervision of the guards. Although this 'freedom' was limited by three rows of barbed wire and manned watchtowers, they could choose whether to sit inside their barracks or go for a walk, stop to talk to someone or simply look around. They were permitted to go to the latrine whenever they needed, even if it was a primitive pit in a remote corner of the zone, covered with wooden planks into which several holes had been cut.[27]

After about two weeks, prisoners were transferred from the quarantine zone to the general zone of Karabas; bustling like an anthill, it was not large enough to keep up with the numbers who arrived during the Great Terror. Hundreds of prisoners were cramped together in large barracks, waiting to be distributed across Karlag. Built from logs, the barracks had huge windows without grilles and doors that remained unlocked, allowing prisoners to move around freely. They were large, damp, cold rooms, heated insufficiently by a Dutch oven burning coal to about ten degrees Celsius. Along the walls there were two rows of primitive wooden double-decker bunks, separated by an aisle about two metres wide. Thick clusters of bedbugs hung from the top bunks, dropping down on their prey on the lower bunks through the spaces between the planks. Some prisoners tried to outsmart the parasites by sleeping fully dressed, with gloves tied closely to their wrists, a headscarf over their hair and a cloth with two small breathing holes covering their face, but the bedbugs were persistent; some even crawled into nostrils.[28]

There was a lively trade in garments among the waiting prisoners. Many only possessed light clothes, and some still had money. But theft was so rampant that many politicals were soon left with nothing but what they were wearing. The criminal prisoners ruled the camps of the Gulag; they despised the politicals and often managed to be in cahoots with the guards, who were indoctrinated to see the criminals as errant but 'honourable' members of Soviet society and the politicals as enemies of the people who had forfeited the right to be considered human. For the criminals, life inside the camp merely meant a continuation of their regular existence in a different setting. A year before Nina arrived in Karabas, the administration had started a campaign against robberies and violence, arresting and shooting dozens of the worst criminals; lists of their names were hung up around the camp as a warning and their possessions were sold in the camp store. But by the time Nina arrived, the situation was as bad as before, not least because members of the administration were profiteering from criminal activities, buying stolen goods at ridiculously low prices through middlemen.[29]

The food in the general zone was even worse than in the quarantine zone. The prisoners received 500 grams of dark bread and soup for lunch. There were no tables: the women ate out of mess tins, sitting on their bunks. In a small booth there was a boiler for heating water, fired with sawdust from a woodworking factory nearby, but the sawdust was damp and burned badly. Often the boiler could be brought to boiling point only once a day; as soon as it was, a long queue formed outside the booth's small window.[30]

All prisoners heading to Karlag had to undergo a medical examination at Karabas to determine their fitness to work. After standing in an endless queue, a doctor would ask the prisoner to put a foot on a bench, feel their calf, and decide whether to put him or her into the first (heavy labour), second (medium) or third (light) category. Administrator-managers of Karlag's different camp divisions travelled to Karabas to inspect the new arrivals, choosing the most able-bodied or those with certain skills. On those days, the prisoners would sarcastically say to each other: 'The buyers have arrived.' The bosses were looking for specialists, above all carpenters, coopers, masons, stove-setters, metalworkers, drivers, engineers, agronomists, cooks, even hairdressers.[31]

∽

14 November 1938

My beloved Kostia!

I am writing you the second letter, I hope you have already received the first one. I am still in Karabas and have now been assigned to a long-distance transport. So it will probably not be my lot to stay here in Kazakhstan.[32]

This could have frightening implications: a long-distance transport meant the mining and logging camps of Siberia, the deadly gold mines of Kolyma, or other camps in Russia's barely inhabitable far north or far east.

Nina was depressed. Reduced from being a charismatic dancer commanding the stage to an anonymous prisoner's number, she increasingly felt that she was fading from her family's and friends' horizon, dissolving into a vast, invisible ocean of faceless convicts:

> Without you, my dear, I am very lonely, more and more so every day . . . your concern and kindness at the time of my arrest moved me more than all that you had done for me in my previous life. Maybe you already forgot me a long time ago or maybe you only remember me occasionally? After all, I will now never dance again, and my career is finished once and for all. I can only write letters and wait for news from you. If only you knew how much I want to find out how you are all living over there.

But her sense of irony was irrepressible. Even now, as she was beginning to understand what her life for the next five years might look like, she could still muster the detachment to muse on whether her experiences might become an extreme form of character-building: 'As for myself, I am alive and healthy, I am feeling cheerful all the same and I am becoming hardened in my loneliness. Probably, when I come out, my character will seriously change, and everything that once seemed to me offensive, everything that once made me cry, all of this is such childish nonsense that it's even simply funny.'[33]

Like many others who found it psychologically unbearable to sit idle, cold and hungry in the barracks or to wander aimlessly around the camp, Nina was anxious to start working. The surgeon Nina Afanasova, who arrived from Leningrad three months after Nina, wrote to the camp administration, asking to be allowed either to work in her profession or to be assigned to general tasks. The German Communist Margarete Buber-Neumann requested permission to work in the laundry in the quarantine zone, calculating that this might give her a chance to wash herself properly.[34]

Nina hoped that work would give her a sense of purpose, and less time to think: 'The main thing is to arrive sooner at the site and to begin to work. Now I'm free all day and don't do anything.' It was also starting to get cold. The day before there had been a small blizzard, but, in contrast to Russia's far north, in Kazakhstan at least the sun did not disappear for months. A light tan was beginning to breathe colour into the prison grey of Nina's face. Someone had lent her woollen socks, so her legs were not too freezing, but she hadn't yet received any packages from home containing her winter clothes. She was torn between the impulse to list her needs and the anxiety that her family would worry too much if she did so. By saying that she was fine she hoped to bridge this gap; yet such assurances, written from the Gulag, would hardly put the recipient's mind at rest.

Suspended as she was in uncertainty, any thoughts about her profession triggered increasingly complex emotions and responses. Nina oscillated between a deeply anchored hope that she would return to her former life and the stage and the realisation that, with every passing day, this became less and less likely. At Nina's level, dancing was not just her profession; it defined her whole being. Her mind kept travelling back to the Kirov, wondering about her friends who were free, dancing and choreographing: 'How are the boys, they are probably working to the full. Vasia* and [???] are probably staging new ballets and Vasia has probably already forgotten my existence.'

Nina knew that she should focus all her mental energy on survival. Given how much it pained her to think that life at the Kirov was continuing as if she had never existed, was it wise to keep hoping, especially as she would probably be in no state to dance even if she survived the camp? One minute she tried to block out the past to ease the pain: 'I try not to think about the theatre and have even reached the point where I have forgotten the theme of the waltz from *Sleeping Beauty*. If I wish, I will probably soon forget altogether that I once danced. And I am not risking moving an arm or a leg, what if I have all of a sudden forgotten how to.' The next, she started dreaming: 'You know, still, somewhere there is a small hope that someday I will again be of use and dance. And to stage ballets, I have now such a large stock of all kinds of movements, what wonderful

* The choreographer Vasily Vainonen.

things I would stage if someday I will be allowed to work in my profession. Well, I will not write more about this, I will hope and believe that everything in my life will still turn out well.'

Writing to Kostia gave Nina strength, even though every letter had to be submitted to the scrutiny of the camp censor and she did not yet know whether her letters were reaching their destination. By the end, Nina sounded again like her old self, tenderly and endearingly self-deprecating: 'Now I have all sorts of instructions for you. First of all, take care of yourself, worry less and think more about me. Isn't it true, I have become, or, rather, remained the same egoist. Well, don't be angry with me, you see, to write to you, even if only nonsense, is great happiness for me. I am kissing you strongly, strongly, my dear. My husband, live, enjoy yourself and remember me.'[35]

∼

By the end of November, Nina had spent almost a month in Karabas. She had written a request to be allowed to stay in Kazakhstan, but it had been rejected. She told her family that she was happy to leave:

My mood is cheerful and good! I am sure that in the future, I will have the possibility to work in my profession. I have a lot of strength and the desire, and that is the most important thing. I read in the newspaper about the performance of Leningrad's ballet in Moscow! So far, nobody is genuinely working on character dance. This is a moral comfort for me. Maybe in the future, I will be able to prove once again the usefulness of my existence. I ask you not to be upset and to remember me more often.[36]

The moment of departure came. Nina packed her few possessions, endured another body search and was marched to the train station. She was herded into an overcrowded wagon, but as she was trying to settle down she suddenly heard somebody call her name: 'Anisimova, Nina Alexandrovna?' She was told to grab her things and was pulled down from the train. Instead of going on a long-distance transport, she would stay in Karlag.[37]

This was a miracle: once Moscow assigned a prisoner to a transport, local camp authorities did not have the authority to take them off the transport. Somebody was watching over her, but nobody in Stalin's Russia acquired a powerful protector by chance.[38]

~

28 December 1938

My beloved Kostia.

Today is the happiest of days for me. I received two letters from you and Valia. They told me already yesterday that there are letters for me, I even dreamed of your envelope written by your hand. My dear, why does my Mamochka not write anything. I even cried, why is she alive and healthy both in the telegram and in your letters but she herself doesn't write a line. This really worries me, but the envelope with the return address calms me down . . . let her write in every letter even if only two words and then I will be fully happy.[39]

Nina was deeply worried about her mother's inexplicable silence; she feared that she had either been arrested or died.

She didn't know that her mother was lying sick at the hospital.[40] But receiving mail from Kostia and Valia marked a crucial turning point. It had taken a while for her own letters to reach her family: her first two arrived in Leningrad at the end of November; her postcard written in late November, informing them of her imminent departure, arrived only in mid-December.[41] As soon as Nina's family heard from her they sent a telegram, but even though her mother's silence tempered her joy, Nina was ecstatic finally to receive proper letters: 'But I am happy for many reasons. None of you have forgotten me, you love me and at home, everything is more wonderful than I thought.' She laughed and cried and had even felt like breaking into a dance.[42]

Kostia had solved the problem of her room by moving into it from his parents' flat: 'Are you really in my big room. Walking around in it, sleeping, working and everything is standing in its place. I really can't believe it, although I don't have the right not to believe you.'[43] To move from his parents' apartment into Nina's communal flat, to choose to live with Nina's mother, who appeared to be a complicated character, was not just selfless but brave. Instead of distancing himself from his arrested love, Kostia was powerfully backing her mother and sister. In contrast, the common-law husband of the actress Tatiana Okunevskaya, another Karlag prisoner, threw Tatiana's mother out of their joint home and proceeded to marry someone else.[44] Kostia's public display of solidarity was even more remarkable given the fact that the family seemed cursed: Valia's husband was also a political prisoner serving time in a labour camp.

Kostia's letter left Nina giddy with love and optimism:

And then your letter is such a long, wonderful one, carrying so much joy and hope. I will re-read it every day and smile until a new letter. Dear Husband, I want to write so much to you that I frankly don't know where to start. Firstly, a big thank you to you for what you have done for Valia and Mamochka. Secondly, I thank fate that I have found you and that I have the possibility to remember and to dream of the future. To remember my first acquaintance with you at my only premiere, or rather, the staging of *Andalusian Wedding*. Do you remember how you invited me to the third row of the stalls and we watched *Esmeralda* and do you remember Feodosiya* how I was appearing indistinctly on the pier and you were on a large, wonderful ship. And Batumi and the dark-brown fox and the wonderful dark-blue sea, the sun, the warmth and everything good, splendid that was. Well, yes, everything will still return and there will be new big memories.[45]

Kostia wanted to give Nina strength. Dancing was such an intrinsic part of her being that he feared she would wither away if her profession was taken from her. In order to live, Nina had to continue to believe in life. She had not yet reached the state where, in the words of Varlam Shalamov, who spent seventeen years in the camps of Kolyma, 'all human emotions – love, friendship, envy, concern for one's fellow man, compassion, longing for fame, honesty – had left us with the flesh that had melted from our bodies during their long fasts.'[46] Kostia's words still had the power to make Nina feel invincible:

* An ancient port on the Crimea.

You write to me about my art. You praise me. Nobody
has praised me in a long time. What I can tell you about
myself is this, no matter where fate will toss me, whatever difficult school of life I might have to go through,
nobody and nothing will destroy my small abilities
(actually, why small?). As a dancer I will of course die
without practice. If I will be allowed to work in my
profession, then maybe in the future you will again be
able to be a bit proud of me. With respect to my second
profession, I am fully convinced that in the future I will
stage a whole series of big, good ballets. If only you
knew how much I want to choreograph. I am absolutely
not devastated but on the contrary full of strength and
the desire to create. If only to keep up with life and to
know everything that is new in art. This depends on
you sending me journals about art, but only when I am
settled . . . Write to me about everything that is new in
literature and theatre.[47]

Nina felt full of creative energy and hope. Sitting in a camp
behind barbed wire, 4,000 kilometres from Leningrad, Kostia
was not just her personal anchor but a lifeline to her own professional milieu. He had written to her about his work, about
his plans to write about a Spanish dancer. Sharing details of his
life, of his mind, made her feel like Kostia's partner, not just a
burden constantly asking for things. Kostia had already posted
her packages. They hadn't arrived yet, but his letter made her
feel like a woman again, making her yearn for luxuries that
went beyond items necessary for her survival: 'You can send
perfumery items. Eau de cologne, perfume, powder, lipstick,

crème and so on. In general, anything you will send will make me really happy.'

Thinking of material items quickly brought her back to reality. There were many basic things she urgently needed: a mattress, or, to be more precise, a sack she could fill with hay and a pillow; a small wash-basin, a bowl, a cup, a spoon; another blanket, galoshes, scissors, tweezers would be good, a thermos would be useful, a mirror and a toothbrush. She said she had 'lost' everything. More likely, it had been stolen – and maybe her request for perfumery items had a more prosaic purpose: to have something valuable to trade with the criminals.

'For the time being, I kiss you strongly, strongly, my one and only and irreplaceable one. Your wife Nina, who is eternally and newly in love with you.'[48]

❧

Nina was sent to Dolinka, a settlement twenty-three kilometres from Karabas housing Karlag's central administration and zones for inmates. As long as their final destination was not too far away, prisoners had to walk in a convoy to their camp division, accompanied by guards on foot or horseback. In winter, the march from Karabas to Dolinka could take from early morning until night. Leaving Karabas, the column of weary souls trudged slowly along endless barbed-wire fences behind which they could make out rundown sheds and small earthen huts, dwellings that looked so primitive that it was hard to believe human beings were living inside them.[49]

At some point, the outlines of Dolinka appeared on the horizon. The flatness of the steppe created the illusion of a fairly large city, but as the convoy drew closer, the 'high-risers' visible from afar turned out to consist of only two storeys. Apart from two such buildings, Dolinka comprised a few skinny little trees and a number of shabby huts. The barbed-wire fence surrounding the settlement was its most impressive feature. After walking along the fence for about fifteen minutes the prisoners reached a guardhouse, which they passed without checks. They were now marching along wide, unkempt streets. Dogs and hens roamed around freely, scavenging for food.

The place was wretched. There were barbed-wire fences even inside the village, subdividing the settlement into different zones. Once the prisoners arrived at the fences designating the zone they had been assigned to, they would enter its small guardhouse. Inside, they endured yet another round of the already familiar procedure: prisoner files were handed over to the officer on duty and checked; each prisoner was body-searched; their belongings were searched; the prisoners were taken to the bathhouse, their pubic hair was shaved, their clothes were disinfected. Later on, a medical-labour commission would check their health and professional qualifications in order to determine what work they were suited for.[50]

⁓

Nina was waiting to be assigned to a permanent job. In the meantime, she had once again been lucky: on some days she worked in the kitchen, a coveted job as it brought the prisoners into close proximity to food. Nina thus had a reason to tell her family good-humouredly: 'I've learned to clean potatoes magnificently. When I return from the camp I will be a jack of all trades and I will be able to help Mummy at home.'[51] Nina's deceptively light tone must have pierced her family's heart, knowing that she would have been writing from a freezing barracks in threadbare clothes. Despite the levity, she alluded to the horrors of camp life at the height of winter to the extent that censorship permitted:

My hands have coarsened, but don't worry, not because of cold or hot water, it is simply very cold without gloves, after all, it is 43 degrees Celsius below zero here. I am in general splendidly worn out. My poor boots are leaking, and one has become completely crooked, the scoundrel, all my stockings have been darned over and over again but continue to tear, my shoes are all worn out. True, I have toughened up very much. Imagine in Leningrad in winter without gaiters, what cries and weeping there would have been. Well, and here I am walking around and doing so comparatively cheerfully. My knitted suit is looking decent, I could even saunter around in it in front of Iordan,* I am proud of it, only on its backside there are two kind of greasy stains. My coat is my salvation. Night and day it warms me faithfully and truly. I look in it like a nag like in Leningrad. It would be good if you could find a short sheepskin coat, many here have one of those. Although, winter will soon be over, but there is still no package ... Tomorrow is the New Year, I will send you congratulations through the snowstorm and cold, mentally of course, and sit together with you

---

* The ballerina Olga Iordan was a classmate and friend of Nina Anisimova's. She was admired by her contemporaries for her charm and elegance.

at the table, eating delicious things and looking at faces dear to me ... In general, I am still a totally new camp inmate, still such an inexperienced and stupid one. But I am gradually learning human wisdom and will come out with a stronger character. I am entirely sensible, am behaving well and am of course, Kostia, not intending on falling in love with anyone. I want a quiet, calm life at the fireplace in my room, together with all of you. To see you, that would be crazy, crazy happiness. But as long as I don't have you, I have to wait, hope and endure. I will write you a little bit about Kazakhstan. There are severe frosts, sometimes there are snowstorms, there is a lot of snow. The people are all wrapped up, warmly dressed. I'm looking with envy at *valenki* [felt boots] and woollen things. If only there will be a package with things and food soon ... The houses here are all white, made out of sun-dried clay bricks, there are very few trees and the big, wide expanse of the steppe. I like Kazakhstan very much for its nature. I am writing a confused, stupid letter, but you will forgive me, I can't write a different one now.[52]

Even Nina could not keep up her cheerful tone, sitting alone while Soviet citizens were getting ready to celebrate the most joyful holiday of the year, New Year's Eve, which since 1935 had been promoted as an alternative Christmas, including a tree but excluding religion. She, meanwhile, slept on wooden planks, wrapped in nothing but her coat.

Nina knew that she might not survive whatever was ahead of her. Even if she did, she might never return to the theatre.

Looking into the abyss, she wanted to make sure that at least her artistic legacy would live on:

> Don't let my partner play the fool, let him take some young dancer, for example Fedrova [sic],* and start working with her. What we have done together in art are very valuable things and one must continue to create and work on character dance, and not sit and fold one's arms. Pass this on to him with these words, it is enough that I have left life, he needs to work and he has all possibilities to do so. It is difficult to find such a wonderful dancer as he is. I am very proud that at one time in my life I could dance with him. Everything that we created together must not get lost, and I totally don't care if a competitor of mine will have success in this matter. If I will return some day, then I will be able still to create many, many new things. I cannot live without creativity. For me, there are only two extremes, either to live in hope of my future growth or to perish, because I cannot understand and comprehend how to live only in order to exist. Pass this on to Serezha [Sergei Koren] and tell him that I believe that he will again begin to dance on the variety stage.[53]

But the time to say goodbye had not quite come yet, not even in Nina's mind. Otherwise, she would not have written in the next sentence:

* Nadezhda Fedorova had performed the solo 'lyrical dance' in Anisimova's first ballet, *Andalusian Wedding*.

Take care of my beautiful white costume, I am still planning on dancing in it. About the sheet music, still, it would be good if it was all copied in two copies, what if suddenly I start to dance, I could need it then. And if it's possible, let Serezha return my march. However, so far this is all my fantasy. I am not even thinking about my specialisation now. As regards exercises, for the present I mustn't even dream about it, there is no place and there will be no time when I will begin to work. But still, send ballet shoes. Know that in my loneliness and great sorrow, I am for the time being still Nina. Only my movements have become slower and my thoughts shorter . . . Yes, let Kostia enlarge the film on which my photo was taken in the white costume and send me one photo. Report everything that is new at the theatre in terms of productions. I read that Chabukiani is staging a Spanish ballet. Now this I'm jealous of. Write to me what Vasia is staging and in general everything everything about my own art. . . . Goodbye, to a New Year with new happiness.[54]

7

The Folly of it All

Meanwhile, Kostia had not yet received Nina's news that she was to stay in Kazakhstan. He had not heard anything from her since her announcement in November that she was about to be put on a long-distance transport. He had no idea where she was or whether she was still alive. Without her, he had nothing to lose, and he made a decision. A few days after the New Year, he loaded a sheet of paper into his typewriter. He would channel his rage into a razor-sharp indictment meticulously laying out the injustice of Nina's case, make sure it reached the NKVD, and live with the consequences:

1.

On the night from 2 to 3 February 1938, <u>Nina Alexandrova Anisimova</u>, soloist of the ballet company of the State Academic Theatre named after S. M. Kirov, living on Kirovsky Prospect No. 1/3 flat 31, was arrested by organs of the NKVD in Leningrad.

On 18 August 1938 the Moscow Special Council passed a decision on her case and, having recognised her as a socially dangerous element, decreed to send her for five years to a corrective labour camp. On 9 September 1938 this decision was announced to N. A. Anisimova with the oral explanation that no concrete guilt whatsoever had been settled on her, that her property would not be confiscated, that the right to correspond and the right to appeal without time limit remained with her.

On 22 September 1938 N. A. Anisimova was sent to Karaganda. Around 30 October she was delivered to the station Karabas of Karaganda region. She remained there or in the nearby village Dolinka until the last days of November. At the end of November she was put down for a long-distance transport. Until today, there is no further information about either her or her location, now, apparently, outside the borders of Kazakhstan.

2.

Five days after N. A. Anisimova's arrest, on 7 February, I managed to talk to Leningrad NKVD employee Gantman, who declared with respect to the question interesting me, her case's prospects: 'We don't intend to let Anisimova go, but to investigate her case, maybe we will release her, maybe we will set some punishment for her, but neither one nor the other will depend on the level of her guilt.'

After this meeting, I sent statements addressed to Zakovsky, Pozern* and to the USSR Procuracy, contain-

---

* Leonid Zakovsky was head of the NKVD/Leningrad region in 1937, from January 1938 deputy commissar of internal affairs and head

ing a characterisation of N. A. Anisimova's personal and creative cast of mind and a series of considerations trying to prove the impossibility of charging her with any article of the Criminal Code, and, in particular, any of the points of article 58. It was perfectly obvious to me that any concrete charge levelled at her would be precisely under this article.

On 22 February, I had a conversation with assistant procurator Izraelit of the Special Department of the Procuracy for Leningrad province, who announced to me that N. A. Anisimova's case was 'complex, it has a number of layers and angles.'

On 27 March I had a conversation with Chief Procurator Rozovsky of the RKKA,* stating my understanding of the essence of N. A. Anisimova's case. On 9 June I had a conversation with Military Procurator Shmulevich of the Leningrad Military District, in which he emphasised that no facts of espionage had been established in N. A. Anisimova's case, but that by virtue of her 'link' to former legal consultant Salomé of the German consulate in Leningrad she had brought about some evil for which, in his opinion, she should receive eight years in a concentration camp.

On 22 September, already after I had found out about the Special Council's decision, I had a conversation with Kuznetsov, head of the 1st Department of the

of the NKVD/Moscow region. Boris Pozern was procurator of Leningrad province, 1937–8.

* Workers' and Peasants' Red Army.

Main Military Procuracy, who declared categorically that
N. A. Anisimova was in no way guilty of anything concrete, that she herself was of enormous value, but that
she had turned out to be participating in several things
taking place around Salomé and that she did not keep her
acquaintance with him within the necessary borders. At
the same time, he acquainted me with several, apparently
fundamental points of Shmulevich's closing indictment,
tallying with the formulation of the indictment's essential accusations which were also contained in the Special
Council's notice.

I have drawn the following conclusions from the
above stated:

1.   Indeed, just as demonstrated in my note from
February, N. A. Anisimova is not guilty of anything
whatsoever, and especially not of anything contained in
article 58.

2.   N. A. Anisimova's conviction for her 'link to Salomé'
by the Special Council was based on the investigation's
extremely terse deductions, Procurator Shmulevich of
the Leningrad Military District completely subscribes
to this opinion.

3.   These deductions consist to a significant degree of
a naked statement of facts, in several instances incorrectly accentuated, oversimplified and corroborated: by
biased information given by one–two individuals from
the depths of the ballet company of the Kirov Theatre
who are interested in compromising N. A. Anisimova and
by the testimony of one 'witness', an individual whose

character is far from trustworthy – the artist Levanenok, arrested already in the month of September in 1938 for his links to foreigners.

Kostia also detailed Nina's family history, including her father's military record, and Nina's accomplishments as a dancer, concluding:

> According to the character of her talent, N. A. Anisimova is a Soviet artist in the full sense of the word, whose whole creative work, imbued with the spirit of genuine innovation, entirely independent, deeply realistic, responds to the basic interests of the Soviet ballet theatre, whose front is really not rich in workers full of creative initiative. In terms of the level of her mastery, she indisputably occupies first place in the ranks of female character dancers in our Union, distinguished by her high level of performance technique and a delicate understanding of the national artistic forms of the nations of the USSR. Neither one nor the other could have been achieved without being an artist who loves her Soviet art and, in it, her country, her people, its poetry, its music, its creativity and its new, Soviet life.[1]

Kostia was pursuing two lines of argument. The first, pointing out to the NKVD the irrational injustice of Nina's Gulag sentence, resembled a suicide mission. What compelled Kostia to address the NKVD as if he was dealing with a security force restrained by a regular legal framework upholding norms such as the presumption of innocence until proven guilty? Was he deluding himself that rogue agents were responsible for Nina's arrest, and that the organisation would act once alerted to their machinations? After witnessing arrest after arrest in his immediate vicinity, surely he could not believe that he was beyond the NKVD's reach – or had anger and despair propelled him into a psychological state where he no longer cared about his own life?

Kostia was not a fervent Communist – neither he nor Nina had joined the Communist Party. He had shared the dreams of Petrograd's theatrical avant-garde and witnessed their obliteration through censorship. He knew that the regime was ready to destroy not just ideas, but also the people who had them. But his persistence and fearlessness presupposed a certain degree of faith in the system he was living in – or at least a hope that it contained the possibility of rational fairness. Kostia and his contemporaries did not have the benefit of hindsight. Nor did they have the option of leaving their country. To live day after day in the terrifying reality of Stalinist Russia, perhaps there was nothing left to do but to cling to hope.

Determined to clear Nina's name, Kostia was ready to ignore the fact that his own history was potentially even more suspect. Although his father had sided with the regime early on, his mother was a hereditary noblewoman. More importantly, his work had brought him dangerously close to influential people who were on their way down, including his former boss at the Committee on Arts Affairs, Mikhail Rafail, arrested on 4 July 1937, but most notably Vsevolod Meyerhold and Olga Kameneva. The latter was Leon Trotsky's sister, and the first wife of the Bolshevik and oppositionist Lev Kamenev, who was sentenced to death at the first Moscow show trial in

August 1936. Kameneva was arrested in 1936 and executed in 1941. Right after the revolution, she had worked closely with Meyerhold on revolutionising theatre at Narkompros' Theatre Division. In 1926 she had been put in charge of the newly founded All-Union Society of Cultural Relations with Foreign Countries, or VOKS, responsible for organising the visits of Western intellectuals and writers to the USSR and for cultivating relations with them in their home countries.

Ostentatiously non-political, VOKS was supposed to seduce Western intellectuals into active support for the Soviet Union.[2] Kostia acted as VOKS representative in Leningrad from 1926 until 1930, hosting numerous foreign cultural luminaries visiting the city, including the Norwegian explorer, humanitarian and Nobel Peace Prize Laureate Fridtjof Nansen, the French novelist Henri Barbusse and the influential American writer Theodore Dreiser. Kostia had welcomed Dreiser on a foggy November morning in 1927 as he disembarked from the night train from Moscow.[3]

From the vantage point of 1939, Kostia's time as VOKS representative was by definition suspicious: working for an organisation headed by the wife of Stalin's enemy Kamenev, he had regularly consorted with foreigners. The NKVD began arresting many VOKS staff in 1936 and continued to do so during the Terror.[4] That Kostia's role largely involved showing off Soviet achievements to visiting foreigners was unlikely to prove much of a defence if he was arrested. Accusing the NKVD of negligence in connection with Nina's case was therefore anything but prudent.

Kostia's second line of argument – that Nina was of greater use to the authorities outside prison than inside – was more reasonable, but this did not make it more promising. Across the Soviet Union, people were appealing to the NKVD on behalf of their scientist or artist friends, trying to convince the authorities that they were not just innocent but were important contributors to Soviet society, whose talents would be wasted if the person remained imprisoned. More often than not, such appeals led nowhere. But Kostia was right: Nina had indeed started to occupy an unusual position in the world of Soviet ballet. He argued that as Nina was a down-to-earth character dancer and one of the few choreographers interpreting the folk dances of different Soviet nationalities, her artistic profile corresponded directly to the ideological demands of the times. Nina's creative personality offered ballet a Soviet path of development, leading away from the aristocratic conventions of the past.

Kostia had participated in the complicated relationship between the intelligentsia and the party since the early days of the revolution. He knew the strategies, the wrestling for control, the attempts at mutual manipulation. He understood the rules of the game and how to present Nina's story. Time had brought the sobering realisation that the Bolsheviks were not visionary enablers of avant-garde dreams but aspiring puppet-masters hoping to enlist art for their own goals. But the Bolshevik regime had nonetheless carved out a special place for artists in its emerging power structures. There was something messianic in its zeal to build a proletarian, socialist civilisation on the vast territory of the largely agrarian former Russian empire. To spread the new faith, the leaders of the cult needed heralds to spread the message. The Bolsheviks firmly believed in the power of art, offering artists privilege in return for active loyalty. But their belief in the importance of art inevitably brought with it a deep fear of its subversive power: who could know what artists were really trying to say, and what people were really thinking when listening to music, reading a book, watching a ballet or looking at a painting?

One of Nina's colleagues would later write about this period: 'In the days of my youth, character dance was astonishingly popular. The female and male dancers of this *emploi* were competing entirely on the same level with the ballerinas and male principals, attracting the auditorium's sympathy to the same extent as they did.'[5] But before Kostia could develop the argument that Nina's work was of vital ideological importance for the Bolsheviks, he had to establish her innocence.

4.

N. A. Anisimova's incriminating 'link to Salomé' boils down to the following.

Mr Salomé, legal consultant at the German consulate in Leningrad over the course of several years, cultivated a very wide circle of acquaintances in the artistic ballet world right until his departure abroad in 1936. The atmosphere providing the possibility for making these acquaintances was created by the special favour Salomé enjoyed with the management of the Kirov Theatre, granting him free access to the director's box, backstage, rehearsals and so forth. The theatre's 'party' leadership's servile obsequiousness vis à vis Salomé went so far that when, at the moment of our worsening relations with Germany, some of the artists acquainted with him tried to put an end to their acquaintance, Salomé expressed his surprise to the theatre's management that 'moral pressure' was exerted on his acquaintances, forcing them to avoid encounters with him, and the obsequious management reprimanded their subordinates for the embarrassment of breaking off acquaintance with an official representative of a foreign government with whom we maintain diplomatic relations.

Kostia was playing on the fact that Salomé had allegedly used his connections to the Kirov's director, a political appointee, to gain – and maintain – special access to the dancers. In Stalin's Russia, life at the top was dangerous. By the end of the Great Terror, three consecutive directors of the Kirov Theatre had been 'unmasked' as enemies of the people, offering Kostia the opportunity to implicate the theatre management in the Salomé affair. Veniamin Solomonovich Bukhstein, director of the Kirov until summer/autumn 1934, was arrested in September 1937 and shot as a spy, terrorist and member of a counter-revolutionary group in January 1938; his successor, Ruvim Abramovich Shapiro, was arrested in September 1936, sentenced to five years of forced labour for 'counter-revolutionary Trotskyite activity' and ultimately shot in March 1938; and his successor, Natan Iakovlevich Grinfeld, was arrested in November 1937 and sentenced to forced labour.[6]

Running the Kirov in the 1930s was not an enviable job. Almost twenty years after the revolution, opera and ballet were still seen as seriously wanting in ideological terms, unable to free themselves of the frothy conventions of their frivolous past. The Kirov looked for salvation in the respectability of the dramatic theatre, inviting leading directors from other venues to supervise its productions in order to improve their narrative and ideological coherence. But this was utterly impractical as it made the Kirov's production schedule dependent on the directors' other commitments. The result was a deadlock: new productions were planned on paper, but often never materialised. The theatre needed to train its own directors, but this was easier said than done.

Within the context of the Great Terror, this unfortunate interaction between political demands and practical constraints metamorphosed into accusations of 'wrecking', intentional anti-Soviet sabotage. The Kirov's in-house newspaper *Za sovetskoe iskusstvo* stated in October 1937: 'The wrecking system of the two previous directors of the theatre – now unmasked enemies of the people – is obviously firmly ensconced in our theatre, if until now the new leadership hasn't lifted a finger to create appropriate conditions to grow cadres of directors inside the theatre.' The singers and dancers were also complaining that the artistic directors of the opera and ballet ensembles were not distributing roles properly, creating a 'completely abnormal situation, where only one part of the ensemble is genuinely working, while the other part is not used'.[7] The theatre's annual report for 1937 put the blame for its significant over-expenditure, despite its failure to fulfil the plan for new ballets and operas, squarely on the shoulders of its former leaders: 'all these violations and hold-ups in the plan fulfilment for 1937 are to a significant degree the result of the wrecking activity of enemies of the people who, earlier on, were leading the theatre.'[8] Scapegoats were easy to find during the Great Terror.

Kostia continued:

N. A. Anisimova was introduced to Salomé by one of the female artists. Playing the balletomane and patron of young talents, after some time Salomé started to invite her over to his house in the company of her comrades from the stage. From time to time, he presented her with small presents and souvenirs. Sometimes he sent baskets of flowers to her home or to the theatre. He didn't do this just with respect to N. A. Anisimova. He did this in relation to a whole series of his acquainted artists, in a number of instances on a far larger scale and constancy. During the period of their acquaintance, he appeared once to pay her a visit on her birthday or name day, sat for half an hour and left.

Salomé had his regular visitors. A number of dancers such as Levanenok, Mikhailov, Georgievsky, Dudinskaya, Kuznetsova, G. Kuznetsov, Trakhtina, Belikova, Latonina and others were his personal friends, they visited his house almost daily, without special invitation, enjoyed very generous presents, even spent the night at his flat, paid court to his wife and so forth. N. A. Anisimova did not belong to this category of Salomé's acquaintances. She was at his place only on the basis of invitations, she was there never on her own, she did not enjoy any personal partiality of his towards her and she did not receive any kind of special presents from him. She stopped her acquaintance with him over the course of 1933. Towards the beginning of 1934, an end had been put to this acquaintance, and she even tried to avoid meeting Salomé by chance at the theatre. Meanwhile, a number of persons continued to maintain the closest connections to Salomé right up to

1937*, unperturbed by the presence of a fascist dictator-ship in Germany, the fact of Kirov's murder and so forth.

Does it follow from all this that N. A. Anisimova, by no means a person in any way especially close to Salomé, played any kind of special role in Salomé's wide circle of acquaintances in the ballet world? Of course not. And the very fact that it was not found necessary to hold a number of people responsible for their acquaintance with Salomé as such, people who were to a significantly greater and significantly closer degree connected to him, is only evidence that this cannot be the reason for the punish-ment of N. A. Anisimova, even though it is in fact given as such. At the same time, the absence of any claim against a number of people who enjoyed Salomé's personal favour completely explicitly and openly, to an incomparably greater degree than N. A. Anisimova, presents itself as an egregious injustice. This is just only to the degree to which the absence of any kind of concrete actions aimed at harming our country permits the possibility of ascribing no special significance to the 'links to Salomé' maintained by a group of ballet youths, who were more-over 'inspired' to this by their management. But we are told that N. A. Anisimova 'is not guilty of anything spe-cific'. Consequently, in this respect, she differs in no way from the rest of her group of friends, together with whom

---

* Kostia appears to have been not entirely certain about the year of Salomé's departure, mentioning both 1936, the correct year, and 1937 in his letter.

she was at Salomé's house. What then, in this case, is the compelling reason for subjecting her to punishment?

5.

The reason for N. A. Anisimova's punishment, a punishment which presently, by force of her profession's specific peculiarities, threatens her whole creative life and promises to put an end to the possibility of further work for her whole life, appears to be an incorrect, biased, erroneously highlighted understanding of her acquaintance with Salomé. The sources of this incorrectness are, on the one hand, an uncritical attitude towards the information which might have been received about her from the depths of the ballet company, on the other hand – excessive trust in the testimony of Levanenok, a witness in all respects not trustworthy. Moreover, the order of the investigation didn't understand N. A. Anisimova's outlook on life and creativity, because from any explicitly unprejudiced view, declaring her a socially dangerous element in the absence of any concrete guilt along the lines of her acquaintance with Salomé is a monstrous contradiction of her entire conduct, her work, her opinions, thoughts and ideological interests.

The atmosphere created around her in the last years shows that biased information about N. A. Anisimova could have come from the depths of the theatre. Starting in 1934, N. A. Anisimova is quickly going up in the world as an artist. She has a series of major stage successes following one upon the other. It is important to emphasise that these successes were successes of a *Soviet* dance artist

168

and choreographer. *The Flames of Paris* and *Katerina* are still forgiven. In these, N. A. Anisimova still stays within the limits of her traditional role – episodic character dance staged in ballets where prima ballerinas still take the central place. But then N. A. Anisimova is given the leading part in the ballet *Lost Illusions*, a role created for a character dancer. Inside the theatre, a storm breaks out in the circle of prima ballerinas. They cannot admit the possibility of a character dance soloist occupying one of the central positions in a production. Under their pressure, under threats of letters to Bubnov* and so on, the producers cut N. A. Anisimova from this part and give it to one of the prima ballerinas, in the process redoing the whole structure of the production in conformity with the possibilities of classical dance. As a result, the part, having been taken away from N. A. Anisimova, is ruined. N. A. Anisimova receives the leading part in the ballet *Partisan Days*. She has the right to get this part since the ballet is entirely built on character and folk dance, and she is its best representative in the company. A long squabble, unprecedented in scale, begins, inspired by two, three people, a squabble that draws in the entire theatre and almost ruins the production. Commissioned by the Ballet Institute, N. A. Anisimova stages the production *Andalusian Wedding*. It is a big success with the public. It is said that a new, talented and

* Andrei Bubnov (1884–1938), RSFSR Commissar of Enlightenment 1929–37, arrested on 17 October 1937, sentenced to death by shooting on 1 August 1938.

fresh choreographer has emerged in the person of N. A. Anisimova. She is there and then invited to stage ballets in other theatres. But when the question comes up whether to revive this ballet the next season and to show it to a wide audience, unbelievable opposition to this arises, evidently originating from the same people. This opposition leads to a situation where the rehearsals fall through, where the conductor, who in spring had led the production, now sabotages the production and so forth. N. A. Anisimova proposes to make a small production – the ballet *Pushkiniana* – for the Pushkin anniversary, with an apotheosis showing Pushkin amid the nations of the USSR portrayed in his works. [Kostia knew about the Kirov's theatrical intrigues not just from Nina. In 1936, he had been appointed assistant to the head of the Directorate of Arts Affairs of Leningrad's city council, attending to the repertoire of the city's theatres and working on the city's preparations for the Pushkin centenary in 1937.] Before the proposal was officially considered it had already excited some sort of incomprehensible bitterness against itself. Informed about this by someone from the depths of the theatre, Tsilshtein,* head of the City Committee's Cultural-Enlightenment Department, gives the instruction not to work on 'such trifles' under any circumstances. N. A. Anisimova and S. G. Koren prepare their concert. The same small group of people foretell its failure beforehand, spread all sorts of rumours, start

---

* Emmanuil Tsilshtein (1902–38), head of the Leningrad Committee on Arts Affairs, arrested 28 October 1937, shot on 17 February 1938.

a conversation about how 'one can also clip Anisimova's wings'. Her arrest indeed clips her 'wings', coinciding with the day on which posters for the performance appeared around town.

A few hours before the NKVD took Nina, the Kirov Ballet's new artistic director, Leonid Lavrovsky, had given a talk to the ballet section of the Leningrad branch of the All-Russian Theatrical Society, outlining his plans for the Kirov for 1938. Nina's senior by four years, Lavrovsky was considered one of the most promising choreographers at the time. He would soon write ballet history with the Kirov's legendary production of Prokofiev's *Romeo and Juliet*,* but on that fateful day in February 1938 he announced what would have been the chance of a lifetime for Nina in a field – choreography – still dominated by men: Lavrovsky intended to commission Nina to stage a new one-act ballet for the company.[9]

So it's not surprising that in this kind of atmosphere, any kind of defamatory and politically compromising material about N. A. Anisimova can come into being! So it's not surprising that this material is channelled in the direction of an old 'link to Salomé', because this 'link' existed already almost five years ago, the contours

* Prokofiev's *Romeo and Juliet* was also an accidental victim of the Great Terror: the ballet was cut from the Bolshoi's repertoire plan after an official administrative review and evaluation culminated in the arrest of the Bolshoi's director Vladimir Mutnykh in April 1937. Mutnykh was executed in November 1937. Piotrovsky, the ballet's librettist was arrested in July 1937 and executed in November 1937 (Simon Morrison, *Bolshoi Confidential*, pp. 292–3).

of its reality are fading, allowing for pretty free accents and embellishments!

Kostia's conspiracy theory was not outlandish. Nina's meteoric rise had taken place in an increasingly poisonous atmosphere. During the Great Terror, people all over the Soviet Union manipulated the manic climate to their own advantage. Why should disgruntled ballerinas be an exception? The regime's insistence that enemies were lurking everywhere meant that anybody could be framed as such – and woe betide anyone who failed to join the verbal lynching. Displaying a lack of enthusiastic vigilance was undoubtedly more dangerous than accusing the wrong people.

Clouds had also been gathering over the head of Agrippina Vaganova, who had been artistic director of the Kirov Ballet since 1931. Many of the dancers who had passed through her strict school and graduated into the company were unhappy, complaining about the lack of new productions and accusing Vaganova of casting only her favourites. The last two years had indeed been frustrating for many. Vainonen was in charge of *Partisan Days* and the company's next classical production, a new version of Alexander Glazunov's ballet *Raymonda*, but fear was slowing down work on both ballets. The classical ballerinas were left to hone their old repertoire, jealously noting who got cast and how often while Nina and Vainonen continued working on *Partisan Days*, delaying work on *Raymonda*.

On 7 December 1937, the ballet company convened a meeting that turned into a political trial. So many dancers were queuing up to attack Vaganova that the meeting had to be continued on 9 December. Of the leading ballerinas, only Natalia Dudinskaya defended her former teacher. The other ballerinas were ready to attack. Vaganova was accused of wrecking: instead of fighting the previous directors, she had hushed up dancers trying to complain about the abnormal working situation. The theatre's new director concluded that the theatre needed to take decisive action.[10]

By the end of December 1937, everything was pointing towards the impending arrest of Vaganova. But she was one step ahead of the game. Vaganova had survived the revolution, and she would survive the Great Terror and the deadly first winter of the siege of Leningrad. Seeing the writing on the wall, she relinquished her role at the theatre and pleaded her case in Moscow.[11] On 19 December 1937, she was honourably released from her position as the Kirov Ballet's artistic director.[12]

Vaganova had had a narrow escape, but in this environment, any action – or inaction – could be interpreted as anti-Soviet and workplace conflicts quickly acquire a deathly dimension. Kostia's supposition that Nina had fallen victim to a theatrical intrigue was thus entirely reasonable, but the classical ballerinas who had attacked Vaganova were unlikely culprits: they all had their own ties to Salomé. The NKVD had contemplated focusing its attention on another of Salomé's favourites, Vaganova's defender Dudinskaya. On 7 January 1938, just a few weeks after Dudinskaya had bravely defended Vaganova, a paper was signed by an NKVD officer decreeing that Dudinskaya and her fellow Kirov dancers Andrei Mikhailov and Galina Kuznetsova should be investigated for espionage. Levanenok had testified that they had maintained close ties to Salomé without giving concrete facts about their 'espionage activities'. Dudinskaya and Kuznetsova escaped arrest. Mikhailov didn't: arrested on 20 June 1938, he was shot as a spy on 3 November 1938.[13]

Judging by Levanenok's trial, the NKVD's stooges inside the Kirov Theatre had made sure that the Big House was well informed about Salomé's wide-ranging friendships. Most likely, no special denunciation had been needed to get Nina arrested, but it is impossible to determine why the NKVD issued an arrest order for her but not for Dudinskaya and Kuznetsova. Perhaps someone higher up was protecting them: Dudinskaya was a rising star, but also a lively, charming young woman, a workaholic who also knew how to enjoy herself. Kuznetsova was married to one of the Kirov's male stars, Dudinskaya's stage partner Vakhtang Chabukiani, who had apparently also visited Salomé's flat. It is striking that Anisimova was the highest-ranking dancer arrested for ties to Salomé: none of the principal dancers who knew him were arrested. But chance might have played a greater part than fame in who escaped detention. Kostia had observed correctly that there seemed to be no logic to the NKVD's arrests among the dancers. He was determined to use this randomness to his advantage, and to show that the secret police had made a mistake in singling out Nina. Resolved to unravel the ties that had bound her, he challenged Levanenok's credibility as a witness.

Levanenok, asked about Anisimova because of such material, out of one motive or the other reaches for her like for a straw. He can heap part of his guilt on her. If he had been asked about someone else and asked within the same context within which he was asked about Anisimova

– he would have said exactly the same about someone else. But he was asked specifically about Anisimova. He draws her close to himself. He connects her name with himself, attributes to her one action, plan, intention or the other. There are no other witnesses. In the investigation's opinion, Levanenok's words completely confirm Anisimova's 'involvement' in something, something in which the whole remaining circle of her comrades acquainted with Salomé could have been found involved in just as successfully.

Nobody, however, asks himself the question why Levanenok could be considered a trustworthy witness, competent in N. A. Anisimova's affairs and moods? He knows her very little. If he has been to Salomé hundreds of times, then Anisimova was there immeasurably less frequently, and she was never there only with Levanenok. In the entire ten years of N. A. Anisimova's work at the theatre, Levanenok was at her place three, four times. He does not belong to her circle of comrades, and, even less so, to her circle of friends. According to the scale of his artistic work, the range of his interests, the character of his acquaintances outside the theatre, his way of life and so forth, Levanenok has nothing in common with N. A. Anisimova. He is a figure who was connected to her completely accidentally. There are neither any psychological, nor domestic, nor any other reasons why N. A. Anisimova should have had anything in common with him altogether, especially in terms of any kind of unseemly schemes or intentions. Levanenok's depositions are nothing but unfounded allegations that have no serious basis whatsoever, but which for one reason or the other have earned trust and encouragement.

Discrediting Levanenok was one thing, but Nina had not actually been sentenced for espionage. In labelling her a 'socially dangerous element', the Special Council had looked not only at her friendship with Salomé, but also at her suspect social origins. The Soviet court system was often more interested in who somebody was than in what the person had done. Kostia needed to dismantle the social argument underpinning her sentence.

6.

The prosecution's closing indictment in N. A. Anisimova's case was made up of several points. One ought to dwell on them.

First: the emphasis in the text of the Special Council's decision on N. A. Anisimova's social provenance as the daughter of a colonel. Now there is a clear example of an incorrect accent put on reality. Yes, N. A. Anisimova was the daughter of a colonel. It was explained above what sort of colonel this was. Why oughtn't one call her the daughter of a commanding officer of the RKKA? Why, finally, oughtn't one classify her according to the position she herself takes in our art, the position of one of the best Soviet ballet artists? Why does she have to answer for the fact that her father was a colonel twenty-one years ago, notwithstanding the fact that then, over the course of ten years of his life he actively participated in the construction of the RKKA and the fight with White colonels and

ABOVE: Nina and a group of students of the Leningrad Choreographic Institute, mid-1920s. First row, second from left: Nina; second row, third from left: the future ballerina Marina Semenova; third row, third from left: Alexander Pushkin, future teacher of Rudolf Nureyev and Mikhail Baryshnikov.

ABOVE: Rossi Street, with the Leningrad Choreographic Institute on the right and the Alexandrinsky (Pushkin) Theatre in the background, 1930s.

ABOVE: A scene from the mass spectacle *The Storming of the Winter Palace*. Kostia was one of the co-directors of this theatrical experiment. Petrograd, 1920.

ABOVE: Kirov Theatre of Opera and Ballet, Leningrad, 1939.

ABOVE: Nina leads the revolutionary masses with the tricolour flag in *The Flames of Paris* at the Kirov Theatre, early 1950s.

ABOVE, LEFT: Nina in *The Flames of Paris*, early 1950s. ABOVE, RIGHT: Andrei Levanenok as a Chinese labourer in the ballet *The Red Poppy*, 1929.

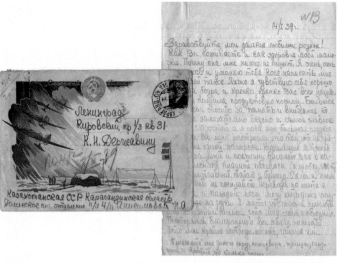

ABOVE: A letter Nina wrote to her family from Karlag in January 1939. The envelope commemorates the Soviet polar expedition of 1937–8.

ABOVE, LEFT: Konstantin Derzhavin, 1930s. This is probably the photo that Kostia sent to Nina in Karlag. There is an inscription on the back of the photo: 'To my dear and beautiful ballerina Nina Anisimova from Derzhavin – from your husband, friend, brother, admirer etc. etc. K. Derzhavin. 23 November 1938.'
ABOVE, RIGHT: Nina Anisimova, 1950.

ABOVE: Karlag's Central Administration, Dolinka.

ABOVE: Prisoners of war, Karlag, 1940s.

ABOVE, LEFT: Konstantin Derzhavin, August 1936, the summer he and Nina met.
ABOVE, RIGHT: Nina and Sergei Koren dancing the Krakowiak from Mikhail
Glinka's opera *Ivan Susanin*, 1946.

ABOVE: Molotov (Perm) Opera and Ballet Theatre, 1940s.

ABOVE: Tatiana Vecheslova, Natalia Dudinskaya, Nina and Alla Shelest walking on Rossi Street, 1940s.

ABOVE: Nina and artists after a performance of *Gayané*, probably in Yerevan, late 1940s.

ABOVE: Isai Sherman (conductor), Aram Khachaturian and Nina working on *Gayané*. Molotov, early 1940s.

ABOVE: Konstantin Sergeyev (Armen) and Nina (Aisha) in *Gayané*. Molotov, early 1940s.

generals? For what purpose was such an emphasis made and such an accent set? In order to put the appropriate 'social' basis under the points that follow and, by doing so, to let the feature of N. A. Anisimova's social danger protrude more relief-like. A method without much conscience, but which in this case apparently appeared to be necessary, because in order to give a motive to N. A. Anisimova's social danger – a notion which, applied to her, takes on a rather strange character – one had to assemble at least some sort of basis out of crumbs.

From the point of view of Soviet ideology, to have roots in the wrong social milieu could be a crime in itself. Across the Soviet Union, people hid their family origins or ties even from their own children. Kostia needed to convince the secret police that even though Nina was born the daughter of a tsarist colonel, she had grown into a loyal Soviet citizen and artist devoted to her country. He was also trying to show that although Nina had made a mistake when she accepted Salomé's invitations, she had matured enough politically over the years to realise when the moment had come to break off contact with him. He turned to the second point made by the prosecution:

Second: <u>N. A. Anisimova was acquainted with Salomé until 1934</u>. Formally, this is true. But in substance, one should have written this: 'Starting in 1933, that is, from the moment of the establishment of an openly fascist dictatorship in Germany, N. A. Anisimova started to put an end to her acquaintance with Salomé on her own initiative, not wishing to compromise herself with a link to an official representative of the fascist government. She had broken off this acquaintance by the beginning of 1934, notwithstanding the fact that Mr Salomé continued to enjoy the theatre management's exclusive individual attention and favour like before, notwithstanding the fact that a number of her friends and comrades from the stage, politically significantly less developed than her, calmly continued this acquaintance until the very departure of Mr Salomé abroad, that is, until 1937, not stopping to visit his house, to accept presents from him and so forth.' Such a formulation would have been completely accurate, objective and, like every objectivity in the given case, advantageous for N. A. Anisimova. But it's perfectly clear that, in that way, the concept of her social danger would have come to naught. Now this is the reason why this correct and objective formulation was replaced with a confused and general intimation whose method of using an accumulation of accusatory information in no ways differs from the intimation of 'daughter of a colonel'.

. . .

It's enough to limit oneself to these examples. They characterise graphically enough this method of superficially stating facts which was applied to N. A. Anisimova. Unfortunately, this method proved effective in its own way. A collection of essentially empty facts created a kind of mosaic of 'links', 'acquaintances' and other connections to figures politically hostile to us. At the same time, the fact has been lost sight of that, for the sake of objectivity, these 'acquaintances' and 'links' ought to have been regarded not on the level of political contact, but on the level of social contact brought about by the conditions of theatre life and theatre routine characterised above. Now this is why it has to be recognised that the conclusions concerning N. A. Anisimova are based on facts which in and of themselves have absolutely no basis. And, once again, the following fact convinces us of this: notwithstanding legal grounds to suspect something wrong in Salomé's relations with the ballet, not twenty, thirty people from this ballet have fallen under suspicion, but seven people, out of which three have successfully come out of prison (Fiurt, Sidorovskaya and Oppengeim), one was compelled to change her place of residence (Medalinskaya), the two remaining ones – to the extent that this can be guessed – find themselves at this moment accused of one or the other article of the Criminal Code, but N. A. Anisimova, who was not found guilty of anything, has found herself in the position of a 'socially dangerous element'. The most characteristic aspect of all this is that, apart from working in the same theatre, N. A. Anisimova herself had no connection whatsoever to any of those people whose arrest was to some degree caused by their connection to Salomé and that those people to whom she was really connected at that time, through close comradely relations on the one hand and their simultaneous acquaintance with Salomé on the other hand, were found to be above suspicion and punishment.

7.

One evidently needs to recognise as socially dangerous that type of person who, under the conditions of our socialist way of life, exerts, or could exert, a harmful influence on those around him by virtue of his inclinations, opinions, conduct etc. From the moment she reached a conscious age, N. A. Anisimova's only inclination was an inclination towards her art. Her only desire was to serve this art with all her strength and to serve it in a way that would be useful for her country. This is why in art, she worked in the definite ideological and creative direction described above. In this respect, she can only be recognised as a socially useful, actively useful person. For how could a person internally alien to our construction, a person alien to our socialist construction, even a person only potentially hostile to the life of our peoples – how could such a person feed so intensively on their creativity, their ideas, their life as N. A. Anisimova did?

In the life of this 'socially dangerous element', there is only one episode that took place five years ago – the 'link to Salomé', an episode which exists in the lives of a great number of other people, people close to N. A. Anisimova in one way or the other or people absolutely not close to her. There is nothing, literally nothing, in her biography either before or after this episode that would attest to her socially negative inclinations. This episode began at a time when N. A. Anisimova was extremely young, when she had only recently emerged from the walls of a closed educational institution, when she found herself leading a theatrical life, a girl in many ways naïve and not very discriminating in a number of questions. Some time passes. She herself eliminates this episode from her life, an episode in which even the most attentive investigation could not detect any criminal guilt. And after five years filled with intensive Soviet art saturated with what is needed, with correct creative thoughts, with work, after five years, during which N. A. Anisimova has grown into a major worker in Soviet art, she finds herself, in the full sense of the word, guilty without guilt.

Her father turns out to be only a colonel of the tsarist army, even though his service record gives evidence of many other things. Her acquaintance with Salomé turns into an element of accusation, even though many maintained this acquaintance and even though many people from her circle had much wider and closer relations and even though she herself put a stop to this acquaintance five years ago, which can only be evidence of her political growth. Official visits, and maybe even only one visit to the building of the German consulate together with several tens of representatives of the artistic world grow into 'visits to the building of the German consulate' and appear as the source of a story about some sort of special personal acquaintance with Walther. Levanenok becomes a person who reports some special information about N. A. Anisimova which no one, above all not she herself, knew, even though he was never in any way close to her, not in life, not in work, not even in their acquaintance with Salomé and even though he is indisputably not a trustworthy witness. Instead of arrests of 'frequent' visitors to Salomé Shmulevich promised in his talk with me, completely random people like Fiurt and Sidorovskaya are arrested. The genuine 'frequent' visitors of Salomé – N. A. Anisimova's friends – continue wondering till now why they haven't been arrested. A person is incriminated with espionage, when the espionage version collapses there is talk about 'some kind of evil' he caused, and finally the conclusion is reached that he is altogether not guilty of anything concrete and he is sent for five years to Karaganda. He is defined as a socially dangerous element, eyes having closed to everything taking place beyond the confines of 'the acquaintance with Salomé' – all his work, his personality, his world view, his circle of real friends and acquaintances and even to the real circumstances of this acquaintance. Eyes are closed to the fact that, already for a long time, this acquaintance hasn't played any role in the biography of the accused, that it has not in any way affected her behaviour, her opinions and that it has not in any way influenced the years of her honest, enthusiastic Soviet work that followed, just as it had no influence at the moment of its existence. On the fifth day after N. A. Anisimova's arrest, I proved to people involved in the investigation that she can't be and never was a criminal. They satisfied themselves of this after two to three months. I would never have allowed myself to raise my voice in defence of a person genuinely danger-ous to our system. I raised it at the time because I knew that N. A. Anisimova isn't guilty of anything. And I am raising it now because I firmly know that she is not a socially dangerous element and that such a definition was affixed to her by the incorrect path of the investigation and mistaken initial directives. It's not difficult to undo the knot that has been tied around N. A. Anisimova if one approaches evaluating her with the necessary attention, feeling of objectivity and impartiality. And then she will have all grounds to be saved from the accusations hanging over her – accusations that are inherently deeply incorrect and based on information that is either incorrect or incorrectly interpreted and illuminated.

Professor K. N. Derzhavin

4.1.1939

On 5 January 1939, Kostia's missive landed on the desk of Junior Lieutenant G. B. Artamanov, a senior investigator at the Leningrad NKVD.[14]

8

Dancing Behind
Barbed Wire

14 January 1939

Greetings, my distant, beloved family!

How are you and how is my Mamochka's health? Why isn't she writing anything to me. I am very, very worried and beg you, Kostia, to write to me what's the matter with her. I personally feel well, healthy, cheerful and strong, I kiss all of you strongly. The other day I received the package with provisions. Many thanks to all of you for remembering and caring for me. Everything is incredibly delicious and the most important thing are the tons of sweets, I have for the time being still a big sweet tooth. But you did upset me by not sending me a single cigarette. I am now a completely avid smoker and therefore beg you to put cigarettes into every package (a package of 100 pieces) or smoking tobacco and paper.[1]

Nina was hungry. A Karlag inmate described the convicts' situation succinctly: they were given too little food to live, but too much to die. Breakfast consisted of bread, hot water and *balanda*, watery soup. Lunch and dinner meant another bowl of *balanda*, supplemented at lunchtime with a bowl of *kasha* (gruel). According to one of Nina's contemporaries at Karlag, bread was 'the most valuable good in the camp' and 'worth more than gold'.[2] Some prisoners immediately devoured their entire ration; others ate small pieces throughout the day; some kept it until the evening so that they would not have to fall asleep hungry. As the only reliable component of the meagre food supply, bread was the most important currency for barter transactions among the prisoners. Most convicts received about 600–700 grams of bread; those unable to work received only 300 grams, an amount so small that it often pushed a convict already too weak to work to the brink of death.

The *balanda* was little more than 'dirt with pepper', a revolting liquid that would have been inedible outside the desperate context of the camps. Anna Edanova, an inmate of Karlag's Akmolinsk division from 1938 until 1946, worked as a cook in the camp kitchen. She did not remember ever receiving meat to prepare throughout those years, beyond the occasional head of a sheep. The kitchen prepared soup for 3,500 women: 'Forty buckets of water, but not a gram of fat, no oil, no meat, nothing but that barley. Sometimes, there was one spoonful of sunflower oil per cauldron.' The soup was so thin that it was easier to drink than to eat with a spoon. The same applied to the gruel often given out for lunch, a thin, watery porridge made of millet, buckwheat or oats. The distribution of food was a moment of heightened tension, fights and arguments: some criminal prisoners pushed to the front of the queue to have their soup ladled from the top where a few drops of fat might be swimming; others kept leaving the queue and rejoining it at the end because they wanted soup from the bottom of the pot, where some of the solids might have collected.

January in the camp was a particularly tough time of year: supplies were coming to an end, leaving little more than frozen potatoes and cabbage. Karlag's inmates grew vegetables, but they rarely saw the products of their labour. Subsisting only on camp fare for a long time was virtually impossible;[3] the packages Nina received from her family were therefore essential for her survival. Nina knew the sacrifice behind every item of food she received. Kostia's family occupied a relatively privileged position, but everybody bar the highest officials was struggling for basic supplies in the Soviet economy of scarcity. There were five long years ahead, but Nina was beginning to learn the rules for survival in the camps. Maybe she was requesting cigarettes not because she had suddenly turned into an 'avid smoker' but because they were valuable camp currency that could be traded for bread and other necessities.[4]

Hunger taught Karlag's inmates to find – or imagine – nutrition in the least likely locations. Compared to other camps in the far north or far east, Karlag had crucial advantages: in addition to a degree of freedom of movement, most jobs offered opportunities to supplement the meagre food rations, despite strict prohibitions. Inmates processing sunflowers scratched the pulp out of the flowers' stems and added it to their soup; those making sauerkraut picked away at the insulating flour smeared between the boards of the giant wooden tubs containing the kraut and ate the juice-saturated substance. Prisoners working outside searched for wild garlic, nettles, berries and mushrooms. Some added shamrock to their soup. Convicts caught hedgehogs and sparrows, ripping off the small birds' heads so that they could impale the tiny carcasses on pitchforks and roast them over a fire. Some trapped and ate rats.[5]

Nina was still anxiously waiting for a package with clothes – hers were desperately worn out – and other necessities. The camp administration didn't provide even basic eating utensils. Knives and forks were forbidden; the prisoners usually had to source their own wooden spoons, inspiring a former prisoner of Karlag to quip that Russia was the country with the most wooden spoons in the world. The prisoners always carried their spoons with them, one of their most important possessions. Small, battered metal pots, clay bowls or old cans, their sharp edges blunted with stones, served as food receptacles. Usually arriving in the camp without anything suitable, prisoners often had to trade in one of their first valuable bread rations for a container and utensil. Some saw an opportunity to express their individuality: sometimes a fellow prisoner could be found who would carve a beautifully decorated spoon in return for bread or other desirable goods.[6]

Keeping clean was virtually impossible. According to instructions given in 1947, prisoners were to be taken to the bathhouse three times per month. Inside the barracks, facilities for washing were less than rudimentary, if they existed at all, consisting of a few shared bowls or containers that had to be filled by hand from a small spout in a water barrel. Female prisoners waited in line for the shared bowls and melted snow in winter for some additional water. Lotte Strub, arriving in Karlag around the same time as Nina, described her daily morning routine using the small amount of water at her disposal, a can holding about 250 ml: 'You used a small amount to rinse the mouth. The second mouthful you let drip over your hands and quickly washed your face and neck. The next small portion, if there was still enough water, was used to wash the armpits and the bosom. And for down below, there was usually already not enough water.' Most women did not have their own towels and had either to use a piece of clothing to dry themselves or dry in the air. Menstruation was especially humiliating: the camp did not provide sanitary products, which were generally in short supply in the Soviet Union at that time. Many women stopped menstruating under the awful conditions, but not all. Some used rags, which were often stolen, but in the late 1930s most women didn't even have that option. They had to live with the demeaning reality of blood running into their pants, stiffening, stinking and itching.

The 'lavatories' were usually wooden huts with a row of holes cut into a plank, or crude beams over which the prisoners had to relieve themselves, often sitting so close to each other that their behinds were touching. The pits were regularly emptied, but the lavatory huts themselves were never cleaned. The prisoners had no paper or water with which to wipe themselves; they often used steppe grass or whatever else they could find outside. During the winter there were sometimes ropes leading from the barracks to the toilet hut; without them, a trip there in the midst of a snowstorm could cost a prisoner his or her life.[7]

Kostia's letter had given Nina enough comfort to allow her loving mischievousness to shine through her worries:

I am more and more convinced that my husband is gold and I love him more and more. I ask you, Mamochka, not to be upset and not to worry. I know that you are very highly strung and that you always cry because of every tri-fle. Now take me as an example. I now possess uncommon composure. I am looking after my health and I'm trying to gain weight especially for you . . . Not long ago I tried out whether my legs are functioning. And I am confident that I only have to start training properly and I will be able to dance like I used to. I am now on a posting where I am doing some light work and as soon as the possibility will present itself I will gladly work in my profession. In general, don't worry about me, as I've already written, I'm strong and in good spirits and confident that I will again be happy and that I will be able to see all of you.[8]

Nina folded the letter and carefully wrote Kostia's name and address on the few dotted lines marked on the envelope, which featured a dramatic scene in various shades of green, blue and red: stormy clouds, four planes flying over four waving Arctic explorers standing next to a snow-covered tent, a few items of scientific equipment and a pole with several red banners. Above them, a celebratory red wreath encircled a red globe dominated by a hammer and sickle; to its left and right were the words 'North Pole'.

The year leading up to Nina's arrest had been one not just of terror, but also of the great Soviet polar expedition. Soviet planes were the first to land on the North Pole, dropping off four members of an expedition tasked with erecting a drifting station – 'North Pole-1' – to collect scientific data over the course of nine months. Like most of her compatriots, Nina had probably proudly followed the progress of the expedition, drifting on an ice floe through the silent darkness of the Arctic Ocean. The scientists had recreated a mini-Soviet Union on their floe, listening to news broadcast by the Comintern station or a concert transmitted from the hall of the Moscow Conservatory, and organising their own spontaneous parade after listening to the October Revolution celebrations on Red Square. Nina's arrest had robbed her of the opportunity to hear about the scientists' dramatic rescue from the melting ice floe and to witness the national heroes' triumphant homecoming on the icebreaker *Yermak* in Leningrad on 15 March 1938, two weeks before her traumatic confrontation with Levanenok.[9] Nina put a stamp showing Lenin's serious face on the envelope. The small envelope and its sender encapsulated her generation's experience: revolution and terror, but also wonder at heroic Soviet achievements that seemed to prove that they were indeed heading towards a utopia of socialist greatness.

～

The Gulag encapsulated these conflicting extremes of Soviet reality. It was intimately linked to the Soviet leaders' messianic world view that they were creating a better, socialist civilisation that would culminate in a Communist paradise, and their Manichean conviction that you were either on their side or against them. Unlike Hitler's *Konzentrationslager*, the camps of the Gulag were not explicitly designed as death camps, even though at least 1.6 million died there, while those who survived often had their lives ruined. But the fact remains that about 20 per cent of Gulag inmates were released every year.[10]

The camps brutally exploited inmates and deliberately destroyed their dignity, but there was an ideological dimension to the Gulag that went beyond the crude economic rationale of slave labour. The Gulag grew out of the Bolsheviks' faith in the power of politics to transform society, a belief rooted in the Enlightenment and the scientific revolution. The Bolsheviks expected this transformation to be violent. For them, the logic of class war necessitated a dictatorship that ruthlessly persecuted members of certain social classes or groups as inherent enemies of the Soviet project. In the Gulag they were given a last chance: if they survived and reformed themselves, they could return to society. Just as iron ore must be smelted before being processed into steel, hard labour was supposed to forge errant elements into loyal Soviet citizens who proudly viewed their toil as an intrinsic part of the Soviet project.

Even the Soviet penal philosophy was rooted in class war: criminals imprisoned in the camps were seen as 'our people', because crime was defined as a remnant of pre-revolutionary class exploitation, a disease that could be cured by the right injection of socialist labour. From the system's point of view, the real enemy was the political prisoner, pushed to the bottom of the camp hierarchy as socially dangerous vermin that could infect healthy members of society. Still, even political prisoners could re-enter society if they survived.

The camps of the Gulag were dotted across the Soviet universe like the islands of an archipelago and, like islands, they defined the landscape of the sea that surrounded them. The world of the camps could be seen as a nightmarish hall of mirrors, reflecting a distorted version of everyday Soviet reality. Both inside and out, people lived in permanent fear of arrest or punishment, experiencing the daily pressures of a chronic lack of safe private space and basic necessities. The Gulag was central to the Soviet project because it was the most extreme expression of the regime's determination to break the individual. The fear of being sent to the camps was maybe the most powerful tool to coax people into compliance.

Officially they were called corrective labour camps. Given its central place in Soviet Communist ideology, 'labour' was not just 'labour' but an ideological statement. Exceeding production targets was a public declaration of devotion to the Soviet enterprise. On the ideological level, the camps' production figures went beyond economic significance: they were indicators of whether the camps were performing their task of re-education successfully. From the outset, the Gulag included a *kulturno-vospitatel'naia chast'* or KVCh, a cultural-educational department whose purpose was ideologically to reform prisoners and inspire them to work better. The KVCh's education campaigns were in theory targeting those it deemed most redeemable: criminal prisoners. But all prisoners were subjected to the same type of political-educational campaigns and propaganda; posters painted by camp artists with slogans propagating the value of labour were omnipresent, loudspeakers extolled the virtue of toil, there were literacy campaigns and political lectures, newspapers were read out loud to prisoners during their short lunch break on the fields of Karlag. To cynics this was a farce, and, for many local camp commanders, a waste of time and scarce resources like paper. But the cultural-educational departments never closed, sending detailed reports of their activities to Moscow just like any other production unit.

The KVCh was also responsible for supporting 'amateur creative activities' (*samodeiatelnost*), officially to contribute to the 'reforging' of prisoners through the performance of ideologically appropriate material. According to a 1940 directive, 'every performance must educate the prisoners, teaching them greater consciousness of labour.'[11]

An undated report from the war years related the existence of 122 cultural clubs across Karlag to Moscow.[12] At least on paper, the KVCh was certainly trying to fulfil its mandate of re-education: in 1947, Karlag's KVCh organised 1,911 concerts, 1,954 educational lectures, 10,404 political lectures, 87,747 collective newspaper reading sessions, 1,300 film shows and 264 wall newspapers supposed to inspire greater productivity and improve camp discipline.[13]

In many of the larger camps, sizeable ensembles staged performances, primarily for the camp administration but also for prisoners. Karlag was no exception, and Nina's hope for artistic work was thus not unfounded. Some camp bosses tried to amplify their own glory by collecting the best prison artists for their theatres, basking in the presence of names that had been celebrated across the Soviet Union. Headed by Boris Mordvinov, leading director of the Bolshoi Theatre at the time of his arrest, the Vorkuta camp theatre north of the Arctic Circle was one of the most famous of the Gulag.[14]

Operating under the auspices of the KVCh, the Gulag theatres were supposed to contribute to re-education, but their success was built on two entirely different factors: a bored camp administration that wanted to be entertained, and thousands of imprisoned artists desperate to perform. Prisoners who had the education or artistic skill to work in the KVCh or to entertain the camp bosses were almost inevitably 'politicals', leading to a paradoxical situation where the inmates deemed ideologically least reliable were responsible for re-educating others. Decrees from Moscow did not allow for this; for example a 1940 NKVD directive stated that prisoners convicted of counter-revolutionary crimes were not fit for re-education and should only be allowed to play musical instruments in camp theatricals, but not to speak or sing.[15] But in reality, most of the artists working in Dolinka's Central Club had been sentenced for anti-Soviet agitation.[16] And this is where Nina found her salvation.

~

Nina's family probably felt the big change in her fortune the moment they pulled her next letter out of its envelope. For the first time, she had written in ink on a pretty sheet of unlined, light-green paper, not in pencil on pages torn out of a school notebook. The quality was a sign of privilege: paper was in short supply across the Soviet Union, and convicts were not allowed to keep a stockpile lest they use it for counter-revolutionary activities.

> My life has come right. I have finally arrived at my post and am working in my profession. You yourselves have to understand how happy I am about this. My days are filled completely. I am working a lot, I have no time, just as it used to be in former times. The club here is very good even though it is small. I already performed, I danced the Spanish Dance, after all, my castanets are with me. I thought my legs would fail me, but it was OK. I am now

> getting ready to start training and want to ask you, Kostia, what to send from my costumes. We are now preparing a Pushkin performance. Gypsies, the scene at the fountain and a concert section. I will have to act and dance.[17]

In Leningrad, fellow dancers had admired Nina for her incredible mastery of the castanets. Previously, ballet dancers had just rattled them in their hands, but Nina knew how to make them speak. When she danced with Sergei Koren, it was as if their castanets were having a conversation. Even their tonality differed: Nina's were chattering in a higher register than Koren's. They had introduced the musical art of the castanets to Soviet ballet;[18] now Nina was performing for her jailers on the small stage of Karlag's Central Club in Dolinka, which, ironically, had also been named after Sergei Kirov.

During the summer of 1934, Kirov had visited Karlag and laid the club's foundation stone. Located in the part of Dolinka reserved for the camp administration and Karlag's free employees, the club had been constructed quickly, opening its doors in autumn 1934.[19] By the time the former Mariinsky Theatre was renamed the Kirov Theatre in 1935 in honour of its assassinated patron, convicts had already been performing on the small stage of its namesake in Karlag. Nina had probably written her letter there. Her new position brought her in close contact with prisoner artists, tasked primarily with painting number tags for the prisoners, bright slogans, placards and propaganda posters extolling the virtues of labour, but also with designing sets and costumes for performances. Members of the camp administration also commissioned the camp artists to create decorative paintings for their homes.

The *vakhta*, the headquarters of the armed guard, separated the prison zone from Karlag's 'capital', the village of Dolinka. By the mid-1940s, convicts had beautified 'free' Dolinka with parks and gardens and even constructed a place for dancing and a restaurant. According to convict lore, there were golden carp swimming in the beautiful fountain murmuring on the square in front of the camp administration. In November 1939, 2,570 out of Karlag's 1,660,342 convicts were living in the Dolinka commandant department, one of its eleven large administrative districts. The districts were divided into fifty-three camp points or *lagpunkty*, each of which operated like a separate camp. These were further subdivided into 191 smaller units, *komandirovki* – specific sheep farms, milk farms, field plots and so forth.[20]

According to the musician Anatoly Karpinchuk, a member and later music director of Karlag's cultural brigade in Dolinka from the mid-1940s, the cultural brigade was supposed to entertain the higher camp leadership living in Dolinka and their families. Cut off from everything beyond the borders of Karlag, the bosses did not want to spend their years of service renouncing all entertainment. Karpinchuk believed that some might have felt a genuine yearning for culture; for others, the performances by *zek*** artists were a way to flatter their own vanity, confirming their status in the eyes of those around them.

Dolinka's Central Club was only intended for performances for free employees and their guests. Provincial party leaders came from Karaganda and Akmolinsk to watch,

---

* Slang for prisoner, convict; *zek* comes from *z/k*, an abbreviation for *zakliuchennyi* (prisoner).

thanking the Karlag leadership profusely for the cultural treat. Camp performers habitually referred to the theatres as 'serf theatres', alluding to the performing companies built up by some of Russia's big landowners in the eighteenth and nineteenth centuries. Both camp and serf theatres were supposed to increase the prestige of their 'owners', to bring them pleasure, while the performers remained at their mercy. The serf theatres on the estates of the landed gentry brought cultural enjoyments, previously only available in Moscow and St Petersburg, to the Russian provinces; in the words of the historian Richard Stites, 'in the wilderness sprang up an archipelago of culture created jointly by lords and their serfs.'[21] Likewise, the camp theatres of the Gulag archipelago took European culture to the remote, inaccessible and inhospitable corners of the Soviet Union; one of the most celebrated arose in Magadan, the gateway to the deadly gold mines of the Kolyma. The artists of Karlag, in turn, sowed the seeds of European culture in Karaganda region, often settling there by necessity after their release, working and teaching art, music, acting and dance to the town's growing population.[22]

For everyday rehearsals and performances for their fellow prisoners, the artists used a small club built of adobe bricks in the male zone. Female artists reported to the guardhouse between the zones every morning in order to be allowed in for the day, but they did not have permission to go anywhere else in the male zone.

The artists were working as professionally as possible, trying to maintain their form; dancers did their daily barre, singers followed their routine of vocal exercises, everyone rehearsed.[23] In later years, costumes were made for each performer of

Karlag's Central Club. A prisoner who had been the private tailor of King Michael I of Romania sewed the tails for the male soloists of the cultural brigade.[24] But for now, Nina had to rely on her own creativity:

> I now want to ask you, Kosia,* to send me my costumes . . . my gypsy, red Spanish or the black taffeta one that's not very cumbersome. The Uzbek shirt . . . and everything connected to my Uzbek costume. The red shawl and some of the rags, so that I might be able to make something here myself. Buy some tulle, it's easy to roll up and put into a package, send some of my sheet music and any kind of small items, for example a wig, adornments, shoes, make-up, a mirror, powder, eau de cologne and so on. You can send all of this gradually, not immediately. You are after all a man of the theatre and you know how to do all of this. Now the most fundamental thing. Even though there are lots of plays here, they are all big classical works. We need a whole range of new plays of small format. For you as a writer, this is a piece of cake. Select suitable plays and send all of this, from classical as well as contemporary material. Some sketches and so on.[25]

There is something macabre about Nina's costume requests from beyond the barbed wire, but they were a powerful demonstration of her will to survive and preserve her sense of self. Like many of her imprisoned peers, Nina was fighting against slipping into indifference. For artists, the determination to

* Nina sometimes addresses Kostia as 'Kosia'.

create culture and bring it to the abyss was a way to survive the camp and its horrors while maintaining a sense of their humanity. If anything, the jarring contrast between their art and their surroundings made them even more sensitive to the sublimity of artistic creation:

> I will try to write in more detail about my whole life and about my feelings in the coming days. I have to tell you that every day, having arrived home from the club, I listen to the radio. This brings me great pleasure. I've listened again to 'Pique Dame'* and am full of the sounds of the brilliant music. I'm now comprehending the whole genius of Tchaikovsky like never before. In general, music is a miraculous thing and I am very sorry that I am not a musician. I so want to write many things to you, my loved ones, dear ones, my family. I am so full now of all kinds of thoughts about art. All my feelings have become much sharper and deeper. On the other hand, I have become calmer and more reasonable.[26]

Many of her colleagues shared Nina's heightened sensitivity to music. The German violinist Arthur Hörmann called the brigade's rehearsals a 'celebration of the soul'.[27] Anatoly Karpinchuk remembered being transported to a different sphere by the coloratura soprano Alla Verbo. Her fellow camp artists adored Verbo, watching her apprehensively from the wings whenever she performed for Karlag's top brass. Verbo

---

* Opera by Peter Tchaikovsky based on Alexander Pushkin's short story of the same name.

was prone to lose her nerves during performances for her jailers, gradually slipping into a different key, only to be rescued from musical disaster by her experienced accompanists. But her colleagues could listen endlessly to her otherworldly voice whenever she was performing only for them:

> In the evenings, in the club inside the zone, whenever there was the possibility just to make music, after a precautionary checking of the club's whole premises to make sure there were no 'freemen' near (away from sin!), yielding to our urgent pleas, Alla sang Mozart's 'Halleluja' . . . 'Halleluja' in this environment penetrated into the soul and lifted it up to such height, to such radiance, that, most likely, a similar perception is hardly possible in the atmosphere of a gala hall usual for everyone else. In order to preserve in oneself this feeling, on such evenings nobody sang or played after this. We quietly dispersed to our barracks, carrying with us a small part of the warmth gifted by Mozart's genius and the singer's talent.[28]

Not only the artists yearned for culture to feed their souls. A significant part of the camp intelligentsia ended up in Dolinka, their education harnessed by the camp administration to ensure Karlag's proper functioning: engineers, scientists, mathematicians, doctors, professors in the humanities and social sciences and so forth. Many of them took great pleasure in socialising with the artists and tried not to miss their evening rehearsals, notably the important biophysicist Alexander Chizhevsky, who was courting a member of Dolinka's cultural brigade, his future wife, contralto Nina Pereshkolnik.[29]

The artists also brought relief to prisoners assigned to hard labour. The popular Russian actress and singer Tatiana Okunevskaya* was imprisoned in Kargopollag, a logging, railroad and industrial construction camp in the sub-Arctic climate of Arkhangelsk region in European Russia's far north. Okunevskaya was assigned to the camp's cultural brigade, travelling through the endless forest to perform for convicts cutting down trees. Once, they were diverted from their planned route because the prisoners in one section had promised to cut down twice as much forest if the singer performed for them:

> As soon as they let us down from the lorry we heard in the frosty silence the thumping of axes, one had to go up a hill, and on the hill in the forest we saw lumberjacks, undressed down to their waist, steam was curling above them, and it roared through the forest: 'Hel-lo!' We walk, swallowing our tears. There will never be concerts like this in my life, where people listen not breathing, their gratitude is incomprehensible, if they had been allowed to approach they would have carried me on their hands to Moscow. In one of the camps they started to chant: 'Freedom to Okunevskaya!'[30]

~

The position of artists in the Gulag thus mirrored their standing in the wider Soviet Union. Both outside and inside the camps, they had access to privileges beyond the reach of

---

* Before her imprisonment in Kargopollag, Okunevskaya served time in Karlag.

ordinary people; in the context of the camps, these could mean the difference between life and death.

At the bottom of the camp hierarchy were the *dokhodiagy*, the 'goners' whose survival chances were at best slim, convicts on the punishment ration of 300 grams of bread because they were too weak to work. Next came the mass of prisoners, malnourished and insufficiently dressed, who were assigned to do general work on rations that depended on the fulfilment of their work quotas. The third category consisted of prisoners allowed to work inside, mostly in technical, engineering, administrative or medical positions, usually assigned a higher category of food ration and better barracks. The *pridurky* – 'trusties' – had physically less demanding, more specialised jobs that were considered essential to the functioning of the camp. Coveted 'trusty' positions ranged from bathhouse attendants, laundresses, dishwashers, cooks, barbers, work assigners and those working in camp repair shops to medical staff, accountants, engineers, designers, mechanics, geologists and so forth. Camp artists working full-time in their profession were included in this category. From the perspective of the camp administration, criminal prisoners made ideal trusties, but since they were generally uneducated and often completely illiterate, certain positions had to be given to educated political prisoners if the production plan set by Moscow was to be fulfilled.[31]

Often, convicts were forced to switch back and forth between general labour and more privileged positions, always in the knowledge that they could be sent back to fields, mines or forests on the slightest whim. Artists involved in the KVCh's cultural activities but not released from general work tried to get tasks that would nonetheless put them into the more privileged category of the *pridurky*. Work assignments also depended on the season: during the harsh Kazakh winters, when snowstorms were racing over the steppe, there was less to be done outside, which meant more time was spent on performances for Karlag's leadership and their families.

The top rank of the camp hierarchy, the professional criminals, the *urki*,* had the best survival chances. Theoretically the prime target of the Gulag's re-education programme, in practice the local camp authorities soon gave up on any attempts at reforming the *urki*, who organised themselves in gangs. According to their moral code, an honest criminal refused to do any work in the camps, living instead by thieving, deceiving and bribing. However, the *urki* were often deliberately put into positions of authority, as *starost*, or elders, inside the barracks or as brigadiers out at work, distributing and monitoring assignments within their brigades. A brigade would only receive its full ration if the quota set for the entire brigade was fulfilled, and the criminals were used to threatening and intimidating the political prisoners to take on their tasks as well as their own duties. The system worked well for the camp authorities, who could lean back in the knowledge that the *urki* would use whatever means of intimidation necessary to make sure that work quotas were fulfilled.[32]

～

Once Nina was assigned to work at the Central Club, the improvement in her status was immediately tangible. She

---

* There are several Russian terms commonly used for a professional criminal: *vor*, *urka* or *blatnoi*.

was allocated a place in a technical barracks, an extraordinary stroke of luck. At the time of the Great Terror, Karlag had capacity for 21,825 prisoners, but by the winter of 1939 almost 32,000 convicts were squashed into the barracks, forcing the camp administration to report to Moscow that, on average, Karlag's barracks were overcrowded by 30 per cent. Margarete Buber-Neumann, a German Communist arriving in Karlag around the same time as Nina,* found there was no space for her and her friend inside the barracks. Instead, they were told to sleep in the humid bathhouse. When they were finally moved into a barracks, they had to sleep together on an old door that had been placed on top of two wooden blocks. Whoever ended up lying on the side with the door handle had lost out for the night.

In the technical barracks, Nina was given a good blanket and even a mattress, an almost unheard-of privilege. She was also put on the food ration for engineers and technical workers and could thus write to her family in May that she was tolerably fed.[33]

In addition, she was given a pair of government-issue boots while her own were sent for repair.[34] An official report to the central Gulag authorities on conditions at Karlag in November 1939 complained that the camp was not able to issue adequate clothing to prisoners: there were leather shoes for only 77 per cent of prisoners. Only 23 per cent of prisoners were given *valenki*, the felt boots that offered the best protection against

* Like Nina, Buber-Neumann was sentenced to five years' corrective labour as a socially dangerous element in 1938. She was sent to Karlag in 1939, then in 1940 she was handed over to the Gestapo, who sent her to the concentration camp Ravensbrück.

the harsh cold.[35] The reality was probably worse than the report, which most likely stated the volume of clothing the camp had received, not what was actually distributed. It also didn't take into account the fact that political prisoners constantly had to defend their clothing against the greedy hands of the criminals.

Working as a camp artist was not all privilege, however. The humiliation of being treated as a serf artist was part of daily life; the threat of punishment at the slightest displeasure was always present. When sick, artists were still pulled from their bunks to perform; painters were told to beautify the private apartments of camp bosses but had to find a way to create colours and materials out of whatever they could source around the camp; bosses 'ordered' artists for their camp divisions from the administrative centre as if they were cattle.

Certain administrators and guards often deliberately targeted artists and members of the camp intelligentsia, punishing them whenever they could. According to Anatoly Karpinchuk, the guards and other Gulag staff oppressed such a prisoner simply 'because he was higher, more educated, more intelligent, finally – simply more upright than they were'. The guards took pleasure in behaving like bloodhounds during searches of the barracks; rolling over the modest bedding, they rummaged through the convicts' possessions and threw them on the floor. Distributing packages provided another golden opportunity for humiliation. Tearing open each parcel, the guards would throw forbidden items on a heap, break open boxes of cigarettes, or mix tobacco with sugar. Some took special pleasure in blowing their nose with two fingers in front of the waiting convict and then rifling through the contents with their soiled fingers.

Karpinchuk felt that there was a particularly painful psychological dimension to the Gulag for artists:

> After my work in the cultural brigade I also had to work in construction, in the mine, in the copper mine, in the brick factory. There I reached the conviction that physical labour blunts the sensation of camp existence. There is significantly less room to engage with the emotional and spiritual perception of the manifestation of violence towards man as an individual, because in collective labour, monotone and inescapable, he takes on himself what is applied to everyone in equal measure. For Karlag's 'Court Artists', it was immeasurably more difficult.[36]

17 February 1939

Hello, my dear, beloved Kostia!

How are you and do you still remember me! I write to you punctually and if you have already got my last letter than you should know that, for the time being, my life has come right. I'm in the 3rd Churbai-Nurinskoe district and am working in my specialisation in the local Central Club.* The attitude towards me is good, I feel

* This letter raises some questions as to where exactly Anisimova was located and worked – Churbai-Nurinskoe District or Dolinka. Several experts on Karlag all agreed that she must have worked for the Central Club in Dolinka: she refers to the club as the Central Club, the scale of work she describes throughout her letters corresponds to that undertaken by Dolinka's cultural brigade, and her postal address was in Dolinka throughout her time in Karlag; but the content of her letters refers to her

again useful and have perked up a bit. The club here is small but good, one can stage any performance here and even small ballets, if there was the possibility. We just had the 'Pushkin Days'. We staged the scene at the fountain, gypsies and a divertissement. It was a success, apart from my basic occupation I had to play Zemfira as well as Maria Mnishek* and, you know what, it turns out I have talent for drama. On the whole, I would like to specialise a bit in this. You never know, it might come in handy.[37]

Nina was settling into her routine as a camp performer. The artists were trying to work as professionally as possible:

We are now preparing for Red Army Day. We have to work a lot, but you know that I love my work and that I know how to work. My health is disturbing me a little bit, because lately I have fever in the evenings and feel intense weakness. It might be malaria or the flu, but more likely it is just intense overwork after everything I've gone through. But I'm now no longer behaving capriciously like at home, where you were all coddling me, I'm holding out and hoping that in spring, with the warmth, my indisposition will pass. I'm living in a technical barracks. They've given me a good blanket and mattress, so I'm sleeping well.[38]

accommodation in a technical barracks in Churbai-Nurinskoe. The most likely explanation is that she commuted between the two.

* The young gypsy woman Zemfira is the main female character of Alexander Pushkin's narrative poem *The Gypsies*. Marina Mnishek is the central heroine of his play *Boris Godunov*.

Most convicts were undernourished and anaemic; many suffered simultaneously from multiple diseases, and little medical treatment was available. Malaria was a common scourge, often leading to serious complications affecting kidneys, liver, brain and blood. Victims were plagued by unpredictable, dramatic fever and shivering fits.[39] The actress Elena Ter-Asaturova endured malaria for the last three years of her imprisonment in Karlag: 'they were eternally dragging me out of the bed not yet recovered and forcing me to participate in concerts.' Ter-Asaturova was healed with acryhin, which turned her yellow, and quinine, which made her temporarily deaf. When she looked into the mirror after her first attack, she dropped it in horror at the unrecognisable image it presented.[40]

Despite her improved circumstances, Nina remained dependent on packages sent by her relatives and continued to wait impatiently for the clothes and everyday items she so urgently needed. She was lonely, yearning for a letter with Kostia's photo that had apparently already arrived in Dolinka, and dreaming about a meeting with him, the biggest reward short of early release that could be granted to a prisoner:

> I personally live quietly without friends, which I don't plan to acquire here, I feel very lonely, even though, as before, there are many people around. I am working on my character, I try not to get offended by anything, not to argue with anyone, and above all to preserve my albeit small, but decent, qualities. Often, when the radio is transmitting something close and dear, for example, they transmitted *Swan Lake* from the Bolshoi Theatre, I listen and cry. But these tears are already calmer, only infinitely sad, sad, sad.

I so very much want to see and know everything new and
big that has now been done in art.[41]

The radio was a link to both the outside world and the past.
Recently, Nina had listened to a transmission of Kabalevsky's
opera *Colas Breugnon*, which had premiered at Leningrad's
Maly Theatre in 1938. Nina had staged the opera's dances.
Inevitably, as she listened she wondered whether her dances
had been removed from opera productions after her arrest,
and how her friends' careers were continuing while she was
locked away:

> And I have listened to Kabalevsky's *Colas Breugnon* how
> is the production going and how are my dances. Is
> *The Bartered Bride** running and have my dances been
> removed. How are things at our theatre, who is having
> success and who, on the contrary, is not getting anywhere.
> Write everything, my dear, for the sake of me, who is
> interested in the ballet. How is Serezha, is he working
> on something and who is his partner, how is Vasia, how
> are the boys. I'm interested in what Volodia is doing
> now, how is his life developing and what is he now in art.
> Please write to me about everything.[42]

Nina asked Kostia again for short comedies and dramas with a
small cast. Her actual list went far beyond those requirements,
however, and prioritised foreign classics – surely not the kind

---

* Opera by Bedřich Smetana. Nina staged dances for a production at
Leningrad's Maly Theatre in 1937.

of plays the KVCh would have deemed successful vehicles for Bolshevik re-education. They included the Spanish playwright Lope de Vega's 1618 three-act play *The Dog in the Manger* about love across class barriers; the French dramatist Eugène Scribe's 1840 five-act comedy *The Glass of Water*, dealing with the conflict between a weak Queen Anne and the powerful Duchess of Marlborough in early-eighteenth-century Great Britain; the Italian Carlo Goldoni's 1753 three-act comedy *The Mistress of the Inn*; and Louis Verneuil's and Georges Berr's 1934 two-act comedy *My Crime*.* In addition, she asked Kostia for new, contemporary Soviet plays that were not too difficult to stage; sketches from the Soviet variety stage; some vaudeville plays; sheet music for the latest songs, if possible also for wind orchestra, and for some of her Spanish dances, for example 'La Corrida' and 'Conversations with Castanets'. Moreover, she asked for her complete Uzbek, Armenian and Turkish costumes, boots, cymbals, a tambourine without decorations, her black or red shawl, tulle and anything else that was necessary – adding to this substantial list the contradictory instruction that he shouldn't send a lot. Other camp artists also prioritised valuable package or luggage space for artistic props; two opera singers from the Bolshoi Theatre and Kharkov Opera brought two suitcases filled with sheet music – but barely any clothes.[43]

---

* Goldoni appears to have been a popular choice for prisoner performances at Karlag. I mention in this chapter that Anna Kniper was involved in staging Goldoni's *The Curious Incident* at the Karlag division Burma. In the second half of the 1940s, Dolinka's cultural brigade managed to turn Goldoni's *The Mistress of the Inn* into a musical. The production did not require a large cast or bulky sets and could therefore repeatedly be shown to the prisoner audience in Dolinka.

❧

A few days later, on 19 February 1939, Nina received her second food package from home, which also included a pair of urgently needed stockings and mittens:

> Tell Mamochka that I'm looking after my things and that I'm trying to be neat. I washed my sole, beige suit, it became clean but lost of course its original look. I've given my boots to repair, they are making *valenki* out of them for me. Some of the underwear I give to the laundry, some I wash myself, my two sweaters I wear in turns and the scarf you gave me is rescuing me wonderfully. The coat is in order, but of course relatively, the lining I stitch up when it tears but the outside is still strong. Send sheets and underwear and I really ask as soon as possible. And many thanks for the powder, it's just a pity that you didn't send perfume, it's so pleasant here if one can sometimes put on perfume. For this reason, send something from my favourite things and when I will be in a bad mood I will wear them so that I feel better.

It was time to go to rehearsal; tomorrow, her letter would be taken to Dolinka, and make its way from there to her 'distant, beloved Leningrad'.

> Write to me, beloved, and don't forget me. I love you very, very much. I kiss you all strongly. I beg you, look after Mamochka and Valiusha. Don't worry about me, I'm cheerful and strong in spirit. Towards spring I will write

an appeal, I will only work a bit and I hope I will deserve
a good reference.

Your Nina.[44]

∾

Nina's next letter was on proper green stationery with a
dark border:

Hello, my dear ones!

I'm sitting in the club and I'm writing you a letter as the
post is leaving today . . . The warm boots are warming
my old, tired legs and Mummy's cardigan is saving me
from the cough. I put on eau de cologne every day and all
things altogether are a big joy for me. There was a lot of
laughter when I put on my skiing costume, a crowd gathered around me in the barracks and everybody discussed
the cut of the costume and the hat and acknowledged that
my husband is a darling.[45]

Not everyone was lucky enough to receive letters from her
spouse or family. Karlag prisoner Sharifa Ustinova remembers
being the only one in her barracks of forty-one women to get
mail from her husband, who was imprisoned in another camp.
Whenever she heard from him, the other women asked her
to read the letter out loud. Some would start crying, moved
to tears by words written to another by a man they had never
met. The women often found it meaningful to read their letters to each other, taking comfort in sharing both sad and
happy news.[46]

Kostia's last letter had calmed Nina's fears over her mother – he had confirmed that she was alive, healthy, and resting in a sanatorium. It had also given her an unintentional fright when strands of hair fell out of the letter as she was impatiently opening it. She then realised that, in a novel attempt to send her a piece of home, Kostia had enclosed some of Stepa's hair! Fear quickly turned to laughter. The thoughtful yet humorous gesture was typical of Kostia. His letters made her feel light and happy.

She hungrily devoured any piece of theatrical news he could pass on. She was lucky: her friends were brave, choosing not to ignore her. Kostia had conveyed her regards to 'the boys', and they were reciprocating them through him: 'Thank the boys for remembering me, I wish them from all my heart complete success and good wives.' Nina asked Kostia to pass on her congratulations to Dmitriev in case he saw him – he had been given a big award: 'I am very happy about his successes and grateful for the fact that, once, he helped me in my theatrical career.' She had read that Vainonen was staging *The Nutcracker* at the Bolshoi: 'Write how the production turned out. In general, I'm very interested in theatrical life and all new productions.' And she would not give up her emotional connections to her former life: coming to the end of her letter, she asked Kostia to kiss her partner Serezha, as well as Stepa.

❧

Spring was coming. During the past months, Nina had seen the steppe at its most terrifying. With the temperature dropping to minus 40 degrees, snowstorms and blizzards wiped away any distinction between the white sky and the endless flatness of the snow-covered steppe. But in spring, the landscape blossomed and the aromatic scent of growing wormwood saturated the air. Fields of delicate iris, wild scarlet, yellow tulips and small blue and yellow flowers swayed gently in the breeze; ground squirrels and jerboas scurried over the low hills; flocks of gazelles ran gracefully through the sea of steppe grass; and proud golden eagles circled high in the sky.[47]

Four years earlier, the avant-garde Leningrad painter Vladimir Sterligov had looked at the same landscape:

> Spring in the semi-desert. Vast expanses. Enlarging them, gently sloping, endless hills are rolling across them – enormous stomachs of giants. The dry spring wind is blowing over them, blowing away the last patches of snow. At the beginning of the world, it was probably just the same here . . . But why is 'cultured Leningrad' finding itself here? How could a member of Petersburg's intelligentsia have imagined that, called an enemy of the people, he would meet spring here? A combination, intolerable even in a delirium . . .[48]

Sterligov and his friend and fellow artist Vera Ermolaeva had both been arrested in the wake of the Kirov assassination and accused of anti-Soviet agitation because they had met weekly at Ermolaeva's flat to exhibit their paintings and to discuss art. Both he and Ermolaeva designed sets for Dolinka's Central Club, joining forces with Petr Sokolov, who at the time of his arrest had worked as set designer at the Bolshoi Theatre.

Ermolaeva, Sterligov, Sokolov and Vladimir Dubinin worked together on a production of Alexander Ostrovsky's classic play *A Profitable Position*, which enjoyed great success with Karlag bosses, run-of-the mill guards and, of course, the prisoners. Sterligov later remembered:

> The free employees were howling out of delight, after this, a miracle followed. An unprecedented event . . . 'The ladies' of the free employees (meaning the wives of the guards) prepared a banquet for us!!! . . . Everything was as in freedom, as if we were free people . . . In the foyer on the second floor, a long table was set . . . Meat patties! Meat patties! Meat patties! (This after brown scum soup made from tortured horses.) Cutlets! Of course not a drop of alcohol. We, the actors, musicians, artists, directors . . . are sitting at the table (all *zeks*), and the free 'ladies' are hosting us. Are serving us . . . Especially captivating was one 'lady' – the wife of the head of the third* department (the most terrible) Kliushin. After the meal she thrust her hand into a bowl of sweets and playfully threw handfuls at us. We were forced to try to catch them.[49]

Sterligov was released in December 1938, but perhaps Nina was able to admire the monumental murals he had painted inside the Central Club, which was renovated every year.[50]

Spring was also the time when corpses collected throughout the winter were buried; in winter, the frozen ground was too hard for digging graves. While Nina was surviving her first

---

* A subdivision of the secret police in charge of intelligence and operational work such as prisoner surveillance.

winter at Karlag, the bodies of 170 Uzbek, Tadjik and Turkmen prisoners had piled up in some washrooms. This specific cluster of cadavers has not been forgotten, because Irina Kulle, daughter of Professor Robert Kulle (a member of the Petersburg intelligentsia shot in 1938), had to write the family names of the deceased on small wooden labels and attach them to the remains before they were taken away on horseback. During that same winter, Kulle had also witnessed how water had been poured over some prisoners who had been executed, turning the corpses into ice statues that were placed inside the prison zone or on watchtowers as a warning.[51]

With the arrival of spring, cultural clubs began closing down across Karlag's many subdivisions in anticipation of the busy agricultural season; artists were assigned to general labour, which usually meant working in the fields. Nina and the artists of Dolinka's Central Club were not ordered to work on the fields during the summer months, but the change in season did alter their routine: a brigade of artists would travel around Karlag giving performances in every department. Some were for free employees and convicts, who were allowed to move around without guards; others were for convicts living inside guarded zones.[52] There were strict limits on what they could stage outside Dolinka, and no pianos were to be found outside the camp's 'capital', limiting the artists to numbers that could be accompanied by accordion. Travelling from north to south and west to east, Dolinka's artists were greeted by radiant faces wherever they went, despite the limited programme. Sharifa Ustinova, a prisoner working on one of Karlag's experimental agricultural stations, remembered the excitement and gratitude when artists from Dolinka came to perform. The prisoners asked for permission to thank them with carrots grown on the station. Permission granted, the women ran to the irrigation ditches, dug up carrots of an especially sweet variety and, using some greens, proceeded to bind 'bouquets' of the carrots. The artists were overjoyed.[53]

The Gulag's professional performance brigades, its amateur music, drama and dance circles and the occasional film screenings presumably achieved little in terms of re-education. For cynics, cultural activities served a simple purpose: refreshing prisoners' minds so that they could work better; but they offered the inmates a vital mental outlet whose significance went far beyond that. For the prisoners, any kind of cultural possibility constituted one of the most powerful tools for resisting the camps' dehumanisation of the individual. Inside and outside the camps, the Bolsheviks never managed completely to bend culture to their own will. Ironically, their belief in the power of art elevated artists to a position where they could use their officially sanctioned platform to do the exact opposite of what they were supposed to do: offer an escape from prevailing ideology into a different dimension where art fulfils its most basic function – to bring joy and beauty, to offer relief from everyday worries and to allow people to connect to their deepest and purest emotions. The fact that this could happen even in the extreme context of the camps showed that, ultimately, art proved stronger than politics. It reminded prisoners of their humanity and their former lives, briefly restoring to them the dignity the camps were designed to destroy and strengthening their resilience.

The urge and ability to make art and to take joy in it is one of the core characteristics that distinguishes us from other animals. Many artists imprisoned in the camps felt the same as Nina: to be alive meant to be able to create art. Working in a pork factory in Karlag, the artist Irina Borkhman used the only paint available – pig's blood – secretly to paint the landscape surrounding her, eternalising a moment of melancholy beauty.[54] The artists' dogged attempts to continue their work were powerful acts of defiance because they demonstrated that a powerless convict could defend the integrity of his or her soul against the regime.

Behind the barbed wire, fleeting moments of wonder were propping up withering souls. Gulag memoirists describe in highly emotional terms the joy brought to them by artists who sang to them in the barracks, recited poetry from plank beds, retold stories or danced, giving comfort to their fellow prisoners during their darkest hours, allowing them to escape reality for a moment. Seeing the deep sadness of one of the women in her barracks on the birthday of her young son, the Ukrainian opera singer Ekaterina Oloveinikova sang for her all evening.[55] For the performers, it was a way to survive spiritually, as well as a powerful act of defiance. But it was also a double-edged sword psychologically: while convicts assigned to general work were forced to focus on their immediate physical survival, the camp artists were reminded day after day of the life they had lost. Anatoly Karpinchuk introduced his recollections about the cultural brigade serving Karlag's Central Club wistfully: 'everything written here is about those whose fate could have and should have turned out more successfully, and whose calling it was to bring happiness to people. In some way they did just that. But, under what conditions and at what a cost!'[56]

The artists' 'summer tour' offered a welcome break from the daily humiliations of camp life. Rolling on horse-drawn carts through a sea of feather grass with yellow islands of blooming Siberian pea-shrubs, past hills and rivulets, surrounded by birds and animals, to feel at one with nature was a precious taste of freedom: 'After "the zones" this was life!'[57]

Spring thus brought a new dimension to Nina's life as a camp artist:

> Dear beloved Kosia!
>
> I received a letter from you the other day and am hurrying to answer you quickly. I only didn't write to you because I am very, very busy. One of these days, our agit-brigade will leave for the spring sowing and I'm busy up to my throat.[58]

Nina's heart was full, she had happy news to share:

> We were given the permission for a meeting. I don't know how this is for you, but when I received the paper with the permission for a meeting I cried for a long time out of happiness. Just think that I will once again be able to see your glorious dear mug and to talk to you. So then, it would be best if you came at the end of May. Then it will be warm here and it will be better for me in terms of timing, I will be freer. You will go to Karaganda where you will receive the permission for the meeting at the commandant's office and there they will tell you how to get to me. And so you will have to come a long and far

way Kosia but you will see me only for a very short time, if you think that it doesn't make sense to do this then don't come I will not be offended one bit. Discuss all this with Mummy and Valia and if you decide to come I am waiting for you and will always wait. I hope you will like Kazakhstan, spring here is very good and beautiful.[59]

Even before the tightening of rules during the Great Terror, Karlag's boss Otto Linin had called visits by relatives 'one of the highest forms of rewarding the inmate for his work and behaviour in the camp . . . not only in production but in daily life'. After submitting her request, Nina had been thoroughly evaluated as to whether she was worthy of such a reward.[60]

But negotiating the limits set to communication with the outside world continued to be a constant challenge: 'Now, my dear, I really want to scold you. Even though you are a very clever and marvellous person you mustn't send me so many packages.'[61] Nina wasn't being disingenuous – she had to ask Kostia to send only one large parcel per month because there was a limit to how many the convicts were allowed to receive; beyond the allotted number they were returned to the sender:[62] 'So, my dear, fulfil my request and don't force me to be upset for nothing. I have after all become much more sensible than I used to be, I have learned (of course not yet completely) to look after my things and to know the value of people. I'm trying to develop for myself a strong and robust character, otherwise it's very difficult to live here. In general, you don't have to worry about me, I'm alive, healthy, I'm learning how to live and I think a lot, a lot.'

But notwithstanding her new-found common sense, there was a certain pleasure in nagging Kostia, as if her life hadn't been turned completely upside down:

> By the way, my little one, a big thank you for the costumes, but you send much that is superfluous and little that is needed. Firstly, what's the purpose of sending a bad suitcase without a lock, it's better to have a strong suitcase with a lock here, in which you can put all your things and close them. Secondly, why send me two Uzbek shirts if it would be better to send one and my good brocade one. Then you sent few of my national costumes and no Spanish one. I would have liked ballet slippers so I can train. Of course you can't send all of this in one package, but you have to think everything through more sensibly. Thank you for the vaudeville but we need contemporary ideological plays and sketches. I'm waiting impatiently for the journal *Folk Art*, I utterly need it and you can always send me printed matter. There you go, you are doing so much for me and I write it's all wrong. But don't be angry and don't forget that I'm in a camp and everything here goes through labour processes.[63]

Nina had also been overjoyed to receive a letter from her friend Zhora, the set designer Georgy Moseyev who had designed her first ballet, *Andalusian Wedding*. This was extraordinary – unless they were related to a convict, people were rarely willing to take the risk to write to someone in the camps since any contact with a prisoner brought its risks. It gave her special satisfaction to be able to ask Kostia to convey her joy to Zhora and to tell him that she would write back.

∿

Spring brought one of the most important Soviet holidays: 1 May, international workers' day. Nina and her cultural brigade performed for the camp personnel more than once that day to mark the holiday:

> I wish you (though late) a happy holiday. On the day of 1 May, sitting in the sun after the matinée, I remembered my home and the faces that are dear to me, I sat together with you and talked in Mummy's room and saw in my mind's eye naughty, wonderful Stepa jump around. On 29 April I received a large, wonderful package from Kosia, so I celebrated the holiday splendidly, the whole day, I ate delicious things and read wonderful plays. Many thanks Kostia that you are not forgetting me.[64]

Nina's thoughts turned to one of the basic conundrums of the Gulag performers: they were expected constantly to renew their repertoire, but they had no access to additional plays or musical scores. Nina had hoped that Kostia could provide a flow of new material, but even she was only beginning to grasp the full extent of the ideological and practical constraints she faced:

> Unfortunately, the plays and sketches you sent suit us little. I know you are making a surprised face because I myself asked for example for *The Dog in the Manger*, but

the issue is that, first of all, we don't have any possibilities to stage it, and secondly, it will be too complicated and boring for our audience. We need worker club's plays, something about sowing and harvesting on *kolkhozes* [collective farms], and so forth. If something from the classics, then it has to reach everyone. On the whole, this isn't difficult for you Kosia, but you can help us a lot because we don't have much literary material. From the sketches you sent one can only stage 'Desdemona's Handkerchief', and even that when there will be time. Large plays will be staged only in winter, so send without fail *Glory* and something else. Many thanks for the book about Yuryev,* I read it with great pleasure. True, you wrote it rather dryly, but it is a wonderful edition and has a completely solid as well as impressive look. I'm proud of the fact that my dear husband writes such good things. Send me everything possible written by you and the magazine on folk art.[65]

Even the amateur clubs in other divisions put on ambitious works in winter. Nina's acquaintance Anna Kniper staged a production of *The Curious Incident*, a play by the eighteenth-century Italian playwright Carlo Goldoni in Karlag's Burma division. Determined to give the classic play the right look, Kniper ran up two flannel caftans with 'gold' embroidery made from brass clippings thrown out in the repair workshop, glued

* Yuri Yuryev (1872–1948), famous Russian and Soviet actor who had leading roles in Meyerhold's plays at Petersburg's Alexandrinsky Theatre before the revolution.

cardboard for hats, wove straw and shepherd's shavings into another hat, sewed a mauve and pink dress from two packets of unpicked gauze and found a way to make wigs with oakum, a tarred fibre used to seal gaps, powdered with flour or chalk. She put green boxes on the stage, placing creeping thyme – the only greenery to be found in the steppe in winter – between the boxes' wooden planks. Kniper cut the thyme into round shapes as if she were a gardener on a country estate, carved 'oranges' out of carrots, and the illusion of Mediterranean orange saplings was complete.[66]

From the early 1940s, Dolinka's Central Club put on genuinely large-scale productions. By 1943, the camp leadership had concentrated all the artistic forces in Dolinka. Working under the direction of Marianna Ler, a former conductor of Moscow's Operetta Theatre, Dolinka's cultural brigade staged well-known operettas such as Emmerich Kálmán's *Countess Maritza* and Rudolf Friml and Herbert Stothart's operetta-style Broadway musical *Rose-Marie*. Elena Ter-Asaturova was the choreographer, working with a large cast on dance numbers at the club inside the prison zone.[67]

∼

Kostia's book had included a picture of the actress N. Rashchevskaia, who had also had some successes directing. Nina started dreaming:

> I often wonder whether I will be able to stage ballets upon
> leaving the camp; here I'm staging solo and small mass
> dances, the majority with singing. I have already danced
> a great quantity of numbers again and again. I must say

that I'm enjoying good success. Our audience loves my dances, but I'm facing the problem of constantly renewing my programme. This is very difficult. I have already danced here again and again almost everything: lezginka, khaitarma, Uzbek, Armenian, gopak, gypsy, all sorts of Russian, Spanish dances, even the panaderos and so forth.* Now recently I did Vasin's† comical Finnish dance, the audience was very pleased. On the whole I don't have music and I get myself out of this to the extent that I can, I also dance the male part and I try to reproduce all numbers I know. I think little about composing dances, but somewhere deep down in my soul I'm of course harbouring the desire to stage big, wonderful ballets. If one day I will have such a possibility, I will stage a ballet about the Kazakh steppes, about shepherds who are herding their sheep and about the wonderful Kazakh girls.[68]

Themselves victims of horrific abuses by Soviet power, the Kazakhs in the area of Karlag had touched the hearts of many convicts. Instead of looking at the downtrodden strangers flooding their ancestral lands with angry hostility, nomad hospitality made it a matter of honour to welcome and help them. Some of the prisoners in Akmolinsk had been horrified when small Kazakh children seemingly started throwing stones at them in the middle of winter. The guards had laughed, taunting

---

* Lezginka: national dance of mountain peoples from the North Caucasus; khaitarma: national dance of Crimean Tartars; gopak: Ukrainian folk dance; panaderos: Spanish dance (Nina is probably referring to the panaderos from Alexander Glazunov and Marius Petipa's ballet *Raymonda*).

† Vasily Vainonen, choreographer of *The Flames of Paris*.

the women that they were hated not only in Moscow, but even by the children of the nearby Kazakh *aul*, or village. The scene repeated itself for several days, reducing some of the women to tears until one of them stumbled, falling face-down on to the small white 'stones'; suddenly she smelled the scent of curd. Carefully lifting one and taking a small bite, she realised that they were *kurt*, a Kazakh dried cheese: the Kazakhs had asked their children to throw food at the emaciated prisoners, despite the risk of harsh punishment if discovered.[69]

I am, as always, writing very chaotically, but you, my dears, understand me and won't laugh. In appearance I am just the same as I used to be, thinner in the face, I run around in my grey suit which I'm already washing for the third time, in a striped singlet, acquired for 'Yablochka',* in my only, worn-down, white shoes and with a leather bag in which I carry with me a mug as well as bits of rusks and my castanets. Of course I have seriously coars- ened, I have learned to defend myself and even to curse. But of course all this hasn't changed me for the worse. I have only started to learn more from the earth how to understand people, nature and work. I've fallen in love with music even more than before and especially with Tchaikovsky. There is less aestheticism in me, so that now for example I would completely tear to pieces *Carmen* as well as Zhorin and even Volodin.† Well, I'm planning

---

* *Yablochka* ('little apple') is a political Russian folk song from the civil war period, presented as a sailors' dance.

† The set designers Georgy Moseyev and Vladimir Dmitriev.

to write Zhora everything about art and about my, as he writes, trembling dances. If he hasn't yet forgotten my existence, then tell him, Kosia, that the first ballet we will stage together with him, of course only if he abandons his idiotic decadence and if he will look for example at *Carmen* not only through his eyes but also through the eyes of the audience . . . Look after yourselves, don't worry about me and believe me that despite all my big misfortune, I try to be robust and strong. I am waiting for Kosia and I kiss you all. Mummy, look after yourself. Your Nina.[70]

9

The Return

Kostia did not visit Nina in Karlag. His appeal to the Leningrad NKVD had somehow achieved the impossible. Prompted by Kostia's letter, Junior Lieutenant Artamanov, senior NKVD investigator, had pulled Nina's case file out of the archive. He read that Nina had been arrested on suspicion of espionage. Artamanov chose to focus on the fact that the investigation had not only failed to prove Nina's involvement in espionage, but that it had rested its case of anti-Soviet agitation solely on the testimony of one person: Andrei Levanenok. On 26 February 1939, 'guided by instructions' given by Commissar Goglidze, head of the Leningrad NKVD, Artamanov recommended transferring Nina back to the Shpalerka prison for a further investigation of her case. His superiors approved his request.[1]

❧

Of course, Artamanov was not acting out of a genuine concern for legal justice. Kostia's letter had been as impeccably timed as a dramatic entrance in a play; his application could not have landed on Artamanov's desk at a better moment. On 17 November 1938, while Nina waited in Karabas to be put on a long-distance transport, the Politburo had adopted a resolution – 'On arrests, procuratorial supervision, and investigative procedure' – that put an end to the Great Terror. The resolution stated that the simplified procedures for conducting investigations and trials adopted during the NKVD's mass operations of 1937 and 1938 'could not help but lead to a host of major deficiencies and distortions in the work of the NKVD and the Procuracy'. A central order had started the Great Terror; now another one brought it to an abrupt end.

Six days later, Lavrenty Beria replaced Yezhov as People's Commissar for Internal Affairs. Yezhov would be arrested in April 1939 and shot in February 1940. Mikhail Litvin, head of the Leningrad NKVD and Yezhov's close collaborator, anticipated what was to come. As Stalin was later to quip: 'For the chekist, there are only two paths: one to promotion, one to prison.'[2] After his daily telephone call with Yezhov, Litvin took matters into his own hands and shot himself on 12 November 1938.[3] He was replaced by Sergei Goglidze, who had served as Georgia's People's Commissar for Internal Affairs under Beria, at the time First Secretary of the Central Committee of the Georgian Communist Party. Called to Moscow to become Yezhov's deputy, then his successor, Beria was supposed to reorganise the NKVD and to rid it of Yezhov's followers.[4] Part of the purge would involve a very limited review of cases to demonstrate that Yezhov and his people had made 'mistakes'; Nina's fitted the requirements like a glove. She was a well-known dancer, occupying a politically uncontroversial but highly respected position in the Soviet social hierarchy.

She had never admitted her guilt, or rather, to put it correctly, she had never been forced to sign a false confession. Accused of counter-revolutionary crimes, she had in the end been sentenced as a 'socially dangerous element', a comparatively minor criminal offence that made it politically easier to investigate her case.

Purges of the NKVD after episodes of enhanced political terror were routine: Yezhov's predecessor Yagoda had also been arrested and shot. There was never any intention to start an extensive review that could undermine the 'achievements' of the Terror. This was about placing a few fig leaves in strategic locations and the opportunity to rein in NKVD departments that had grown enormously powerful during the Terror – within limits. As soon as local NKVD departments complained about overly eager efforts to investigate their excesses, Beria appealed to Stalin, who promptly sent a telegram to relevant party and NKVD bodies, explicitly stating that the Central Committee had allowed the NKVD to use torture from 1937 onwards. The perpetrators could breathe more easily: that telegram provided absolution. It made clear that Stalin fully supported the results of the Great Terror, backing the people who had achieved them.[5] There would be no justice for the victims.

∾

By the end of May 1939, seven months after she had arrived in Kazakhstan, Nina was back at the Shpalerka. On the 30th, a clerk filled in the usual personal form for her. This time Nina listed Kostia as her husband: her family was no longer limited to her mother and sister. A receipt for her sparse belongings, handed in for 'safe keeping', recorded her possessions: two suitcases holding three dresses, one pair of underpants, one pair of knitted stockings, two corsets, two pairs of small scissors, eleven sewing threads of different colours, a few other items, and thirty-nine roubles and sixty-eight kopeks.[6]

Two weeks later, on 15 June, Nina was taken to Artamanov. The interrogation started at 12.15 p.m. and lasted for over two hours. The protocol was short, providing a record of questions and answers that could be read out loud in three minutes. Artamanov asked Nina whether she confirmed the evidence she had given during the investigation of her case. Nina responded in the affirmative, with a few minor qualifications: the record of her interrogation on 5 February stated that, of all the dancers, Mikhailov, Levanenok and she had been closest to Salomé. Nina now clarified that she had only been closer to Salomé than others in the sense that she, Mikhailov and Levanenok had been his most frequent visitors. But she had visited Salomé on average no more than twice monthly, not every six days, as originally recorded, and only until 1934, not 1935. She had seen the German consuls Walther and Sommer only once each, at official banquets. Nina also pointed out that she had been accused of memorising and giving false testimony. Artamanov asked Nina why these inaccuracies had not been corrected at the time. Nina responded that she had pointed them out, but that the investigator had said that they were not essential; she had acquiesced and signed the protocol. Lastly, Artamanov asked Nina about Roman Galebsky. Nina responded that he had been an acquaintance of her father who had returned to the USSR from abroad and been ordered to leave Leningrad in 1935 to a location unknown to her.[7]

∿

The NKVD now called in four witnesses to testify to Nina's character: the ballerina Tatiana Vecheslova, Nina's dancing partner Sergei Koren, her friend the artist Georgy Moseyev and Antonina Shkodenko, a neighbour who had lived in Nina's communal flat from 1932 until 1935. Her colleagues from the Kirov proved worthy witnesses. Called in on 21 June, Vecheslova's witness interrogation lasted forty minutes. The twenty-nine-year-old ballerina was one of the most popular stars of the Kirov Ballet. In 1934, she had been the first Soviet ballerina to tour the USA.

Vecheslova told the investigator that she and Nina had known each other since 1922: they were not just colleagues but visited each other at home.[8] In her memoir, Vecheslova later described how she, Nina and other young ballet students had passed magical summers together in Detskoe Selo, now Pushkin. In 1921, the school had been given access to a dacha to get the children out of Petrograd and into nature during the summer holidays. The school worried about the health of its young charges, whose small bodies had to cope with the extraordinary demands of their training and frequent night-time performances while struggling with the hunger, cold and fear of the civil-war period.

The dacha was no ordinary cottage. In the 1850s, Countess Zinaida Yusupova, heiress to the legendary Yusupov fortune, had commissioned the construction of a large villa in the fashionable town that had grown around the tsars' Catherine Palace. The students continued their ballet train- ing at the dacha, performing almost every Sunday for the local population, but there was also time to get lost in the grounds and in their imagination. Walking through the park, the students sang old Russian songs and their favourite melodies from ballets and operas, composed poems, and dreamed up whole performances. One summer they were engrossed in a production staged entirely by the students: 'Among the Flowers' included both spoken narrative and dance. Nina had a leading role as the grandfather-gardener, and the future ballerina Marina Semenova played the role of her granddaughter Margarita. The other students were flowers, grasshoppers, bugs, midges and various garden creatures, while Vecheslova danced the part of a butterfly. Later Vecheslova fondly remembered twelve-year-old Nina in her role:

> Nina Anisimova was magnificent in a Ukrainian shirt, in grey summer trousers, in a broad-brimmed straw hat, under which one could make out a grey beard and whiskers. But Nina was also the artist. She painted the poster, invitations. In the future, this talent of hers manifested itself in more serious creativity. Already as a dancer, and later choreographer, she drew costume sketches, painted studies in oil. With the years, her multifaceted nature opened up in an unusually interesting way.[9]

Perhaps images of these happy days were passing through Vecheslova's mind as she answered the investigator's questions. Her responses were straight and to the point; given the circumstances, that in itself was brave. The fact that Vecheslova was testifying for Nina, and not the other way around, could after all be put down to little more than luck. Like Nina, Vecheslova had suspect social origins. Born into an aristocratic family, her father had served in the Imperial Army; to make matters worse, her uncle, a former colonel in the Imperial Army, was now living in exile in Yugoslavia.[10] She had also attended Salomé's evenings. And in the early 1930s, the ballerina was married – at least in the Soviet sense of a common-law marriage – to Viktor Gran, a slim, elegant man fourteen years her senior who was then the senior administrator of the Leningrad Philharmonic. But Gran had a dangerous past: during the civil war, he had been a warrant officer in Admiral Kolchak's army. He was arrested on 26 October 1937 as a member of a White Guard officers' terrorist-diversionist-spy organisation. Gran was more than lucky: even though he had genuinely fought on the side of the Whites during the civil war, he was released after only two weeks and his file was closed.[11]

Asked to characterise Nina from a professional perspective, Vecheslova described her as a talented dancer, honest and conscientious. She testified that she and Nina rarely talked about politics, but that their limited political exchanges demonstrated her Soviet convictions: 'One time, I and Anisimova N. A. were among those artists who visited the flat of the former legal consultant of the German consulate, Salomé. After the murder of S. M. Kirov, Anisimova N. A. said to me in a conversation that she understood the environment of that time, that she thought having visited Salomé's flat had been her mistake and that she would put an end to her acquaintance with him.'[12]

∿

One day later, Sergei Koren was called in as a witness. Artamanov interrogated Nina's partner for forty-five minutes, from 2.20 until 3.05 p.m. Koren stated that he had known Nina since about 1926, but that he had got to know her more closely after becoming her dance partner in 1935. Koren called her one of the most capable and talented leading character dancers, pointing out that she spent her spare time studying and staging the national dances of the peoples of the Soviet Union. Artamanov then cut to the chase: 'What can you say about Anisimova N. A.'s counter-revolutionary activity?' Koren's response was unequivocal: he knew absolutely nothing about this. He had never heard Nina say anything counter-revolutionary, nor had anyone ever said anything negative about her in this respect; he only knew Nina as a person of Soviet convictions. They had talked about politics extremely rarely, but when they did Nina had talked positively about measures taken by the Communist Party and Soviet government. Responding to Artamanov, Koren confirmed that Nina had been among the many ballet dancers who had visited Salomé's flat. Koren himself had been there maybe twice, at semi-official banquets. Nina had not stood out in any way among the artists present; neither she nor any of the others had held any political conversations with Salomé.[13]

～

Next in line was Antonina Shkodenko, a twenty-four-year-old woman who classified herself as a worker. Shkodenko's interrogation took place on 7 July 1939 at 9 p.m., a more ominous hour, but also lasted only forty-five minutes. Shkodenko had lived in Nina's communal flat from 1932 until 1935. Shkodenko testified that she had communicated extremely rarely with Nina, who apparently 'almost never walked out of

her room. I almost never happened to talk to her.' Artamanov
asked Shkodenko to report what she knew about Anisimova's
family. Shkodenko responded with communal flat gossip:
apparently, Nina's mother had told one of the women in the
flat that her husband had been a former colonel in the tsarist
army and that he had had an estate close to Peterhof that had
given him an annual income of 46,000 roubles. Shkodenko
further reported that Nina had often been visited by fellow artists, but she only knew the surnames of the dancer Iordan, and,
if she remembered correctly, of the dancer Oppengeim. The
get-togethers in her room had continued late into the night,
but Shkodenko had never been present at them. Asked whether
she knew of any occasions when Anisimova had expressed anti-
Soviet opinions, Shkodenko could report that Nina had never
said anything anti-Soviet in her presence, and that she had
never heard anything negative about her in this respect from
any of the other parties in the communal flat.[14]

∾

The last witness, Georgy Moseyev, was called in on 9 July and
interrogated from 8.45 until 9.30 p.m. Moseyev was a friend
of Vladimir Dmitriev, who had initiated him into the world
of set design. Moseyev and Nina had met in 1935 when they
collaborated on Nina's first ballet, *Andalusian Wedding*. He
had visited her flat to talk about work, and they had remained
acquainted right up to her arrest in 1938. He had been brave
enough to write to Nina in Karlag. Like the other witnesses,
Moseyev testified that he knew nothing about Nina's counter-
revolutionary activity and that he had not heard anything
in this respect from mutual friends: for him, Nina was a

completely Soviet person who had never behaved in a politically negative way in his presence. Moseyev was dismissed
after hailing Nina as a leading character dancer, stating that,
from a professional point of view, he could only speak positively of her.[15]

Two days later, on 11 July, Artamanov summed up his findings. He had examined Nina's file and the accusation that she
was guilty of anti-Soviet agitation. Throughout the investigation, Nina had not admitted to any counter-revolutionary
activities; the only 'evidence' was Levanenok's testimony,
which he had later rejected at his trial, declaring that he had
been forced to sign a confession. Her character witnesses had
nothing negative to report. Artamanov drew the following conclusion: Anisimova's conviction had been based on Levanenok's
testimony, which he had subsequently withdrawn; Anisimova
had been acquainted with consulate employees to the same
extent as a number of other dancers who were at liberty; the
investigation had not proven that Anisimova had engaged in
espionage. Artamanov recommended petitioning the NKVD
Special Council to review Anisimova's case and release her
from custody. Artamanov's superiors confirmed his resolution
five days later, on 16 July 1939.[16]

～

Two months later, on 20 September 1939, Nina was still in
prison. The wheels of the NKVD were turning tortuously
slowly.

She had been ill, though was now feeling better and training every day inside her cell, but the uncertainty was taking its
toll. Nina was reaching the end of her strength. At least she

could communicate more frequently with her family than in Karlag. Kostia had written that they all loved her, that he was always thinking of her and imagining all her dances – how much he wanted to see them: 'I wish you to be healthy and to feel well. I kiss you lots of times, my beloved and priceless, talented wife.' Even her mother had written to her: 'My dear darling girl, I kiss you strongly and hug you, I'm thinking of you all the time and am in thoughts with you. Mummy, who loves you.' Valia had added her own message, ending playfully: 'Stepa is bowing deeply to his mistress.'[17]

Her family also dropped off small parcels with food. Letter after letter, Nina dutifully reported on the progress of her recovery.[18] On 1 October, Nina wrote:

My dear Mamochka!

Thank you very much for your letter. I am awfully happy when I receive news from you. To know that you are alive and healthy is everything for me. I kiss you strongly, strongly and beg you not to worry about me. I am recovering and hoping for a better future.[19]

The suspense was taking both a physical and mental toll:

Dear Kostia.

Many thanks that you are not forgetting me. Every time I receive a letter I want to write a lot. I write – I tear it up, I write again and there is no way I can write a good letter. I beg you not to be mad at me . . .[20]

But there were also moments when she felt strong enough to dream about the future: 'If you want to know what I am now thinking about a lot, then it is about staging a good ballet if everything will be well.'[21]

~

On 30 October, Kostia wrote to the academician Alexander Baikov, one of the Soviet Union's pre-eminent scientists, a metallurgist and chemist who also served as a deputy to the Supreme Soviet:*

> Dear Alexander Alexandrovich,
>
> I hereby beg you not to deny the possibility of your personal petition to the responsible authorities and, in particular, to the People's Commissar of Internal Affairs of the USSR Comrade L. P. Beria, concerning the speedy decision of the case of my wife – soloist of the ballet of the State Academic Theatre named after S. M. Kirov, Nina Alexandrovna Anisimova, sent as part of a review to the Special Council in Moscow already in mid-July of this year.
>
> In the deep conviction that the result of the reinvestigation undertaken here by the investigation department of the NKVD can only be fully positive for her, I beg you not to deny my petition, since a further delay in the case's examination under the conditions of detention

* The Soviet Union's legislative branch, a bicameral body established in 1937 to replace the Congress of Soviets.

would inevitably gravely affect her health as well as her
qualification as ballet dancer.

Respectfully,
K. N. Derzhavin

I join my son's petition

Academician N. C. Derzhavin
Leningrad, 46. Pr. Kirov, 1/3 apt. 31
30 October 1939.[22]

All over the Soviet Union, people were trying to use their
personal connections to improve the lot of an arrested family member, usually to no avail. Every single letter written
in defence of a prisoner was an act of bravery. Like Baikov,
Kostia's father Nikolai Derzhavin was an academician who had
occupied a leading position in Leningrad's academic world. It
was a connection Baikov responded to. There was no guarantee
of success, but Baikov acted immediately. On 1 November he
wrote a handwritten letter to Beria, passing on Kostia's request
to the commissar:

To the Commissar of Internal Affairs of the USSR
Deputy of the Supreme Soviet of the USSR
Comrade L. P. Beria
Deeply respected Lavrenty Pavlovich,

I beg you to consider the attached application from
Academician N. S. Derzhavin, who is asking to acceler-
ate the examination of the case of his son's wife, the artist
N. A. Anisimova. This file has already been examined in

Leningrad and, according to information received by N. S. Derzhavin, it has received a favourable decision, which was sent for a final decision to Moscow to the Special Council.

With comradely greetings.
Deputy of the Supreme Soviet of the USSR
Academician A. Baikov
1 November 1939[23]

Baikov enclosed Kostia's petition. Three days later, on 3 November, Beria wrote a curt note on Kostia's letter: it was to be passed on to Ivanov, the head of the secretariat of the Special Council, and a judgment would be made.

Events now overtook each other: if the official documents are correct, the Special Council had already reviewed Nina's case on 29 October and decided to limit her sentence to the time she had already served.[24]

On 11 November, Nina wrote on a piece of paper the date and one short sentence: 'Today is the day of my release.'* The ink of some of the letters is slightly runny, as if a few tears had fallen where she had written the words. It is the only surviving indication of Nina's emotions that day.

~

Nina had walked out of the prison gates – but the stigma of the sentence still hung over her. Would she be allowed to stay in Leningrad and return to the Kirov? More often than not,

* This paper is the last sheet included in the collection of her letters from prison and Karlag.

prisoners released from the camps were not allowed to settle in any of the major cities. More strings must have been pulled behind the scenes. Beria wrote another curt instruction on Baikov's letter on 20 November: 'To Sp. Co.' Nina's case was returned to the Special Council. On 23 November, the council overruled its decision of 29 October to limit Nina's sentence to the time already served. Instead, it revoked its 1938 judgment and officially closed her case.[25] Her name was cleared; she had been declared innocent. She was finally, genuinely free.

～

Nina was extraordinarily lucky. After Beria had taken over, only a few prisoners had been recalled from the camps for further investigation, and fewer still had subsequently been allowed to resume their former lives in Moscow or Leningrad after their cases had been officially closed. It was thanks to Kostia that Nina had been one of the few.

Having survived the Gulag, Nina was permitted to return to her family, to her theatre, to the profession that defined her life. Nina went back to the Kirov, presenting a certificate issued by the Leningrad NKVD stating that she had been held at the Shpalerka from 2 February 1938 until 11 November 1939 and that she had been released because her case had been closed. There was no mention that she had been sentenced to five years of forced labour or that she had served time in Karlag. As part of her return to work, Nina had to fill in the usual paperwork. How was she to answer the question of whether she had ever been arrested and sentenced to a punishment? She limited her response to the statement that she had been arrested on 2 February 1938 and released on 11 November

1939 because her case had been closed. This was to be the first and last reference to her ordeal in her work file. No further mention of her arrest was made on subsequent forms kept in her personal file at the theatre.[26]

On 23 December 1939, exactly six weeks after her release, Nina stepped back on to the stage of the Kirov on the arm of Sergei Koren. They were reunited in the lively Krakowiak from Mikhail Glinka's opera *A Life for the Tsar*, performed at the time under the politically more appropriate title *Ivan Susanin*. The theatre cast her in her old soloist parts as if nothing had happened: on 25 December, Koren and Anisimova performed the Spanish Dance in *Swan Lake*. They also speedily introduced her into new repertoire. On 4 January 1940, Nina performed for the first time the flamenco dance in Chabukiani's *Laurenzia*. Partnered, as always, by Koren, she shared a stage with Tatiana Vecheslova, who was performing one of the ballet's leading parts that night. *Laurenzia* had premiered on 22 March 1939, while Nina was facing the snowstorms of the Kazakh steppe.[27]

Nina plunged into her work. Three months after her release, on 17 February 1940, she and Koren gave a full evening performance of national dances they had staged at the Philharmonic, featuring themselves and a sizeable group of dancers. It seems unlikely that they put together so large a production in such a short time from scratch; the programme was probably based on the concert that had been cancelled in the wake of Nina's arrest. The dancer Natalia Sheremetevskaya – aware of Nina's arrest and time in Karlag – later wrote about the evening:

> The programme was very interesting. They used new
> devices in the Spanish dance – sharp accents of the torso,

like a 'hiccup', which had first been demonstrated in the Soviet Union by a Spanish dancer of American origin, Pauline Koner. But it seemed to me that Anisimova's dance had changed – it had lost the unrestrained happiness that had previously been characteristic of it, a kind of bitterness and fury had appeared.[28]

Commenting in the Kirov Theatre's paper *Za sovetskoe iskusstvo*, Marietta Frangopulo had a different response to the apparent change in Nina's dancing:

A certain nakedness of N. Anisimova's temperament, which was observed in her performance before this concert, has now disappeared and the artist presents the dance in good taste and a sense of measure. Her expressive face is interesting in its changes, in its emotionality. The slender, supple wrists of her arms are noble and beautiful. The fluidity of the lekuri* alternates with the impetuous rhythm of the Armenian-Kurdish dance, the melodiousness of the serenades, the temperamental bolero. But in everything there is a presence of superb taste.

To those reading between the lines, the review's final paragraph was a tender welcome to the artist who had returned, a tribute to her incredible physical and psychological strength: 'Responding to the greetings and comments of their comrades who had gone backstage after the concert, N. Anisimova and S. Koren say that they are full of strength and that they plan

---

* A Georgian dance.

to work further and to show the public again their creations. We wish them, and everybody who participated in the concert, new creative achievements and successes.'[29]

Nobody would have dared to say so openly, but many, if not all, of her colleagues were aware that the NKVD had taken Nina. Nina would not have been inclined, or allowed, to talk about any of her experiences, least of all about her time in the Gulag, but some members of the company – notably Koren and probably Vecheslova – knew. It seems likely the theatre's leadership decided to turn a blind eye, accepting the official story of an extended imprisonment in Leningrad without asking too many questions. Frangopulo realised better than anybody else what Nina must have gone through: of Greek origin, she had been arrested as part of the NKVD's Greek operation on 29 July 1938 and confined in an overcrowded cell for ten months. She was released on 29 May 1939 and her file was closed for lack of evidence.[30] The Kirov immediately opened its doors to her but Frangopulo, who was eight years older than Nina, shifted her professional focus to ballet history and curatorship after her imprisonment.*

Despite the extraordinary speed and apparent ease of her professional comeback, it must have been immeasurably hard for Nina to return to her former life. She had to learn to live with her memories. Ex-prisoners describe how the fear of arrest

---

* Frangopulo formally danced with the company until 1947, but her focus shifted to writing and collecting historical ballet artefacts, a passion which would ultimately lead to curating. Her first major written work about her former teacher Leonid Leontiev was published in 1939, the year of her release from prison. Works on Agrippina Vaganova and Nina followed in 1948 and 1951. Frangopulo began to teach ballet history at the school in 1940 and would go on to found the school's museum.

stayed with them for decades. Every casual goodbye carried the potential of being final. But knowing how to mask your emotions in public was a necessary survival skill in Stalin's Russia. Shortly after her release from prison, the poet Olga Berggolts appeared to be working as usual, compiling her poems in a small book and dropping them off at the newspaper *Izvestia*, but almost every night she dreamed of the prison, her arrest, the interrogations. Three months after her release, Berggolts wrote: 'I still haven't returned from there. Left at home alone, I talk aloud to the investigator, the commission, with people – about prison, about my shameful, cooked up "case". Prison is the response to everything – poems, events, conversations with people. It stands between me and life . . .'[31] Two months later she wrote: 'The sensation of prison is now, after five months of freedom, sharper in me than during the first period after release . . . They pulled out my soul, they rummaged through it with fetid fingers, they spat on it, they defecated on it, then they shoved it back inside and they are saying: "Live".'[32]

Perhaps it was a little simpler for Nina: whereas Berggolts had believed fervently in Communism, Nina's passion was her art. Ideology still formed the wider context of her work and could not be ignored. But its impact and demands were less direct – dance and music could not be tethered to a propaganda message to the same extent as the written word.

Nina's ability to reclaim her position within the Kirov was remarkable. Maybe her inborn resilience was strengthened by a profound understanding of how lucky she was. She knew how close she had been to death, how unlikely it was that she would ever return to Leningrad and the Kirov, even if she had survived. Walking through the stage door, she knew that Mikhailov and Levanenok had most likely disappeared for good, even though she probably did not know they had been executed. During the time of the Terror, even the closest relatives of executed victims were usually not given the truth: instead, they were told that their beloved had received ten years of forced labour without the right of correspondence. Many would only find out what had happened in the 1950s.

The Special Council had also declared the Maly Theatre dancer Tamara Medalinskaya a socially dangerous element because of her acquaintance with Salomé and sentenced her to five years' exile. On 9 May 1941, Medalinskaya appealed to have her case reconsidered, noting that five other dancers arrested for attending parties at Salomé's – Oppengeim, Anisimova, Sidorovskaya, Molodinskaya, Fiurt-Raikova – had all been freed: Sidorovskaya, Oppengeim and Fiurt-Raikova without ever receiving a sentence. Medalinskaya's appeal was denied with the curt note that there was no basis for reconsidering her case.[33] Unlike Nina, she had no one to appeal on her behalf.

Kostia had fought valiantly for Nina's release, but the fight and the times had left their traces. In June 1939, while Nina was still in prison, waiting for a resolution of her case, Kostia's old idol Meyerhold had been arrested. A few weeks later, his wife, the actress Zinaida Raikh, was stabbed to death in the couple's Moscow flat. Meyerhold was shot in February 1940; his apartment was assigned to Beria's driver.[34] When a student of Kostia's visited him at home in March 1941 to discuss a seminar paper about the seventeenth-century Spanish playwright Pedro Calderón, he found the atmosphere heavy: 'A large room, a deep armchair, half-darkness. No topics that distracted from Calderón. Nobody walked into the room. No tea was offered. Melancholy.'[35]

The Kirov's support enabled Nina successfully to reassert her place within the company. When a small book of friendly cartoons of the company's leading lights was published in 1940, Nina's caricature took its place among them, lovingly characterising her as Spanish whirlwind while recognising her work as choreographer.[36] In June 1940, Nina was awarded the medal 'For Labour Distinction', which bore the signature of Mikhail Kalinin, head of state of the Soviet Union.[37]

The Kirov was backing Nina, but she also had a state to serve – a state run by a regime that had almost killed her.

～

In August 1939, while Nina was still waiting in prison, Stalin had agreed to a non-aggression pact with Hitler. A secret protocol divided up Eastern Europe between Hitler and Stalin in case of war, placing Eastern Poland, Finland, the Baltics and Bessarabia within the Soviet sphere of influence. By the time Nina walked out of the prison gates, she had stepped into a world at war. Hitler invaded Poland on 1 September 1939: the Second World War had begun. It was only a matter of time until Hitler would turn further east. In the meantime, Stalin was aggressively trying to build buffer zones in the Union's western borderlands. A few weeks after Nazi Germany had invaded Poland, the Red Army annexed formerly Ukrainian and Belorussian lands in Eastern Poland. About three weeks after Nina's release, the Soviet Union went to war with Finland, whose border it considered too close to Leningrad for comfort. The Winter War with Finland lasted three months and ended with Finnish territorial concessions.

In June 1940, Soviet troops occupied the three Baltic republics. Close on the heels of the soldiers followed dancers sent to entertain the troops. Two brigades of artists were from the Kirov and Pushkin Theatres; Nina and Sergei Koren were part of the second one, which gave twenty-eight concerts over the course of eighteen days. A Russian journalist wrote breezily about Nina's performance in Dzintari, a neighbourhood in the Latvian resort of Jūrmala popular with Russian aristocrats in the nineteenth century: 'The gypsy dance performed by the ballet soloist Anisimova ... roused stormy applause from the audience, exceptional in its perfection and in the striking talent of the character dancer. When you see her a second time, then you are even more able to appreciate the subtlety of her facial expression and her fiery temperament.'[38] Within the highly ideologised context of Soviet life, Nina's reassertion of her public role as a Soviet artist may have helped her recover her sense of self-worth: she had rejoined Soviet society as a useful member of the collective.

Nina had not lost her power as a performer. She continued to be praised in reviews. But it was her imaginative passion for pushing the boundaries of character dance as a means of choreographic expression that made her unique. A long article about character dance in general, and Anisimova and Koren in particular, summed up their exceptional contribution to Soviet ballet: despite the ideological changes wrought by the revolution – character dance continued to be confined to its old supporting role in ballets: divertissement dances whose emotional expressiveness was usually limited to an exotic, temperamental storminess. Though their work was based on the steps and forms unique to specific national dances, Nina and Koren went far beyond showcasing national dances by infusing them with their own meaning. What they brought to the ballet stage was not ethnography, but an artistic vision that illuminated character dance with a poetic capacity to manifest the full range of human emotions, from sadness, joy, wistfulness and tragedy to humour, something often difficult to express in classical dance. For every piece, they searched for a new vocabulary to convey emotional experiences common to all mankind, exceeding the traditional role of character dance – to add a little local colour. Their Spanish dances had absolutely nothing in common with the 'Spain' of the ballet stage: their famous 'Spanish Suite' was based on an enormous amount of research. The unusual precision of their movements, their astonishing mastery of the castanets, their deep emotionality won them recognition. They complemented each other, Koren's sharp daring providing the perfect contrast to Nina's lyrical dramatism. Both were extraordinary actors, but Nina's musicality was outstanding: her movements were not a response to music, they were born from it.[39]

At Karlag, although she had dreamed of returning to the stage, Nina's artistic hopes were increasingly focused on choreography. Her aspirations were unusual in more than one way. Choreography was, and remains, a field dominated by men. Nina was lucky that the company was still headed by Leonid Lavrovsky, a young but already well-established choreographer. On the eve of Nina's arrest, Lavrovsky had publicly announced that he wanted to give her a chance to choreograph a piece for the company. His decisive move to cast her in her old roles within weeks of her release showed a willingness to help her, regardless of what had happened. This was brave: support for a former prisoner could be interpreted as an anti-Soviet action during a future crackdown, especially as people who had been apprehended once were more likely to undergo the same ordeal in the future. It was also a bold step professionally: despite the ideological emphasis on national and folk art, very few choreographers were seriously interested in exploring the possibilities of character dance at the time.

In March 1940, Nina published a passionate article in the Kirov's paper, bemoaning the fact that character dance remained confined to the sidelines in ballet productions. The ideological demand that ballet librettos become more realistic and performances more like danced dramas meant that in some new pieces there was no place for character dances at all if they did not fit tightly into the storyline. Nina felt that character dance was still undervalued at the Kirov; she yearned to experiment with its artistic possibilities, but it was impossible to do so without the theatre's support. Alluding to the missed opportunity of fully exploring Ukrainian dance in the Kirov's recent work on *Taras Bulba*, a ballet based on Nikolai Gogol's novella about Ukrainian Cossacks, she ended her article with a battle cry for daring creative statements.[40]

Nina was about to be given the chance to make such a statement. In the pre-war years, several national *dekady* were held at Moscow's Bolshoi Theatre, festivals showcasing the art of the national Union republics. In October 1939, it was Armenia's turn to bring its art to the capital. During a friendly conversation with the Armenian composer Aram Khachaturian, the Armenian Politburo member Anastas Mikoyan suggested that the composer write a ballet based on a libretto about the life and work of Soviet border guards and kolkhozniks (collective farm workers) recently written by the Armenian director Gevork Ovanesian. Khachaturian had never written a ballet but rose to the challenge. He collected folklore material in Armenia and wrote the score. Yerevan's Spendiaryan Theatre of Opera and Ballet* successfully performed *Happiness* at the Bolshoi on 24 October 1939 and Khachaturian was awarded the Order of Lenin. But despite the ballet's public success, the composer felt that there were shortcomings in the libretto and score.[41]

These flaws did not deter the Kirov Theatre from jumping at the opportunity to stage a ballet set in a Soviet fraternal republic, especially one with a score by a major Soviet composer. The theatre approached Khachaturian and invited him to start working on a revised production with a new libretto – to be written by Kostia. It is not clear at what point the theatre approached Kostia and Nina, but discussions to produce Khachaturian's ballet at the Kirov seem to have started soon after *Happiness* was shown in Moscow. The earliest letter in the Kirov's archive about the ballet dates from 3 January 1940.

By November 1940, the theatre had officially included the ballet in its repertoire plan, with a premiere scheduled for spring 1941. Initially, Nina and Sergei Koren were supposed to choreograph the ballet jointly, but by December Nina was being referenced as sole choreographer. On 31 December 1940, while Kostia was working on a new libretto, Nina described her artistic vision for the ballet in the Kirov's paper *Za sovetskoe iskusstvo*. After describing how she wanted to rework the rhythmic and movement material of Armenian national dances for the stage, she wrote: 'I personally would like our *Happiness* to be a production that is sunny in its colours, youthful,

* Situated in Armenia's capital Yerevan, the theatre was named after the Armenian national composer Alexander Spendiaryan.

spontaneous in its expressiveness.' The production ticked an important ideological box: for the last couple of years, the Kirov had been adding productions designed to celebrate the culture of Russia's fraternal Soviet republics.[42]

By April 1941, Kostia's new libretto was finished, and Khachaturian had agreed to rework the score.[43] Ovanesian's original libretto had told an ideologically sound but dramatically boring story about Karine, a young kolkhoznik, and Armen, a border guard. The ballet celebrated the happiness of life on a kolkhoz until intruders from across the border threaten the socialist peace. A fierce fight ensues, but the border guards ultimately triumph, and the ballet ends with kolkhozniks and border guards united in a hymn to the great leader of all peoples, Stalin.[44]

Kostia and Nina completely changed the plot. Of all the patriotic, ideologically sound themes they could have chosen, they juxtaposed a thoroughly Soviet wife beloved by her community and her good-for-nothing husband whose selfish conflict with the collective foreshadows a descent into crime. Was this an inverted form of their own story? In real life of course, Kostia had fought to prove his beloved's innocence, though her behaviour had by no means been flawless from an ideological point of view. Nina was not guilty of any counter-revolutionary crimes, but she lacked the kind of finely tuned socialist conscience that would have kept her away from someone whose social origins and outlook were decidedly alien to the Soviet regime.

During her final weeks at Karlag, Nina had written to Kostia that, deep in her soul, she still had the desire to 'stage big, wonderful ballets', and that she was dreaming of staging a ballet about the Kazakh steppe, its shepherds and 'those wonderful Kazakh girls'.[45] In *Happiness* there would be no Kazakhs – but there were Kurdish shepherds, who save Karine and her small daughter from her evil husband, and a Kurdish girl, Aisha, to be danced by Nina. There were also narrative threads linking back to Nina's work for Karlag's cultural brigade. Here as well as there, she was supposed to make the regime's ideological message visible on stage. At Karlag she had asked Kostia to send her material about harvest and kolkhoz scenes. Kostia's new libretto eerily mirrored her request: the curtain opens on a happy cotton-harvest scene on the Armenian kolkhoz.

The plot contrasts Karine's good-for-nothing husband Giko, who refuses to work and gets tempted to deal in contraband goods, with Kazakov, the brave commander of the local border guards. After Giko threatens his wife and she discovers his illegal activity, she runs away from him with their young daughter. They flee into the night and are found by Kurdish shepherds. Meanwhile Kazakov and his fellow guards confiscate the illicit goods and search for Giko and his criminal gang. Giko heads for the border when he suddenly finds himself face to face with Karine. She tries to stop him from escaping but he grabs his daughter from her and threatens to throw the child into the seething waterfall beneath them. Kazakov is hiding nearby and rescues the girl, but Giko manages to break away and stabs Kazakov in his chest. The people throw themselves on Giko and the border guards lead him and the other criminals away.

Kazakov recovers, and he and Karine are united as everyone celebrates the end of the harvest season. The closing scene combines Armenian, Kurdish, Russian, Georgian and

Ukrainian dances, the set depicting them surrounded by the blooming spoils of this happy and triumphant land.[46]

~

Kostia's libretto read like any ideologically sound Soviet film script. But Soviet artists were accustomed to instilling their own ideas and values into even the most trite plots. Nina outlined a more universal vision in the Kirov's newspaper in March 1941, as rehearsals got under way:

> The theme of the ballet is given in its title. Its heroes reach happiness through obstacles, by fighting with evil they meet in their lives, by overcoming obstacles that stand in their way. This is the theme of any fairy tale, of any folk legend, but in our ballet it comes to life based on material taken from Soviet reality, in the figures of people from our country. The participants in the action are Armenians, Kurds, Russians. The theme of happiness is developed in contrast with the theme of moral inadequacy which leads to crime. A feeling which the ballet theatre has not paid attention to until now occupies a big part in the life of the ballet's heroine: the feeling of maternal love.

Ballets usually told their stories in historical or fantastical settings. Nina wanted to find poetry in the reality of everyday Soviet life.[47]

Rehearsals were beset by the usual problems: the leading soloists were overloaded with the daily repertoire and rehearsals on other new ballets, Khachaturian was sick with the flu and struggling to finish reworking the first act according to schedule. There was much to be done to the original score: as Khachaturian would later put it, he had to 'de-kulakise' it.[48] But on 29 May 1941, two years after Nina had returned to the Shpalerka for further investigation, the ballet company held a meeting to discuss her work on the ballet's first act – and to decide whether it showed enough promise to be continued. Evgeny Radin, the theatre's director and a political appointee, opened the meeting. If the tone of his opening words was anything to go by, Nina had little to worry about:

> Comrades, I want to make *Happiness* the basis of my speech, both in the sense of the work by the composer Khachaturian, as well as in the literal meaning of the word . . . So let us begin with *Happiness*, the work of the composer Khachaturian and the librettist Derzhavin . . . I love Khachaturian's music . . . and if we accept the libretto then this means that we also trust the librettist; if we instruct N. A. Anisimova to stage the ballet, that means we also believe in her. But nonetheless, I have to say that I did not expect anything like this . . . Because I remember one viewing of *Taras**– back then, I didn't understand anything, I didn't believe anything . . . Today, I understood everything and believed everything . . . because it is very simple and very literate . . . it is done with real taste . . . That is why I personally have the audacity to say, after

* *Taras Bulba*, a ballet in three acts, composed by Vasily Solovyov-Sedoi and choreographed by Fedor Lopukhov. It premiered at the Kirov Theatre on 12 December 1940.

viewing the first act and individual pieces from another
act today, that it seems to me the piece is well staged.[49]

His praise meant a lot. Although the theatres were publicly
enthusiastic about fulfilling the state's ideological demands,
behind closed doors even a political appointee like Radin would
sometimes throw up his hands in frustration at the tension
between ideology and artistic preferences and standards. For
years the Kirov had tried, sometimes desperately, to avoid for-
malism (too much dance for its own sake) and to make its ballets
more like danced theatre. But the desire to promote realism,
using logical, comprehensible plot development, had sometimes
led to pedestrian productions of limited choreographic interest.

Similarly, the demand that Soviet art should be national
in form and socialist in context had resulted in a number of
'national' ballets set in more 'exotic' locations linked to the
Soviet empire – there had already been Vainonen's 1937
Partisan Days, set among Cossacks; Chabukiani's 1938 *Heart of
the Mountain*, set in eighteenth-century Georgia; Chabukiani's
1939 *Laurenzia*, an indirect act of solidarity with Spanish
Republicans during the Civil War; and the Ukrainian *Taras
Bulba*. Some people in the company were by now fed up with
national themes, but the regime's demands had to be heeded.

The Kirov had fought hard to survive the revolution. If
it wanted to continue, it had to contribute to the drive for
ideological education. Radin was among those who had not
expected much of the company's new 'Armenian' ballet, but
he knew they had to include such productions, regardless of
artistic merit. His speech suggested that, in this case, Nina had
pulled off something remarkable:

We talked, we heard the following kind of conversations: 'There we go, Armenia, the East, Georgia, again exotica, I'm sick of it. Everyday dramas, everyday comedies, again the East, again exotica, I'm sick of it' . . . Here we have something totally different, here there isn't the exotica that everyone feared. True, the action takes place in Armenia, but I don't care where: in Armenia, Georgia or in another Soviet republic, all this could really happen. Yes, this is true, and this serves one goal – to educate our audience, our people, to teach how one should live, how one should work, what one should learn, what one should not learn, how to behave like a real Soviet citizen in our times, in our Soviet country. All of this is already achieved in the first act. Much has to be said in favour of the director,* even though this comrade has only appeared at the front in the role of a new director-choreographer, we are just putting her forward for this work, but she has stepped forward demonstrating full knowledge of this field, knowledge that is very literate, interestingly thought out and interestingly executed.[50]

Radin was using the combative language of the day, likening the theatre to an ideological battleground. Nina was the choreographic commander, and she had just demonstrated that she knew how to lead her troops and handle her weapons. There is a certain irony here, considering what Nina had already survived: fate had forced her to learn how to create art and reflect

---

* Radin means the choreographer.

upon its meaning within the lethal and ideological context of the Gulag. Perhaps this experience had prepared her for the task of balancing a comprehensible Soviet plot with an artistic vision without sacrificing its integrity.

As choreographer, Nina was searching for a language of movement that fused national dance and classical ballet. She was trying to put national dances *en pointe* without losing their special flavour. The result was interesting, artistically convincing – and challenging. The dancer Leonid Leontiev, who had participated in Diaghilev's Russian seasons, pointed out that more rehearsals were needed: 'One must say, comrades, that this work is utterly unusual for us, that is, I want to say that the movement, the colour of the movement, the character of the movement, the style of the movement is not usual for us, therefore the rehearsals need to be more frequent.'[51]

Nina had a loyal champion in Lavrovsky, the Kirov ballet's artistic director, who had just created his masterwork, *Romeo and Juliet*. Lavrovsky had kept his promise to give Nina a platform to choreograph for the Kirov. His faith in her had given her strength at the beginning of the rehearsal period, when there were still many doubters and pessimists who did not believe that her attempt to stage *Happiness* could be successful. But the first viewing had gone well, and Lavrovsky could announce to his company:

I am taking the same position that I took in the beginning: I believe in the production, I believe in Anisimova's staging, I continue to believe in it today. Which positive and negative ballet qualities have we seen today? First of all, we were present at the birth of a very interesting and valuable choreographer; secondly, there are grounds to believe that we are getting a very interesting, original and sufficiently exciting production.

Moving on to the demonstration itself, one must say that we have seen valuable and pleasant things in the dances. How can one characterise it? One must say, the choreographer Anisimova has her dance language, it is fresh, it is hers, it does not resemble anything seen or remade. Musical elements are all the same, but every musical composer has his own musical language in which he speaks. The same applies to the language of choreographer Anisimova. This is a very valuable, basic quality, based on which one can determine that this is a choreographer, and not a railway coupler.[52]

Kostia and Nina also spoke. Kostia claimed modestly that, compared to the other creative elements of the production, the libretto was the weakest link, but he was working under less than ideal circumstances because Khachaturian was lagging behind in his musical revisions. For him this libretto posed a special challenge: here was a tale of contemporary Soviet life and he had to create a plot that presented a poetic version of reality. *Happiness* was not a story about love, but of something bigger: the tensions between the collective and the individual. The clash between Giko and the collective lay at the heart of the whole production.[53]

The last words belonged to Nina, notably worked up by the occasion and disarmingly open about her own shortcomings – though unafraid to comment on those of others:

Comrades, I want to thank you for the fact that, two days
ago, when everything was really not going well for us, you
nonetheless showed a good result today ... This really
helps me, because I'm too young a choreographer. I am
always helped a lot by Comrade Lavrovsky ... I don't
have the same discipline as Leonid Mikhailovich,* I am
young and less experienced, less wise than he is, I lose
it more quickly than he does. When one has to work in
a situation where one dancer is sick, the leg of another
hurts or something, I start to fret. The gopak has to be
danced in a squatting position, and when the men arrive
and limp they can't dance in a squatting position. I fret,
I worry a lot, and you can help me a lot. I have a lot of
strength. A lot of creative enthusiasm. By your help I
don't mean praise, but support. When I see Vecheslova or
Dubkova, that they are absorbed in their work, that their
eyes are burning, I feel better. But when a person comes
and only fulfils his work in the necessary order because
he is required to work from one until four o'clock, then
this diminishes the success.[54]

Nina ended with a promise to try to justify the trust the ensemble was putting in her.[55]

On 15 June 1941, the Kirov officially signed the contract
engaging her as choreographer for *Happiness*.[56] Her dream
seemed about to come true. But storm clouds were gathering
in the west.

* Leonid Lavrovsky. Lavrovsky was actually only four years older
than Nina.

10

The Great
Patriotic War

S even days later, on Sunday, 22 June 1941, at around
3.30 a.m., the largest invasion force in history surged
across Soviet borders without a formal declaration of war.
Stalin had ignored warnings received from the Soviet ambassador to Berlin, military intelligence, the British government
and Richard Sorge, a German double agent in Tokyo. There
had been eighty-four intelligence notifications; he had
dismissed all of them. After initially refusing to act on the military's insistence on putting all frontier troops on full battle
alert, he only agreed to give the necessary order at 00.30 a.m.
When he was called at 4 a.m. with the news that Kiev, Minsk,
Vilnius and Sevastopol were being bombarded, there was no
further escaping reality. At noon, the people of Leningrad
gathered in stunned amazement around the public loudspeakers blaring out Commissar for Foreign Affairs Vyacheslav
Molotov's formal announcement that their country was at

war. Stalin didn't speak to the nation until 3 July, eleven days after the invasion.[1]

On that first day of war, Kirov dancers received an order to join brigades performing at draft centres and recruiting offices; over the first three days, 158 artists of the theatre gave twenty-three such concerts.[2] That same evening, the Kirov Ballet performed Marius Petipa's *La Bayadère*. The company's first wartime performance went well; the auditorium was full and the audience allowed themselves to be swept away by the ballet's dramatic story. But backstage everyone was agitated and anxious. People were silently sitting in the producer's office, listening to the announcements on the loudspeaker.[3]

The war immediately forced the Kirov to change its repertoire. The theatre had just staged Wagner's *Lohengrin* as a cultural gesture honouring the Molotov–Ribbentrop non-aggression pact, but the performances planned for 24 and 27 June now had to be replaced by *Ivan Susanin*, a production in which Nina and Sergei Koren often danced the Krakowiak. Performances continued, but audiences began to dwindle; before long, a performance of *Swan Lake* had to be cancelled after only twenty tickets had been sold.[4]

In July, rehearsals for *Happiness* started again, but gone were the days when tired or unenthusiastic dancers were Nina's main problem. Her friend the ballerina Olga Iordan later remembered how the dancers were mobilised as part of the country's defence drive, just as rehearsals were resuming: 'During alarms, work and rehearsals ceased and we descended down the stairs to the producer's room or the corridor. But the alarms passed calmly. We still only grasped the war with the intellect and did not feel it directly.'[5]

Everyone at the theatre had to bring a gas mask to work.[6]
Whenever they were not rehearsing, everybody, from the theatre's leading ballerina Galina Ulanova and the tenor Georgy
Nelepp to older artists, congregated in the Kirov's set design
workshop on Pisarev Street. They were producing gigantic
nets intended to camouflage the city's high landmarks, to stop
them being used as orientation guides during bombardments:

> From 1 July, we were all mobilised for defence work: we
> tore up loofah in the decoration hall on Pisarev Street,
> connected it with tufts and sewed it on nets. We knew that
> this work was necessary for the defence of the city. The
> work was done cheerfully – even though the hands were
> busy, the tongues were free: we joked, laughed, sharpened
> witticisms addressed to Hitler and his 'Napoleonic plans'.
> It seemed as if the war was taking place infinitely far from
> us and would never reach us.[7]

Nina and her partner Sergei Koren joined a brigade performing for the Baltic Fleet, giving nine concerts for the
'pilot-falcons' on airfields and next to fighter planes ready
for take-off. Neither the sirens, which frequently sounded in
the middle of the artists' improvised performances, nor the
roaring of the planes could stop them. Waiting patiently for
the all-clear, they continued, at least outwardly unperturbed.
The soldiers wrote to them in gratitude, proclaiming that only
Soviet performers would bring concerts like this to troops at
the front.[8]

Artists also guarded the theatre building at night. Mobile
camp beds were put up in the backstage Napravnik foyer,

between the gilded columns of the artists' box, in changing rooms and corridors. Olga Iordan and her fellow dancer Nikolai Zubkovsky carried chairs to the theatre gates on the Kryukov canal, where they sat wearing their gas masks, quietly listening in the silent night. At the end of July, a special train was assigned to evacuate children whose parents worked for Leningrad's theatres; the Kirov ballerina Olga Mungalova and the Maly Opera soloist Vasily Azbukin were in charge of the group. There was little time to load everything on to the train and the artists lugged heavy chests on their backs, sweat running down their faces. Everyone hoped that they would be separated only briefly and nobody had packed warm clothes, but a tearful anxiety still prevailed on the platform. Sobbing children had to be detached from their parents and placed inside the carriages.[9]

It was a hot August. The Germans were advancing on Leningrad, but few in the city understood the extent of the danger. The authorities kept their announcements deliberately vague; cities were falling one after the other, but major defeats were not divulged for several days. Instead, the twice-daily bulletins by the Soviet Information Bureau, which had a total monopoly on war reporting, focused on individual acts of heroism, featuring, in the words of the war correspondent Vasily Grossman, stories along the lines of 'Ivan Pupkin killed five Germans with a spoon.' Hitler, meanwhile, had told the chief of staff of his Army High Command that Moscow and Leningrad should be completely levelled and made uninhabitable to avoid having to feed their populations through the winter.[10]

It was time to start planning for the Kirov's new season, but nobody knew whether the theatre would reopen. The administration remained silent and rumours abounded, including the possibility of evacuation. Kept deliberately in the dark like the rest of the city while German troops advanced relentlessly, the Kirov finally announced in mid-August that it would open on 23 August, with the opera *Ivan Susanin* as usual, followed by *Swan Lake* on 24 August. In the words of the dancer Natalya Sakhnovskaya: 'Everybody roused themselves, sighed with relief. Telegrams were sent to the hinterland to artists who had evacuated with their children with summons to the assembly of the company.' Within the new parameters of the last two months, life seemed set to continue. Nina rehearsed *Happiness* on stage, convinced that the season would open as usual. And then, on 15 August 1941, the Kirov's director announced at a general meeting that Moscow had given an order to evacuate the theatre.[11]

～

The state's decision to devote enormous resources to evacuating the Soviet Union's most important theatres was extraordinary. The German invasion had taken the regime by surprise, rendering its plans for an offensive obsolete. A Council for Evacuation had been established on 24 June 1941 to move resources and workforces vital for the war effort: industrial assets, livestock, skilled workers, political and administrative cadres. Approximately one-eighth of all industrial assets were dismantled and moved over vast distances, to be reassembled beyond the enemy's reach in the Urals, Siberia and Central Asia. Evacuation trains followed the same railway routes that were transporting prisoners to the remote camps of the Gulag. Over 1,500 large-scale enterprises, including over 100 aircraft factories, were evacuated. Trains running in the opposite direction carried troops from east to west, to replenish an army that would sacrifice about 8.7 million soldiers in the fight against Hitler, compared with casualty rates of approximately 383,700 British and 407,300 US soldiers.[12]

Evacuations were driven by practical considerations. The main goal was not to save lives, but to preserve the USSR and its wealth. This was divided into four categories: industry, culture, the state and party apparatus, civilians. Naturally the authorities wanted to evacuate key industrial, political and administrative workers and assets. It is understandable that the greatest treasures of the Hermitage were taken to safety on 1 July 1941 in a special train guarded by a carriage full of soldiers and two flatbeds with anti-aircraft batteries and machine guns. Their destruction or looting by German forces would have been a great material loss, and a propaganda coup for the enemy. But it is far from obvious why the regime assigned valuable train transportation to dancers, opera singers, musicians, costumes, instruments and stage props at a time when the future of the country and the whole Soviet enterprise was at stake.

As the historian Erina Megowan has persuasively argued, the answer lies in the unique position of culture as a central pillar of Soviet identity. The Soviet state treated the arts as a key asset worth saving from the outset, even before it had become clear how much of a contribution they could make to the war effort at the front and in the interior in terms of boosting morale at a time when it was virtually impossible to offer material incentives.[13]

At this moment of existential crisis, Soviet culture would demonstrate that it was the state's greatest asset for projecting soft power. After decades of ideological confrontation, the Western democracies and the Soviet state were united by necessity in the face of Hitler's ruthless ambitions. With little else in common, Soviet culture became a way for the Western allies to sell their sudden partnership with the Soviet Union to their public. While German forces were committing unspeakable crimes against civilians, the Soviets were resisting fascism not just with the gun, but also with the actor's voice, the dancer's grace, the conductor's baton and the violinist's bow, reinforcing the regime's claims of cultural superiority over the barbaric Nazi invaders who looted and destroyed art as they advanced.

A new symphony by a troubled-looking, bespectacled Soviet composer offered a bridge between east and west. As soon as the Soviet authorities realised that Shostakovich had started working on it inside the besieged city of Leningrad, they evacuated him and his family to Kuibyshev, where he completed it. Shostakovich's searing musical response to the invasion was not only a highly significant moment for Russia: a microfilm of the score was taken outside the Soviet Union, transforming it into an international symbol of cultural resistance against Hitler. *Time* magazine put a socialist-realist-style portrait of Shostakovich on its cover, depicting a determined-looking composer wearing a fireman's helmet before a backdrop of red and black bombed-out ruins, a few notes floating behind his head. The caption read: 'Fireman Shostakovich. Amid bombs bursting in Leningrad, he heard the chords of victory.' Throughout the 1942–3 season, many of the symphony's performances across America were accompanied by calls for the opening of a second front.[14]

But these events still lay in the future when Nina received her orders to evacuate with the Kirov Theatre.

∾

Nina and her mother only had a few days to pack. The Kirov's evacuation plan included family members, but Kostia and Valia both decided to stay in Leningrad. Kostia was waiting for a decision about the wartime future of his academy, Pushkin House, the Institute of Literature of the Academy of Sciences. Valia was planning to help Kostia organise the family's possessions before evacuating with him.

The prospect of another separation was terrifying. Once more, a train would take Nina to the east – the Kirov employees were being sent to Perm, or Molotov as it had recently been renamed.* Once more, the couple did not know for how long they would be separated and whether they would ever see each other again. The Kirov was planning to evacuate about 1,600 employees and 2,000 family members over two days, but in the end not everybody left. Some artists stayed behind because they had frail family members for whom the difficult journey was too dangerous; some fell sick, forcing them to miss the first train.

On 19 August, at Moscow station, eighty-three goods wagons and three regular passenger carriages were waiting on two

---

* Perm was renamed Molotov in honour of Commissar for Foreign Affairs Vyacheslav Molotov's fiftieth birthday in 1940. Reflecting the unofficial habits of the time (and Nina's and Kostia's correspondence), I have used the names Perm and Molotov interchangeably. The name of the city formally changed back to Perm in 1957.

tracks. The Kirov was evacuating not just people and their possessions but also costumes, sheet music, lighting equipment and props, although sets had to be left behind.[15] The equipment and most of the artists were loaded on to the same type of cattle wagons commonly used to transport prisoners. Previously, Nina was unsure whether she would survive the transport to the camp and the camp itself; now she did not know whether their train would be hit by enemy fire, whether she, her family and friends would survive the war, or whether her country would fall to the enemy.

On the approach to Mga, a small settlement about an hour south-east of Leningrad that served primarily as a railway station, the train came under bombardment. The artists were instructed to jump out of the wagons as quickly as possible; they threw themselves on the ground, seeking cover among the low shrubs of the railway embankment. Parachutes floated down from the sky, bearing flares to enable the Germans to take better aim. As night became day, the performers pressed themselves flat against the earth, feeling it tremble under the explosions. The Kirov's train was one of the last to leave the city. After several days of heavy fighting, the Germans captured Mga on 31 August, cutting the last railway line connecting Leningrad to the outside world.[16] There would be no further evacuation trains – the siege ring was about to close.

～

Kostia knew that Nina's journey might be dangerous, but he probably had no idea how narrow her escape had been. News from the front was deliberately vague and Nina was an old hand at self-censorship, always aware that mail would probably be checked. As the siege tightened around him, Kostia wrote to Nina in composed ignorance of the losing battle that was raging around Mga: 'Here, there is some calm after several tense days. Evidently, the Germans were driven back a fair amount. We will hope that from here, everything will go even better.' Thanks to his father Nikolai Sevastianovich, Kostia and Valia had been included on the evacuation list of the Academy of Sciences, but they were still waiting for a final decision about their departure:

> The question about the Academy of Science's departure will be decided one of these days. I and Valia are already included in the lists. Ostensibly, we will go to Central Asia, maybe even to Alma-Ata. In any case, this is my plan: no matter where the Academy of Sciences will go – I will go to Perm, and Valia together with the things will go to the Academy of Science's destination under the protection of NSch [Nikolai Sevastianovich] and M Iv [Maria Ivanovna].* In Perm we will decide what to do.

Kostia wanted to find out whether Nina might be able to work at the theatre in Alma-Ata. Most likely he calculated that living conditions in a republican capital much further to the east might be better than in Perm, especially since they would be living with his influential father: 'If this won't happen this way, then we will think about other variations. In any case, all my energy will be used for the purpose of setting you up as well

* Kostia's parents.

as possible, and, most importantly, together with us. This is why I really beg you to endure, if possible, all difficulties of the journey and not to lose heart. Everything will be settled well, and if possible better.'

Unaware that it was already virtually impossible to get out of Leningrad, Kostia and Valia were preparing for their departure. Kostia had taken all their valuables to his parents' flat, which would be looked after by relatives or friends who would live there while Kostia's family was away. Only the heavy furniture remained. Kostia had asked the police to keep an eye on their own flat and to make sure that the communal management didn't get up to any mischief, but they were also looking for a caretaker who could act as a temporary tenant to make sure nobody claimed it while they were evacuated.[17]

On 30 August, Kostia wrote to Nina that he had received her telegram from a town not far from the Moscow region, and that he had then heard that the theatre had arrived in Perm. Kostia was agitated, but resolved to outwardly maintain his usual composure, determined to convince himself that there was a plan despite the deeply unsettling uncertainty of their situation.

Over the next couple of days, Kostia received an express telegram from Nina, letting him know that they were well set up.[18] But the process of settling the Kirov and its 3,000 or so employees and their families had been anything but straightforward. When their train finally arrived in Molotov on 29 August after a gruelling journey that took ten days, since there were stops at every station, the local authorities tried their best to prevent the theatre from remaining in town. They frantically telegraphed Moscow, complaining that the Kirov had arrived without permission.* In theory, the bodies overseeing the evacuation – the Committee for Artistic Affairs and the recently established Council for Evacuation – had to obtain approval from the relevant administration before evacuating an institution to a given city, but apparently the Kirov did not have the necessary papers. The city officials forbade the company from disembarking, ordering the train to remain on its track. The artists had to wait for several days in impatient, puzzled confusion until they were finally permitted to leave the train. Enlisting Moscow's support, the Kirov had managed to arm-twist the city authorities into accepting the situation.[19]

Across the eastern reaches of the Soviet Union, local authorities were dreading the enormous challenge of housing and feeding the evacuated employees of various enterprises and institutions, but they had no choice. A flood of evacuees and hardware poured from European Russia into major urban areas in the Urals, Siberia and Central Asia. Perm was the second most important city in the Urals. It had been the regional capital before the revolution, but after the civil war the capital of the Urals district was changed to Ekaterinburg (now Sverdlovsk).

During the Second World War, the Urals became the basis of the Soviet defence industry, producing about 40 per cent of all industrial output. Sixty-four factories were moved east to

* There is some speculation that the Kirov was originally heading for Novosibirsk, but remained instead in Molotov because of the personal preferences of the theatre's artistic director and chief conductor, Ari Pazovsky, who had been born and raised in Perm. The fact that Kostia names Perm as the theatre's final destination in his letters before Nina had arrived seems to indicate that this story is false, and that the Kirov was indeed headed for Perm from the outset.

Molotov. Throughout the war, evacuees arrived in the region from the occupied territories, including over 379,000 from Leningrad alone. Locals were forced to take them in; some found space in dormitories or other buildings; others had to make do with huts or dugouts. Molotov also hosted several *sharashki* (the Gulag's secret research and development laboratories, which exploited the expertise of imprisoned scientists).

Molotov was already home to one of Russia's oldest opera theatres, which had its own small ballet and opera company. Struggling with funding cuts necessitated by the outbreak of war, the company was away on tour in Chkalov (now Orenburg), a city near the border with Kazakhstan, when the Kirov arrived. The Molotov Opera was trying to find enough cash to bring its touring company back home, but by the time the artists returned they were in for a shock: the Kirov had taken over their theatre. The opera house only had room for one ensemble, and Moscow explicitly prioritised the major Moscow and Leningrad theatre companies. If necessary, smaller local companies had to be disbanded for financial and logistical reasons. On 11 September 1941, the city authorities decided to do just that, moving a group of soloists to the Kirov. Shortly afterwards, the Molotov Opera's property was transferred to the Kirov.[20]

Not surprisingly, the Kirov's reception in Molotov was not at all what it had expected. As Tatiana Vecheslova remembered: 'The city received the theatre not very hospitably. We were obviously not expected . . . We thought that the arrival of such an ensemble would be a cause for happiness in town, but much changed during wartime: the prime concern was to wash, feed, settle.'[21] Molotov was already overcrowded with evacuees, but, following an urgent government telegram from Moscow, the artists were distributed among private flats, dormitories and a hotel. Nina and her mother were put up in the three-storey, centrally located dormitory of the Pedagogical Institute. Those lower down the hierarchy were less lucky: they had to make do with any spare space that could be found, in clubs, houses of culture or even in the theatre's foyer, orchestra pit or auditorium. 'Separate apartments' were improvised out of the stage curtain, the cloth for the wings, boxes, planks and old decorations. Some even had to remain at the station, sleeping on their suitcases until they received an order giving them the right to occupy a small corner in a private flat. Chorus members and extras were housed far from the town centre in Motovilikh. The route back from Perm led them through a desolate area inhabited by wild dogs and wolves. After performances, fearful of being attacked, they only dared to make their way home in large groups.[22]

Perm's pretty opera house stood in the middle of a small public garden. But the Kirov dancers' already low spirits became even gloomier when they realised its stage was barely a quarter of the size of what they were used to. The company was determined to open its first Molotov season on 13 September with Glinka's *Ivan Susanin*, as was its tradition. This left barely two weeks to paint new sets and adjust the production for a much smaller stage, which they managed to enlarge a little by sacrificing two rows of the stalls.[23] The ballet company was scheduled to perform *Swan Lake* on 14 September, but the rehearsal studio was so small that only half of the corps could fit into it. The narrow space sported two dingy console mirrors and an old piano whose third leg had been replaced by a stool.

On opening night, the theatre showcased its best artists: Perm's public could hear the tenor Nelepp sing the leading role in *Ivan Susanin* and admire Tatiana Vecheslova dance a waltz in the opera. But the local population remained hostile to the newcomers and the response was icy. After Natalia Dudinskaya and Konstantin Sergeyev danced the first performance of *Swan Lake*, featuring Nina in the Spanish Dance, the curtain was lowered to the deafening silence of a half-empty auditorium. The artists were completely dejected, questioning the meaning of their profession during wartime: "'Who needs our ballet?', we thought. "Blood is flowing all around, the cities of our homeland are surrendering one after the other to the enemy, refugees are sitting for weeks in stations, and we will dance and try to prove that someone needs our art!'" Some of the male dancers felt there was something shameful and offensive in putting on make-up and colourful costumes to stage a production in front of suffering people.[24]

The town leadership soon found a cunning way to attract audiences, however: at a time of strict food rations, they gave the theatre permission to sell rolls and ice cream without ration cards during the interval. Enticed by food, people realised that they liked what they saw on stage and continued coming long after the buffet had closed. Performances started to be sold out a month in advance. The frost that year was even worse than usual, but the freezing cold could not deter the Kirov's new fans from queuing patiently for tickets. The locals were also intrigued by the aura of big-city life that surrounded the artists: their clothes were completely different from what they were used to. One young fan remembered decades later how she and her friends had admired the elegant garments

Konstantin Sergeyev and Feya Balabina had sewn themselves, secretly watching the dancers for hours reading on a bench on Theatre Square.[25]

Many artists were eager to make a more immediate contribution to the war effort. Fourteen-year-old ballet student Yuri Grigorovich tried to leave by boat in order to join a pilot school, but he and a friend were soon caught. Grigorovich went on to become one of the defining choreographers of post-war Soviet ballet. Vecheslova and many other dancers signed up for hospital duty, barely taking off their stage make-up before rushing half starved to the wards, staying on duty overnight and then returning straight to the theatre in time for morning rehearsals. Vecheslova was haunted for a long time by the image of a soldier whose gangrenous leg had been amputated. He had turned to the dancer with entreating eyes, pleading for water, suddenly breaking out in delirious swearing. Vecheslova gave him a drink. The soldier fell quiet as she stroked his head, his eyes tightly closed, his remaining leg jutting out of the bed's rails. He was dead.[26]

❦

Whatever difficulties Nina and her colleagues were experiencing, Kostia was going through worse. On 4 September, a few houses down from Kostia and Valia, Liubov Shaporina wrote in her diary:

> Hunger is beginning straight away, that's what people in
> the queues are saying, for me, it arrived long ago. From
> 1 September, they reduced the bread norm: for employees
> from 600 to 400 gr. per day, for dependants to 300 gr. On

the 2nd, I went in the morning to buy oil and sugar, they only gave me 100 gr. oil, I wasted half an hour on this and then two on 200 gr. sugar, they are not giving out more. No groats whatsoever, no pasta, no lentils.[27]

Writing a day earlier, Kostia told Nina exasperatedly that they still didn't know whether the Academy of Sciences was leaving. All the papers were in order, but a decision was put off day after day:

My dear Ninochka, I really miss you, but I comfort myself only with the fact that you are together with the theatre and that you are further away from the events that are unfolding. Here, you would be very worried and you would fret. I love you very, very much and beg you not to forget me. You are for me the only happy and good thing that exists in my life. Look after Mummy, remember me and Valia. Stepa is healthy and eats for two. I hope that we will soon see each other. One must wait through this difficult time in Perm, and then everything will be good.[28]

As a member of the intelligentsia, Kostia had, at least theoretically, a greater chance of overcoming the restrictions imposed on movement during wartime: the Academy of Sciences could issue him a *komandirovka*, a document to travel to a specific location for personal or business reasons.[29] Kostia was determined to get one to travel to Perm to see Nina before long, still seemingly unaware that leaving Leningrad was effectively no longer an option. Rumours about the Kirov circulated; Kostia had heard that only a part of the company would stay in Perm while the rest would be sent elsewhere. He missed her desperately:

> Please, don't forget us, and you, Ninochka, don't forget your husband – I love you very much and I am sure that everything will be fine and that the two of us will again begin to live as one should. People say that Perm is not a bad little town. If this is the case, then I am happy that you are there. It is not too far from us and one doesn't have the feeling that you have ended up in some remote place.[30]

∽

The air raids on Leningrad were about to begin. Throughout August the days had been interrupted by sirens, but there had been no bombardment. On 8 September, the composer Gavriil Popov visited Shaporina. He was playing the piano when it started. From the window, the pair witnessed the desperate fire of anti-aircraft guns, a white cloud growing quickly from the roofs, gilded by the setting sun, and from below a black belt of smoke: 'It did not resemble smoke to such an extent that I didn't believe for a long time that this was a fire. According to rumours, gas depots and the Badayev provision depots were burning. The picture was grandiose, of staggering beauty.'[31] The rumours were right: oil storage tanks, a creamery and the thirty-eight wooden Badayev warehouses storing a significant part of Leningrad's food were on fire. Later that night, at 10.34, there was a second raid. That same day, the Germans took Shlisselburg, an ancient fortress town built where the Neva begins to flow out of Lake Ladoga. The siege ring had closed.[32]

Valia wrote to Nina and her mother on 22 September. Four days earlier, the Germans had dropped 528 high-explosive bombs and approximately 2,000 incendiaries on Leningrad in one of the worst daylight raids the city would experience. A bomb hit the Kirov Theatre's right wing at 9.05 p.m. Alexander Beliakov, head of the part of the company that had remained in Leningrad, had managed to avert an even worse disaster. Beliakov slept in an anteroom leading into one of the theatre's opera boxes. Unable to go back to sleep after the bomb, he had noticed smoke emerging from the orchestra foyer just in time to extinguish a fire that could have destroyed the theatre.[33]

Valia was hardly ever home, working at the hospital in the evenings after finishing her regular working day. Nina's beloved dog Stepa had become a real burden: he was alone all the time in the flat, and they had nothing to give him to eat. Shaporina recorded in her diary on 20 September that she had consumed just 250 grams of bread that day (her daily ration had actually been reduced to 200 grams of bread) and four sugar cubes with tea. Kostia and Valia were mostly sleeping at another flat that felt safer. Every morning, Valia had to run home to take Stepa for a walk and feed him. She had reached the end of her tether, frustrated that Nina had not taken the dog with her, unlike many others on the evacuation train. Kostia was now trying to find someone to take him in, but Valia was not sure he would survive that long:

> It would really be a pity to kill him. He has grown very thin . . . What do I write you about our life? We live only day by day, one doesn't want to think about the future . . .

Kostia really misses you Nina, I try to look after him, but this is really difficult. He is rarely home, spending most of the time at ... or at his institute. On the whole, we are still alive and healthy, which is the most important thing ... Take care of yourselves and we will hope that we will see each other. Nina, look after Mummy. I am very happy that you left.[34]

On 26 September, Kostia reported to Nina that he and Valia were all right, even though there were by now many 'inconveniences'. At least his parents had managed to get to Moscow, but for reasons unknown he was not able to leave with them. Shaporina recorded on 22 September that many belonging to the 'golden fund of the intelligentsia' were flown to the town of Tikhvina, 200 kilometres away.[35] The only way to leave Leningrad now was by plane – or across Lake Ladoga. The NKVD was evacuating its prisoners to labour camps on barges across the lake, packing so many prisoners into the hold that many died. By the time the barges reached the shore, corpses filled the decks.[36] Kostia carefully placed a delicate pressed flower within the folded page of the letter and sealed the envelope.[37]

He did not know that a change in German strategy had occurred. Hitler wanted to swallow up all of European Russia, extending the Reich to Archangel on the White Sea and Astrakhan on the Caspian Sea with its valuable oil resources. He intended to destroy existing cities and to replace Moscow with an artificial lake.[38] But since the planning stages of Operation Barbarossa (the code name for the invasion of the Soviet Union), there had been a difference of opinion about whether it was strategically better to capture Leningrad or Moscow first: Hitler insisted on Leningrad, while chief of General Staff Franz Halder wanted to focus on the capital, Moscow. The start of the operation sidelined the argument, but by mid-July the disagreement gained new momentum when Wilhelm von Leeb, commander of Army Group North, responsible for the assault on Leningrad, asked for more troops and equipment. By 5 September, Hitler agreed that if Leningrad wasn't captured within ten days, Panzer Group 4, a key armoured component of the invasion army, would be redeployed south to link up with the troops pushing towards Moscow. On 24 September, von Leeb requested permission to switch from the offensive to the defensive. Only fifteen kilo-metres from the Hermitage, his troops could move no further. The strategy for capturing Leningrad changed from ground assault to a classic siege with air assault: mass starvation and the destruction of water supplies were central components of the plan. Hitler was fighting a war of annihilation. Once captured, Leningrad was to be razed to the ground.[39]

Cut off from his family and isolated in a town that was rapidly heading for death and starvation, Kostia wrote to Nina on 6 October 1941:

> I am writing you a letter almost every day in complete hopelessness, convinced that you are not receiving them. The last I received from you was the telegram sent on the 20th. Since then, already for sixteen days, absolutely nothing! Imagine how worried I am and how worried

Valia is. After all, we don't know anything apart from the fact that you settled in Molotov and that you plan to start working. Are you healthy? Is Mummy healthy? In general, do you even exist or have you left for somewhere.[40]

Memories of their separation during Nina's imprisonment kept crowding in: 'all this reminds us of the period of your departure, and Mummy was lying sick at the hospital and we waited with anxiety for the outcome of all events.'[41] Kostia asked Nina to telegraph once every day if she had the money, even if it was with only one word: 'This would calm us down and support us morally.' They had moved Stepa to his parents' flat in the vain hope that the people living there would be better able to look after him during the day.

Whether through fear of the censor or because he was anxious not to worry Nina, Kostia did not even hint at what they were really living through. Instead, he focused on her well-being: 'Remember that I and Valia are thinking of you every minute and are living in the hope to be again together. We know that it is probably difficult for you in a new, alien place, but don't lose spirit. Try to somehow live – that is the most important thing. I kiss you strongly, strongly, my dear, I wish you health and a courageous spirit. Don't forget me. Write, telegraph.'[42]

Communication was indeed difficult, even more than it had been when Nina was in Karlag. Nina had received Kostia's letters of 30 August and 3 September on 14 October.* When

---

* Nina doesn't specify the months but only gives the days: 30th and 3rd. There are letters from 30 August and 3 September in the archival file, but not from 30 September and 3 October. The long delivery time also seems realistic.

she wrote to him on 15 October 1941, she exclaimed exasperatedly: 'I am very upset that you are not receiving my letters.' She and her mother sent news regularly. Nina could not fathom how quickly life in Leningrad had unravelled. If she had, she would not have asked him to bring some tea, sugar and tobacco once he joined them.[43]

Kostia was finding it increasingly hard to cope:

> It is very difficult, my dear Nina, to bear the loneliness. If it wasn't for Valia and Stepa, I would completely descend into desperate depression, because not a single person that is close and dear to me is now with me. I really want to work and be useful, but now my work here does not have direct and necessary value, all of it is intended for the future, and because of this I'm in a very difficult moral state, I envy the most modest of your artists, who are doing something that is needed and of use to people. But I will not distress myself with these thoughts. I firmly believe in a better future, in our friendship and love and in the happiness of our country, which will emerge from all the trials that have befallen it.[44]

He tried to enter Nina's world by studying an image of the Molotov Opera Theatre:

> As far as I understand, it stands in a garden or on a boulevard and before it is a big vase with flowers. Everybody who has been to Molotov generally has a favourable impression of it. I look at this postcard and I try to imagine your productions and your performances. This

is pleasant, but at the same time also bitter, because I would really like to see you with my own eyes, to hear your voice and to firmly press you to my heart.[45]

The tables had turned: Kostia was now the one locked in a living hell, not sure whether he would survive and see Nina again.

～

Nina had indeed sent the promised telegram, consisting of one word: 'Telegraph'. Kostia received it on 16 October 1941 and telegraphed back, hoping that Nina would get his response soon: her telegrams usually reached him within a few days. He was still determined not to share their existential struggles with Nina, but Valia was less restrained. On 20 October she wrote to her mother and sister a much more candid letter about their increasingly difficult situation. The first snow had fallen early that year, on 15 October. Ice was beginning to form on the canals.[46] It was already terribly cold; Valia was sitting at work wrapped up in her coat, a hat, galoshes and gloves. She had caught a serious cold that was not improving, but she could not allow herself to stay at home in bed and rest: if she lost her job, she would be put into a lower ration category. As it was, there was hardly anything to eat.

Every night, Valia returned hungry from her work at the hospital to their cold flat. The burden of looking after Stepa while holding down two jobs and housework was weighing deeply on her. But moving Stepa to Kostia's parents' flat had almost ended in disaster: one night, during an air raid, when everyone was running down to the basement, Stepa escaped into the streets.[47] Two days passed before they found the painfully thin dog by chance, roaming on Vasilievsky Island's Central Avenue: 'After this story we took him home and I have now decided not to part with him, whatever will be will be. Whatever I myself will eat I will give to him. When he disappeared Kostia and I quarrelled and I even cried, as, de facto, he was given away because of me, because it was very difficult for me to have both jobs, plus the household and Stepka.'[48]

The dog's escape had been lucky in more ways than one. Vera Kostrovitskaya, who had graduated from the ballet school three years before Nina and become a teacher there, was also stuck in Leningrad.* She wrote at the beginning of her siege diary: 'In a city where there are garbage pits, cats and dogs, a person won't go hungry,' adding: 'We all delicately conceal from our neighbour that we eat cat meat; we refer to it simply as eating "chat".'[49] Even the most beloved household pets were eaten, caught by desperate people in the streets or by their owners who had no other way to survive.[50]

Hunger was destroying the last vestiges of humanity. On 26 October, Shaporina went to a market in an unsuccessful search for bread: 'The people are terrifying. This is a kind of Bruegelesque caricature of people. Everybody is looking for food, bread, cabbage leaves. Ragged, with yellow, emaciated faces, noses that have become pointed, sunken-in eyes.' A small boy, perhaps eight years old, had tried to get into the queue for tea, but a fully grown man had seized him and hurled him away from the door. The little boy had fallen head over heels on to the ground, but had jumped back on to his feet, trying

* In the 1920s, Kostrovitskaya had been married to Nina's friend Volodia Dmitriev.

with a roar to thrust himself towards the door again to get into the line. The women would not let him in and there had been shouting and howling: 'Terrible. Unhappy people. Soon we will start to swell up like in 1918.'[51]

Valia had moved into her mother's room, as had Kostia, because his was too cold to live in. Some strangers had moved into hers. She was weighing her future options, in case Kostia managed to evacuate but she didn't. She knew that her chances of survival would dwindle dramatically if she ended up living on her own.[52] It was painful for Valia to watch Kostia. His letters hinted at his state of mind, but she saw every day how much he missed Nina. They should all have left together.[53]

∽

By the end of October, Leningrad's power stations had started to run out of fuel. Before long, electricity was only supplied for a limited number of hours, if at all. The city's inhabitants had to make their own lamps and the small *burzhuika* stoves of the civil war period reappeared, fired by whatever wood could be found across the city. Snow was only cleared from major roads; other streets became impassable apart from narrow, well-trodden paths. The water supply was also failing; water had to be fetched from ice holes cut into the frozen canals and the Neva by the fire brigade.[54]

My dear Nina, it is very boring and empty without you. I simply cannot go into our room because, before I do, my heart contracts. I have dragged all necessary things into the dining room, where Valia and I are living, and only drop in there for individual books. I'm thinking the

whole time that this is a difficult dream and that suddenly
I will wake up – and everything will again be in its place.[55]

There was little work at the institute and Kostia was mostly at
home, trying to research, read and write. In the mornings, he
put on the samovar and drank coffee. Hardly anyone dropped
by. There was no one he could talk to, not even Valia, who
returned each day exhausted from work. He planned to visit
the Directorate on Artistic Affairs about a *komandirovka*; his
father was doing the rounds in Moscow. There were many
promises, but still no tangible solutions.[56]

~

By the end of October, the cold was becoming unbearable,
rations were shrinking even further and private stocks of food
were becoming depleted. Valia wrote again on 31 October
1941. 'We are so far still healthy but suffer very much from
the cold. It is cold everywhere, at work, at home and on the
street.' She was irritated by Nina's sensitivity, which affected
her now as if from a different dimension: Kostia had sent a
telegram that had mistakenly been signed 'Kolia', not Kostia.[57]
Kolia was either a friend or relative who frequently visited
Valia and Kostia, spending the night at their place.[58] Nina had
fussed over the wrong name; her older sister explained that
it had been a simple mistake, the telegraphist had not been
able to read Kostia's handwriting: 'In general, it's not worth
fretting about such trifles, there are things that are much
more important.'[59]

Winter had arrived. Every day there were promises that
the heating in the flat would be turned on, but, according to

Kostia, it continued to be 'very fresh' in the rooms. He did not have a lot to report. His parents had arrived safely in Kazan, evacuated with the institutes of the Academy of Sciences. As for himself, he spent most of his time buried in his books; they helped him to focus his thoughts. He tried to dream of better times:

> Every day, I remember different episodes from our life – wonderful journeys to the south, travels, theatrical experiences and so on and so forth. It is very difficult and bitter to again live through separation and not know for how long. I hope not for too long. We will be alive, healthy – we will meet again in our rooms and again settle down to interesting work, and work, of course, there will be a lot of.[60]

Nineteen days later, on 20 November, rations were cut for a final time.[61] The first, most deadly winter of the siege was about to begin.

11

Gayané

Against all the odds, Kostia and Valia managed to get out of Leningrad. Most likely they were evacuated by plane towards the end of the year, thanks to his father's connections; mass evacuations across the Ice Road over Lake Ladoga were only ordered on 22 January 1942.* Kostia brought Valia safely to her mother and sister, but he himself didn't stay for long. After a brief rest in Perm, where he recovered enough to give a lecture connected to the theatre's revival of *The Flames of Paris*, he travelled on to check on his parents in Kazan. He hoped to return to Perm by the end of March.[1] Once again, the couple were separated, leading Nina to write in worried exasperation:

* They definitely left Leningrad before 11 January 1942: Nina mentions that Volodia had written a postcard on 11 January 1942 confirming that everything was fine at their flat, indicating that Kostia and Valia had already left (Pushkin House, f. 859, op. 1, d. 21, l. 2).

2 February 1942

There is still no news from you from Kazan. I hope
that you will write to us as soon as you arrive in Kazan.
Without you, it has become very sad, cold and hungry
here. I hope that you are healthy, that you are no longer
fainting. According to Valia, with your departure, domestic as well as material well-being has disappeared. Your
proverb is 'a giving hand doesn't become thin' but we are
greedy and we are having a hard time. Well, but in general
everything is all right. We celebrated my name day, everybody visited me, we sat until around three! According to
Serg. Serg. [sic] it was even chic. The Napoleon* turned
out not very tasty, but everybody ate it, even Radin
tried it.[2]

Nina was worried about Kostia's health in general, and his
heart in particular.[3] He had fainted several times: 'I really beg
you to go to a doctor and to find out about your health and
don't drink coffee.' The three women sat together in the evenings; Nina was working on a cardigan: she was hoping that by
the time Kostia returned, it would be finished.[4] All three relied
on him not just for practical, but also for moral support. Valia
added underneath Nina's letter: 'It has become empty after
your departure. We live as we used to, we try not to argue and
to live harmoniously.' Even Nina's mother, a reluctant correspondent, added a few lines of her own: 'It has become very

* A classic Russian cake.

empty and boring after your departure, we live in the hope of seeing you soon.'[5]

Nina was very busy. The Kirov was preparing a special event for the twenty-fourth anniversary of the Red Army and she had been entrusted with the choreography of the entire production.* In the first half, the Kirov Opera's soloists and chorus would sing folk and contemporary songs. In the second, the Kirov Ballet would perform classical numbers and character dances.[6] Initially, Nina had not been overly enthusiastic about the project, but she knew it would have been awkward to refuse.[7] But as she worked against an almost impossible deadline – the performance was to take place on 23 February – her professionalism began to take over. She admitted to herself that, so far, the result was not bad. But she still dreamed of returning to *Happiness*. Khachaturian had written to her; he was in hospital with a stomach ulcer, but he was clearly thinking about their ballet and his score.[8]

On 10 February, Nina at last received a telegram from Kostia in Kazan. They could now go about their daily lives more calmly, even though conditions had become more difficult. Nina was especially irritated by the lack of anything to smoke.[9] Valia wrote to Kostia separately, confiding things that Nina wouldn't. One time, a colleague named Parashin had received a card from Kostia while they had not (theirs would arrive a day later). Nina had been very angry and upset. They were also struggling more for provisions without Kostia. The burden of feeding their family fell on Valia and their mother, as Nina left early in the

---

* Andrei Lopukhov and Mikhail Mikhailov were staging a few individual numbers.

morning and returned around midnight, working feverishly on the concert. She was at least entitled to more food as a result of her additional responsibilities: directors, conductors and choreographers were in the second category of rations.[10]

But conditions remained strained. Every artist got about three metres' living space. A fourteen-square-metre room would usually be divided by a curtain so it could be shared by two families. With the exception of a few principals, everybody had regular tasks offstage: artists helped to sort and store potatoes and regularly formed a long human chain from the banks of the River Kama to unload firewood brought by barge to heat the theatre. The cold could be more terrible than the hunger, but everybody was struggling to obtain enough food. Many dancers sold their Leningrad clothes or traded in their vodka rations on the black market.[11]

∾

On 18 February 1942, Nina and Kostia were both writing to each other. Sitting in Kazan, Kostia put his pen to paper:

18 February 1942

Dear Nina, Maria Iosifovna and Valia!

Forgive me for writing letters to you so often, but in the evenings I am seized by such longing that I would like to converse with you even if only this way. Please, if this isn't so difficult for you, write to me more often, and, if possible, in more detail about everything that is happening. Every letter from you is for me and for everyone a great joy.[12]

Kostia's daily life with his parents was quiet and monotonous, making him long for news of Nina's work:

> I am imagining what is being done in connection with the preparation for the concert! In the first place, I would probably get it from Nina for not being able to also develop some activity in this matter. I'm only worried that Nina will curse at and quarrel with different people during the work process because of her volcanic temperament. Now, more than ever, one has to restrain oneself to the utmost and not create ill-wishers for oneself. Vainonen's example is very instructive in this respect. But I am comforting myself with the thought that Nina understands this perfectly well and that she is conducting herself in the necessary and suitable manner.[13]

Kostia found it difficult to be separated from Nina yet again, but his parents needed him. His mother was suffering from terrible neurological pain; a doctor had been consulted but to no avail, and it was difficult to obtain medication. As for his father, he was missing serious academic work. So, for that matter, was Kostia. The Academy of Sciences had been set up in a somewhat disorderly fashion in the beautiful but rundown building of Kazan's local university. An air of languid apathy pervaded the place. They were surrounded by worthy and respectable people, but father and son felt that there was no one to whom they could unburden their souls. In his desperation, Kostia sometimes sought out the company of a fellow evacuee, Kleiner, who had flown with him to Kazan, but Kleiner was primarily preoccupied with finding a way to get back to Moscow. He behaved as though he had been moved into a dog kennel, and conversations with him had the corresponding character. They had heard almost no news from Leningrad, but now rumours were starting to trickle in about academics who had starved to death.[14]

Nina had already finished eight pieces for the twenty-fourth anniversary of the Red Army, including a Scottish jig to music by Beethoven and a Moldovan dance with costumes by the Soviet avant-garde artist and stage designer Nathan Altman; Altman had returned to Leningrad after eight years in Paris in 1936, and was now also in Perm. She had also staged a sailors' dance that 'promised to be interesting if the men portraying Englishmen manage to keep everything in the necessary style'. Everybody approved of a Russian factory number she had set to music by Khachaturian, culminating with all the cast on stage:

> Altogether, there are sixteen ballet numbers in our part, the ballerinas all dance splendidly . . . Because of this concert I'm terribly tired and am barely moving. But knowing that I have a rich fantasy and that our theatre is really splendidly preparing for the Red Army Day gives me the strength to endure all of this. I don't know, my dear, maybe I am boring you, but I really wanted to tell you everything and this is very difficult on paper. We are now sitting at the table, I am writing and Mummy and Valia are discussing household questions. We argue little, Stepa is moaning like previously at the table in expectation of scraps and sometimes he makes puddles. Mummy is very angry at him and talks about killing him.

In general, life in the dormitory has changed little, it's all the same people in the corridor and all the same conversations. I have now smoked some cigarettes because they have given us five packages of good cigarettes; today they gave me, Lopukhov and Mikhailov eggs, mandarins and chicken. So today is a rich day.[15]

Meanwhile, more dancers had arrived from Leningrad, bringing tragic news: many of those left behind had died, while others were ill. Olga Iordan was lying in the Astoria, which had been converted into a hospital, though Serezha at least was alive and healthy.[16]

∿

The day before the concert, Valia's mother-in-law, Maria Grigorevna Kontorovich, collapsed on their doorstep. Mikhail Efimovich was Valia's second husband. An important engineer, he had been arrested and sentenced to forced labour during the Great Terror. Maria Grigorevna, evacuated from Leningrad and heading for Tashkent, was in such a bad condition that she had to get off the train at Molotov. After living through the first, most terrible winter of the siege, she was in extremely poor health and painfully thin. The three women were trying to help as best they could: Valia slept on the floor and their mother shared her bed with Maria Grigorevna. Only Nina was sleeping 'like the mistress' on her own. Every day, they had to collect the special ration Maria was entitled to as a newly arrived evacuee, consisting of bread and a good lunch.[17]

It was an additional strain for the household, and Valia in particular was missing Kostia's tempering influence: 'Nina is visibly not very pleased, but dear Kostia, what can I do? It is such a difficult time now that it is impossible to refuse shelter, especially to Mishin's mama; she said that if she hadn't got off the evacuation train she would have died on the road, the doctor on the train ... confirmed this ... Everything would be easier if you were here. Our Mummy frets all the time and is angry at life.'[18]

But there were also happy, even triumphant moments. The concert for Red Army Day was a resounding success, especially the second half. Nina proudly reported that this was the first time since *Partisan Days* that the Kirov had staged a contemporary one-act ballet: 'I am hurrying to boast to you that after the end, Radin saluted all the artists and wished me much happiness in my supposedly new career. Everyone clapped and I was very pleased. Coming home I even drank a vodka.'[19]

The stress of the previous weeks took its toll on Nina. She caught a cold and strained some ligaments, though Valia's wry assessment was rather different: 'Nina is resting on her laurels and relaxing after her big and very successful work for Red Army Day. Your misgivings concerning her stormy character were almost justified, but luckily everything was checked in time.'[20]

Kostia, always the astute strategic thinker, immediately grasped the importance of this success for her further career. The threat of war was a unifying and galvanising force, and while others were fighting, many artists were looking for a way to feel relevant. Nina had found herself at the centre of the Kirov's first new wartime production marking a political date. In only two years, she had travelled the long road from imprisonment as a socially dangerous criminal to the heart of one of the country's most important cultural institutions, entrusted with important ideological work during the Soviet state's most existential crisis.

Reflecting on how her recent success might improve her position, Kostia wrote astutely:

> I am very happy about your success and think that it will have serious significance for all your further work at the theatre. I am sorry that I couldn't be present at your celebratory evening, but I thought about the whole evening and tried to imagine it. One ought to really value the fact that, in spite of all kinds of difficulties, you have the possibility to move forward in your work and to gain for yourself more and more recognition.
>
> I think that we won't have to wait that long until the end of our trials and that the first new work upon the theatre's return home will, of course, be entrusted to you, because Lavrovsky as well as Chabukiani and Vainonen have compromised themselves in the most serious way both in public and creative terms. Our times are ones of a profound re-evaluation of people and their moral and ideological cast of mind. With respect to you, this evaluation can only be the most positive and it will play a big role in the future.[21]

The artistic director – and leading choreographer – Leonid Lavrovsky had basically abandoned the Kirov: instead of leading the company into evacuation, he and his wife, the ballerina Elena Chikvaidze, had gone to Yerevan. Vakhtang Chabukiani – one of the company's stars and another successful choreographer – had left for his native Georgia. With the more established male competition gone, the coast was clear for Nina.

Kostia, meanwhile, was worn out by daily life. There was no electric light or water in their accommodation; his mother's eye now needed medical attention as well. He had to tell Nina that most of the items she had asked for could not be obtained in Kazan either. He thought about tobacco day and night, managing to acquire a small quantity of *samosad*, home-made tobacco, which was all that was available. He and his father moistened it with mint, which gave it a pleasant taste and smell when smoked.

Slowly, more evacuees from Leningrad were arriving. The head of administration and housekeeping of Kostia's institute had just arrived. A former joiner or painter, he had subsisted on joiner's glue, boiled into a jelly to which he had added laurel leaves, pepper, drying oil and bread fried in glycerine instead of oil, drinking the concoction with his tea in place of jam.[22]

Nina, meanwhile, was hoping to use her elevated status with the theatre management to secure a place on a train for Maria Grigorevna. Letters were being exchanged with a certain Liusa – either Maria Grigorevna's daughter or daughter-in-law – in Tashkent, but the woman said it was impossible to get her a permit, urging the Anisimovas to keep her in Perm. But Nina did not want the responsibility of caring for an additional person: she confided to Kostia that even though it was terrible to send Maria Grigorevna alone on such a long journey, it was even more terrible to keep her with them. Although sweet and quiet by nature, Maria Grigorevna had been so weakened by the siege that she had to lie down the whole time, making it impossible for either Valia or her mother to lie down to rest.

In the end, Maria Grigorevna was dispatched to Stalinobad. Nina was happy that it was just the three of them again. She bought an ottoman and a spring mattress in anticipation of Kostia's arrival to make sure they would all have enough space to sleep.[23]

~

Our life is flowing as usual, any day I will harness myself again to work because we have to prepare a completely new programme for the 1st of May. We are now all meeting and deciding how to do this concert. I don't know what I'm now being entrusted with, but if it is everything that we have planned, then there will be a lot of work. Pazovsky* takes part keenly in ballet matters and is trying to raise the level of the libretto Radin initially proposed. There was a stormy meeting, I rushed out of it all in tears like a fool, but then everything calmed down and the libretto became much more interesting. You know me Kostia, after all, I cannot not say what I think, and in my opinion it is better to achieve the best artistic product than to keep silent and stage pell-mell. Of course don't tell this to anyone, but I find it difficult. In peacetime, Lavrovsky entrusted me with a whole ballet and believed in me, and now everything needs to be done at once . . .

* Ari Pazovsky (1887–1953) was the Kirov Theatre's artistic director and chief conductor from 1936 until 1943.

I am trying to be calm and to conduct all my work like a
sensible, experienced stage director.[24]

Nina was busy again – she was working at the Satire Theatre
at the Red Army House to earn some extra money, rushing
back to the theatre for meetings followed by concerts in the
evening.[25] Things weren't easy. Valia wrote to Kostia: 'Dear
Kotik, Nina has written almost everything about her affairs,
I can add that she is sometimes in a very nervous mood, it
then starts to seem to her that people want to offend her or,
mainly, go around her. I try to convince her that this isn't so,
but you succeed in this better. On the whole we live quietly,
argue rarely and all three of us really miss you.'[26]

A core group of artists was working on the May Day concert, international workers' day. Nina had again been entrusted
with responsibility for the choreography, but she was ambiva-
lent about it, having had no hand in choosing the libretto.
Nina was used to the regime's ideological demands, but she
did not enjoy having her artistic imagination harnessed to
a project dictated entirely by management; she craved creative independence. This was difficult work, on an extremely
tight schedule.[27]

The libretto contrasted three different May Day celebrations: before the revolution, before the war and during
wartime. The pre-revolutionary scenes depicted the old
maevka, the greeting of spring with walks and picnics that had
evolved into illegal political meetings before the revolution.
The pre-war May Day celebrated Soviet life and agriculture
with national and classical dances; the wartime version featured
the Kirov's leading ballerina, Galina Ulanova, culminating in a

tragic yet heroic finale using the 'Internationale' anthem. Nina struggled to explain to Kostia the challenges the production posed, and missed his advice: 'In my opinion, this is interesting but very difficult. I don't know whether you have understood anything from my muddled explanations. Like Marietta* says, I need you like Freya, carrying fresh apples to the gods. How necessary your thoughts are to me.'[28]

April arrived, and still there was no end in sight to their separation. Kostia's mother was still unwell. Nina and Valia were concerned about their own mother, who had lost a lot of weight:

> Mummy is looking very badly, we try not to agitate her, but this is very difficult because she gets angry because of a trifle. Valia was again a bit sick, now she is better, she has started going out. I work towards the 1st of May, I don't know whether I have enough imagination because the work is very difficult but I somehow have little energy in my head. I will try nonetheless to do everything![29]

Alongside her work as a choreographer, Nina continued dancing her usual repertoire. At least her hard work was paying off, and not only professionally. By now she had been moved up to a worker's ration card, so the family could eat to their

* Marietta Frangopulo.

full satisfaction and get enough bread.[30] But Nina was completely exasperated by her seemingly never-ending separation from Kostia, prompting her to respond with irritation to two letters from him:

> You write that you are worried about not having received news from us; I already told you that it is difficult for me to write to you for two reasons. First of all, I miss you very much, even though I understand perfectly well that it is difficult for you to come and that I have to wait. But it's already obvious that for our whole life, we will write more to each other than we will talk to each other. The second reason is the dreadful race for the 1st of May. I work a lot and parts of the job are still untouched. At home everything is fine. We live quietly, modestly, sometimes we argue and always about trifles. I am urging Mummy to fret less but this is very difficult, she doesn't understand . . . Our mood is average, without you it is dull, and somehow I have nobody to consult with and I can't take comfort in your wise decisions. Well, what can one do, one must wait. I hope that by the time of your arrival, I won't be very thin but that I will already have taken a rest after such difficult work . . . I kiss you strongly and wait. I am behaving well, I worry whether I will manage to finish all the work in time. Stepka also kisses you, he is fat like a pig. Write more often, my dear, I will also try to write to you. I kiss you. Your Nina.[31]

Nina was under enormous pressure. There was very little time and much that hadn't been finished yet:

I cannot call this job real creative work like my *Happiness* was for me. There is so little time that I don't even manage to spend a day on a number I'm staging. One piece of music meets another and everything gets mixed up in my head. I am very tired, and I have grown very thin. I really miss you, I miss your clear and logical thoughts and your genuine strict judgement . . . As I already wrote to you, this time my work is expressed as a whole one-act ballet in three pictures with the participation of all four ballerinas. It is very difficult to work with them because despite all their great mastery they look very trite . . . often my older leaders are also not principled. For example, there was the case that Galia Ulanova, who was supposed to depict a girl partisan in the third part (to a prelude by Rachmaninov), got sick. This has to be a very heroic and tragic figure, with large, strong Duncanesque [Isadora] gestures and pathos, transitioning into an angry, militant 'Internationale'. I had thought to put on Shelest, who recently arrived together with Agrippina Iakovlevna*. . . from Leningrad. But this wasn't to be, Vecheslova decided to dance herself and called me together with Baratov to Radin and suggested her candidacy . . . I, Kostia, have recently become very principled and I spoke out for Shelest, saying that Tania was short. Of course, nobody supported me, and on the contrary all declared the opposite. My opinion remained my opinion, expressed very delicately. Since I am the executor of an order, it is my business to obey, but in front of the troupe I will at least

* Vaganova.

be right. Walking out of the office, everyone started to assure me that there is nobody better than Shelest ... But I have now become much calmer and I decided that they know my opinion as choreographer, and the rest is their problem.[32]

This letter appears to be the last one Nina sent to Kostia in Kazan, so it seems likely he had arrived in Molotov by the time of the May Day production. It culminated in pure melodrama. Vecheslova, who had got her way, performed the part of a 'Woman-Mother', whose grief over a child's death at the hands of the Nazis turns into a violent thirst for revenge. As the audience joined the artists in singing the 'Internationale', the performance turned into a 'popular patriotic demonstration'. A review of the evening bore the apt title 'Art Calling for Revenge'.[33]

∽

Nina was now a central figure at the Kirov. Her ability to deliver on an extraordinarily tight schedule raised her standing within the theatre's hierarchy. Unbeknownst to them, this type of agitational work was of course not new to her: as part of Karlag's cultural brigade, she had worked on programmes organised to celebrate political holidays and participated in agitational work during the spring sowing campaign. Nina's quick creative imagination was at the heart of her success as a choreographer, but her experience in the Gulag also put the difficult conditions of wartime evacuation into perspective.

Compared to dancing for her jailers, harnessing her choreographic talent to the Kirov's ideological duties at a moment of national crisis was straightforward: Nina's work was supposed to help her audience digest the experience of war by inspiring a deep sense of Soviet patriotism. Wartime had distilled the different, often conflicting demands made of the Kirov Theatre's repertoire into one essential goal: mobilising the population in the fight against the enemy. Before the war, the clash between artistic aspirations and ideological censorship often led to a deadlock; wartime solidarity created a new sense of unity, allowing even artists like Shostakovich and the writer Boris Pasternak to feel a sense of release after a disastrous decade of increasingly stringent censorship and terror.[34] Maybe Nina felt the same. A clearly definable, external enemy offered a common cause and the (false) hope that the horrors of the past could be overcome.

Nina and the Kirov artists personified the Soviet Union at its best, instilling pride in their audience for a culture that was worth defending. But for Nina, the former convict, her professional achievements carried a special private significance: her rehabilitation as a dancer and choreographer was a triumph over the system that had almost destroyed her. Her work was not about upholding the Soviet dream; what she wanted was to dedicate herself to her art as a fully respected member of the society she had been born into.

Among the dancers, there was a strong sense that they needed to justify their evacuation. While they were living and creating in Molotov, their loyal Leningrad audience had been left behind to starvation and bombs. In June 1942, Nina Palagina, a ballet devotee, wrote an impassioned letter to the dancer

Feya Balabina, wife of Konstantin Sergeyev, who would create the role of Armen in Nina's ballet. Palagina poured out her 'terrible anguish without the Mariinsky Theatre' to the ballerina, whom she had met only once:

> Feya Ivanovna, you cannot imagine HOW difficult it is to live in Leningrad, TO SEE THE MARINKA, but . . . not to see the LENINGRAD BALLET. You both cannot imagine WHAT THE THEATRE AND BOTH OF YOU MEAN IN MY LIFE. I had a friend with whom I went to the theatre; we had common tastes, you also know her by sight, Ganusovskaya also introduced her to you on that day; now my Vera has died, and I am left alone as my husband is in the army . . . the only thing left is the hope that one day this savage war will end, that everything will be as it was in the old days, that the ballet will also return, and together with it also you, Feya Balabina, and Konstantin Mikhailovich. I swear to you by the memory of my mother, of my friend, that nothing here is life, nothing gives more support than the thought that after the war you will return to Leningrad . . . I am telling you simply and openly: I can only live under the condition that I can go and see and hear the LENINGRAD BALLET . . . [35]

No wonder the theatre felt that it owed something to those anxiously waiting for its return to Leningrad. There had been no proper premieres during the Kirov's first season in Molotov, and the twenty-fifth anniversary of the October Revolution was coming up, assuming an even greater significance given the backdrop of war with fascist Germany. The Kirov planned two new productions for the big date: Marian Koval's opera *Emelian Pugachev*, about the eighteenth-century mass uprising led by the Cossack Pugachev, and Nina's ballet *Happiness*. As that was perhaps not the most appropriate title for a major production during wartime, the ballet was now called *Gayané*, after its newly named heroine. The action was moved to the eve of the Great Patriotic War against Nazi Germany.* The most important plot change concerned the nature of Giko's crime: instead of conspiring with smugglers, he accepts a bribe from foreign spies to set the collective farm's cotton warehouses on fire.

Kazakov becomes a regular army commander, while the Kurdish shepherds are transformed from exotic but benign figures into more ambiguous ones. A subplot involves Nina's character, the young Kurdish girl Aisha: she is in love with Gayané's brother Armen, but some of the Kurds don't want Aisha to consort with a man from a different nationality and faith. In the kolkhoz, Giko has done his job and set the cotton warehouses on fire. Gayané denounces him and in the ensuing stand-off he threatens his daughter's life in the flames. Kazakov rescues her but Giko manages to stab Gayané in the chest before he is caught.

By the end of the ballet, war has broken out. The Red Army soldiers are ready to leave for the front under Kazakov's command. In a wild dance, the Kurds present him with a shining embossed sabre. A recovering Gayané asks Kazakov to take

---

* The term 'Great Patriotic War' was used in the Soviet Union to refer to the Second World War. It continues to be used in post-Soviet times.

her along as well, but he leads her to her daughter. She will help the front with her work in the hinterland. He embraces her before rushing off as the soldiers leave. Gayané, her parents, her daughter and Aisha start to pick cotton. The kolkhoz is working again: for the war, for the homeland, for victory.[36]

∿

Nina had hoped that the dancers would be enthused by her work and contribute their own ideas, but her openness to input from others often came across as disorganisation. Waiting to be taught what they were supposed to do, the dancers were exasperated that she seemed to be coming to rehearsals unprepared. More frustratingly for them, she was fusing the classical dance they were all used to with her own interpretation of the Armenian spirit. Responding to the fast, changing rhythms of Khachaturian's music, Nina instinctively moved her limbs in different rhythmical patterns, but what came naturally to her seemed like a book of seven seals to others. Frustrated and bored, the dancers turned to each other to chat. The theatre's director, Evgeny Radin, was well aware of a general lack of discipline within the ballet ensemble, but even he was shocked by the disorder: at one rehearsal he counted how many times Nina had to say 'quiet' and got as far as twenty-nine.

Nina's hope that the horrors of Karlag had instilled in her some stoicism had not materialised. Quick to lose her temper, she shouted at her colleagues, regardless of the customary rules of politeness. Some were seriously hurt by her outbursts, but many simply shrugged off 'The Plague', the nickname they used even to her face. In the hallways, the dancers came up with another name invented by one of the company's wits:

310

Ninochka-Finochka, a rhymed pun likening her to a *finka*, a type of Finnish knife popular with Soviet men in general and criminals in the big cities in particular.[37]

But work was progressing. Khachaturian had arrived in Perm to finish the score. In later years he reflected on this period:

> I lived in Perm on the fifth floor of the Hotel Central. When I remember that time, I think again and again how difficult things were for people back then. The front demanded weapons, bread, tobacco. Bread, warmth – the hinterland. And art, the spiritual food, everybody needed – the front and the hinterland. And we, the artists and the musicians, understood this and gave all our strength. I wrote about seven hundred pages of the score of *Gayané* in half a year in the cold, tiny little hotel room, where an upright piano, stool, chair and table were standing. So it is even more meaningful to me that *Gayané* is the only ballet on a Soviet theme which has not disappeared from the stage in almost a quarter of a century.[38]

Luckily, Nina got on well with the famous composer and their collaboration went comparatively smoothly. According to Tatiana Vecheslova,

> quite often, we gathered at Khachaturian's to laugh, joke. Once, he hosted us with a bottle of red wine that had been preserved God only knows how – during those times this was an unheard-of rarity. Aram Ilych was a cordial, cheerful person. He was inspired seeing how the

talented N. Anisimova was dancing ... He could rouse
the most indifferent dancers with his music. His rhythms
set people on fire, woke them up to life.[39]

For his part, Khachaturian was impressed by the Kirov.
Speaking to the ensemble at a company meeting held on
12 September 1942 to discuss the production, he announced:
'I have to admit that I am in love with ballet, and, especially,
with the ballet of the Kirov Theatre. Watching what the ballet is doing, I, as someone experienced in art, am moved to
tears ... One doesn't have to give compliments to a brilliant
ballet company, but I am flattered that my ballet is being done
at the Kirov Theatre.'[40]

Khachaturian would later muse whether the straightforward nature of their collaboration could be partially explained
because he was new to the ballet world and flattered to be
composing for the Kirov, making him more amenable to concessions. In the future, he relentlessly defended the integrity
of his ballet scores, even when fighting a lost battle. Working
with another volcanic choreographer, Leonid Yakobson, on a
production of his ballet *Spartacus* for the Kirov in 1962, the
two artists even came to blows. The premiere was hailed as a
success, but they did not speak for years.[41]

On 12 September, the company held a major meeting
about Nina's ballet. Kostia gave a detailed description of the
new libretto, and then it was Nina's turn to speak. She was
nervous – and frustrated. She felt that the dancers did not
understand what she was doing: they had all been raised in
the Russian classical ballet tradition, a fusion of the old French
and Italian schools. While that tradition remained the basis

of *Gayané*, the flavour and style of her choreography had
nothing in common with the classics. This was not about putting authentic Armenian folklore on stage: rather, driven by
Khachaturian's complicated rhythms, she was trying to create
a language of movement infused with her interpretation of
Armenian culture, scented by the old traditions of the east and
of antiquity. The choreography needed to reflect Armenia's
location at a cultural crossroads linking ancient Greece and
Persia. She wanted her dancers to understand Armenia's spiritual make-up, and for that she demanded again and again that
their movements needed to flow like water. She did not need
the strict form of *Sleeping Beauty*, but the fluid freedom of
motion explored by the pioneering dancer Isadora Duncan.
She was agitated: how could she make the dancers understand?

> I will talk with difficulty, I am very nervous and it is hard
> for me to express my idea. The rhythm that exists in our
> ballet demands from us a very precise and clear expres-
> siveness of gesture. Right now, I have a small number of
> people who have grasped this. Maybe this isn't working
> because you don't want to get it or because this is the
> beginning of the work, but many don't play and don't
> feel the musical line. You need to feel, to understand
> that if you are portraying an Armenian woman, she can-
> not turn around sharply, she cannot abruptly turn out
> her arms, she always remains in the shape of a running
> doe. She can be cheerful as well as coquettish and will
> still remain in the poetic form possessed by the eastern
> woman. She will always seem a bit mysterious. The ges-
> ture of the Armenian man is very impetuous, all gestures

need to be in character and preserve the plasticity of the turn, but unfortunately very few were showing this at rehearsal.[42]

Nina needed her dancers to understand not only the style and rhythm of her choreography but also the characters they were portraying. Gayané was a far cry from most romantic ballet heroines. She was a contemporary, suffering Soviet woman pushing against the boundaries set by the old culture she had been born into. Nina imagined her as better educated than most of her fellow kolkhozniks, a Soviet wife and mother fighting for her right to independence and happiness. She was proud yet kind, trying to avoid a public scandal with her husband. She did not fall in love with Kazakov at first sight, but meeting a man who respected her as a woman inspired her to move beyond the confines of her traditional marriage: she had been married off by her family to a man she didn't love. After discovering her husband's betrayal of the collective, Gayané was able emotionally to walk away from him for the greater good of society – and for her daughter, whom she was ready to defend like a tigress.[43]

The conductor Pavel Feldt came to Nina's help. Comparing Khachaturian's music to other ballet scores written in recent years, Feldt was struck by its danceability; listening to it, you were compelled to move. But the music was rhythmically complex:

> Aram Ilyich makes use of an unusual rhythmical wealth, these 6/8 which are divided into two and into three. This creates an unusual impression and one must say that Nina

314

Alexandrovna has understood this with great intuition,
she manages very well to move the legs and arms at the
same time, if one dances two, the other dances three and
I think that everyone rehearsing needs to look closely
exactly how Nina Alexandrovna herself is doing it. She
does this with unusual sharpness, she is very concentrated
and whoever rehearses without concentration will lose
the rhythm.[44]

Another colleague, Boris Shavrov, added a political and
ideological dimension:

Comrades, today, the report by Informbureau has
brought us the following news, that on the order of the
High Command, the city of Novorossiisk has been abandoned by our troops. There is a war, a brutal war, a war
with a brutalised, terrible, cruel enemy – German fascism.
According to the wish of the party and the government,
our theatre was evacuated to the deep hinterland on an
equal footing with other enterprises for major and necessary work for the defence of our homeland.[45]

Staging a successful production, one good enough to stay in
the repertoire, would justify the theatre's evacuation.[46] But not
everyone was able to ignore everyday concerns in favour of
loftier thoughts about the Kirov's ideological duty. Shavrov
was not happy with some of the principal dancers:

[The principals are] still insufficiently understanding
and internalising what moment we are living through.

They have shut themselves up, they pay more attention to their own affairs, not looking at what is happening around them and not even reading the paper, because in the papers they write about the titanic work the country is carrying out. An individualist mood, which must not have a place in our work, is showing through the work of our soloists. It seems to me that our leading workers need to forget a bit about the norms and conditions of peaceful times under which we were existing in Leningrad ... I think that our comrades will understand the responsibility and the tasks facing the theatre, and, especially, the Kirov Theatre and reconstruct their work. They will have a greater feeling of patriotism, a feeling of duty to the homeland. They will become less sick and allude less to their sicknesses.[47]

As the theatre director Radin was aware, stuck in Molotov, most artists feared they were no longer relevant. But this was a delusion: local and central party and Soviet organisations were constantly checking what the Kirov Theatre was doing. Across the Soviet Union, the Kirov continued to be seen as a symbol of Soviet opera and ballet. At such an important anniversary, everyone's eyes would be on them. *Gayané* had to show audiences that the theatre had been worth saving: 'We have to tell the Soviet spectator what we have done in twenty-five years; what we have done, what we have learned. What we have done in a year, when tens of thousands of people-patriots have given their lives so that we could work, that we could create.'[48]

Earlier Radin had told Nina that, in her place, he would demand support from the theatre's leadership to improve discipline or else refuse to work. Though he wasn't blind to her flaws, she had his full backing:

> We know that Nina Alexandrovna is an astonishingly highly strung person, that she often comes to rehearsal not ready. But – she is a talented person and we cannot drop people . . .
>
> It is impossible to create a work under such conditions. I sincerely feel with Nina Alexandrovna. I counted twenty-nine times that she repeated 'quiet' . . . How can one so disrespect a production on which you are working. Surely I don't deserve your lack of consideration and disrespect, that you allow yourself to do this in my presence.

Nina was not the only one unable to control the unruly dancers – over sixty had showed up late to the company meeting. The lack of discipline called for desperate measures: Radin thought Nina should fire people if they didn't work properly. But he also stressed that Nina needed to control her temperament. Her reputation with colleagues did not help, allowing her to hide behind her nicknames instead of doing anything to change the situation: 'Well, what do you want – I am The Plague.' Nina had to take some responsibility for organising herself better and improving the tone of her communication with her dancers.[49]

The dancers were not genuinely opposed to Nina. But the work was difficult, and she was impatient. Lidya Dorfman, who had graduated from the school two years before Nina, probably expressed the thoughts of many:

This terrible year we have lived through has played a really big role for the ballet and the libretto has become significantly more interesting . . . About Nina Alexandrovna I want to say that she is so talented, what she is doing is so interesting, that I feel sorry and it hurts me to see what nerves she is wasting. What seemed impossible earlier has now become possible. If one would have shown these scenes to us earlier, we would simply have laughed . . . The style she has found to open up this remarkable music is very difficult for all of us. Nina Alexandrovna has to show it to us more often. A very difficult task has fallen on to her shoulders. We have to hear the music with the orchestra, to really fall in love with it. There needs to be more patience with us. There is no distrust in her from our side.[50]

Events at the front added a special piquancy to *Gayané*'s geographic setting. Since the spring, German forces had been pushing southwards, advancing towards the Caucasus. The oil fields of Baku in Azerbaijan, across the border from Armenia, were the ultimate prize of Germany's operation 'Case Blue'. Hitler thrust an enormous force east along the Don River bend to protect the left flank of the forces pushing down into the Caucasus, but its purpose soon transformed into another major offensive: the troops were fighting to capture Stalingrad, the large industrial base on the Volga whose name carried great symbolic significance. One of the turning points of the Second World War, the Armageddon of the eastern front would last almost six months.

During the battle for Stalingrad Nina was creating her ballet. On 20 October 1942, she published an article in *Za sovetskoe iskusstvo*, outlining her ideas. She ended on a patriotic note:

> Exerting its last strength, German fascism is now breaking towards the sunny Transcaucasus, towards the blooming valleys of Georgia, the oil fields of Azerbaijan, towards the fruitful gardens and the rich earthy depths of Armenia. Our production is a brotherly greeting to the heroic peoples of the Caucasus, currently repulsing the rabid onslaught of the fascist horde.[51]

Nina and Khachaturian worked feverishly, responding to last-minute demands made by the theatre's top brass.

Two days before the general rehearsal, Radin had called Khachaturian to his office and told him that he needed to add a dance to the last act. Khachaturian refused point blank, but when he returned to his tiny hotel room, he started thinking. Radin had asked for a fast, warlike dance. Khachaturian's stomach ulcers were acting up at the time. His hands impatiently played a chord; he started repeating it at random and a musical outline started to take shape. Khachaturian repeated the insistent ostinato in another tonality, added the theme of a lyrical dance from another scene as a contrast, and set to work. He started at 3 p.m. By 2 a.m., the Sabre Dance was finished. At 11 a.m., the relentless sounds of the dance were filling the small rehearsal studio. By the evening, Nina had staged the dance for Aisha (her character) and a group of sabre-wielding Kurds. It would become both Khachaturian's and her own most famous creation.[52]

Its success was more than the composer had bargained for: a jukebox hit in the United States in 1948 and a number-one hit on the *Billboard* best-selling records by classical artists that same year, the Sabre Dance became one of the twentieth century's most popular classical tunes, recognised by millions of people from films, cartoons, adverts, the circus and video games.[53] The composer could not have imagined that his rushed work would come to haunt him:

> There is one unruly and boisterous child in my musical family – the Sabre Dance from *Gayané*. To be honest, if I had known that it would gain such popularity and start to elbow aside my remaining works, I would never have written it! Somebody abroad has publicised me as 'Mister Sabre Dance' . . . This even makes me angry. I think this is unfair.[54]

On 7 December, the usual commission of artistic professionals, party and city authorities met to scrutinise *Gayané* and decide whether the ballet was ready to be shown to the public, artistically and ideologically. It received a resounding stamp of approval. For the last twenty-five years, the authorities had pushed for plots based on contemporary Soviet life, but Soviet theatres had repeatedly found themselves trapped: works with ideologically sound, contemporary storylines tended to be artistically bland, naïve or stylistically too modernist for the cultural watchdogs. Finally, *Gayané* had struck the right chord. The local officials were more than pleased that the Kirov had managed to create such a successful production under difficult conditions, reflecting some of its artistic glory on to the

GAYANÉ

provincial town while providing a much-needed ray of light
for the city's hard-working population. Everybody felt that
once the war was over, the theatre would have something to
bring back to its Leningrad audience.[55] Nina's dream was about
to be realised.

~

Just before dawn on 9 December 1942, there was a sudden,
frantic commotion along the corridors of the Hotel Central
across the road from the theatre. 'Comrades, our theatre
is burning!'

Racing down the stairs of the hotel, the artists were outside the theatre in an instant. The door was wide open. As
they entered the vestibule, smoke enveloped them while a
thick crust of ice covered the floor. Fire hoses curled up the
stairs, which were swollen and icy: it was a December night
in the Urals and temperatures had dropped to minus thirty
degrees Celsius. Rushing upstairs, the dancers found Evgeny
Radin shouting frantic orders. Smoke wafted from the costume
storeroom on the lower level into the auditorium, smother-
ing the stage. Four dancers dragged the battered piano out of
the artists' dressing rooms above the wardrobe room, which
was burning. Flames licked at their feet through the cracking
floorboards. Just after they managed to save the instrument,
the floor collapsed.

Downstairs, under the stage, the old seamstresses were
wailing. Before the revolution, they had dressed legends like
the ballerina Anna Pavlova. They had survived the civil war,
hunger, the Terror: they would not stand aside and watch a fire
destroy their treasures. Flinging themselves into the flames,

they tried to save the burning costumes. Meanwhile, on the second floor, one of the singers was throwing one garment after the other out of the window.

It looked as if the whole theatre might burn down. High above the stage on the fly tower, Yuri Mankovsky, a small, agile ballet dancer who had been with the Perm Ballet before joining the evacuated Kirov, flitted over the grid, wielding a large kitchen knife. Mankovsky knew the theatre well. During intermissions he worked in the fly system, the theatrical rigging apparatus used for changing sets. Now he swiftly cut the ropes holding the curtain and the velvet wings. Quick hands rolled up the dusty material after it had fallen on to the stage, bringing it to safety.

Miraculously, they managed to extinguish the fire. Everybody assembled on stage to hear for how long the theatre would be closed. But Radin's authoritative voice rang out firmly: 'We will dance *Gayané* tonight.'

Ropes were stretched across the set workshop under the theatre's roofs. Partially charred but usable costumes, which had become frozen in the operation to save them, were hung across the ropes; dark, sooty water dripped from them into large tubs. In the freezing auditorium, ballet tights were hung to dry on the banisters of the boxes and the backs of the chairs in the stalls. An army of people washed the corridors, staircases, foyer and the stage. Some of the dancers sat mending costumes along the corridors leading from the stalls and the dress circle. Artists huddled on the floor amid pitchers and pots, repairing sets. In the courtyard, more costumes were slung over ropes to dry. The musicians formed a human chain, passing along orchestral scores and piano reductions from the storeroom beneath the stage, undamaged by the fire. Armed with a crowbar, others hacked away crusts of ice, searching for unharmed chests of costumes as though digging for treasure; they struck gold, recovering several of them underneath the ice, dirt and soot. The men's outfits for *Gayané* were mostly recovered from the flames, but the women's and the sets had been destroyed. The dancers had to resort to costumes used in *Heart of the Mountain*, a ballet set in eighteenth-century Georgia. Garments that had survived the fire were put to dry in a machine for ridding clothes of lice. The visual result was a mishmash of jarring artistic styles, but the performance could take place.*

When the audience entered the auditorium in the evening, they did not recognise the theatre. The light of the chandeliers barely penetrated the clouds of smoke wafting through the higher parts of the auditorium. Ticketholders for the circles and gallery had to crowd into the aisles: the stage could only be seen from the central part of the stalls. The artists' box was crammed full. Everyone wanted to be present as the theatre returned to life after its narrow escape from total destruction. Those dancers who couldn't squeeze into the artists' box stood wherever they could find a space.

Pavel Feldt walked swiftly up to the conductor's stand, a medal gleaming on the lapel of his black tails. He lifted his wand. A mighty fanfare transitioned into an energetic melody. Through the smoke, the action on stage looked as though it were taking place inside an aquarium. Mankovsky later

---

* The local authorities soon granted the theatre special funding to create new sets and costumes.

remembered: 'It was terrible. And it was beautiful.' Led by Natalia Dudinskaya (Gayané), Konstantin Sergeyev (Armen), Tatiana Vecheslova (Nune), Nikolai Zubkovsky (Karen) and Nina (Aisha), the cast gave it everything they had. Sergeyev danced in a yellow silk shirt with an enormous black burn mark on the back. Comrade Yemelyan Yaroslavsky, the Soviet Union's leading anti-religion propagandist, had remained in town for the premiere of *Gayané* after travelling there to watch *Emelian Pugachev*. He liked the performance, and even complimented Sergeyev on the authentically dirty look of his soiled kolkhoznik shirt, unaware that he wore it not by choice but by necessity.

The stage had not completely dried, a freezing draught came in through broken windows, some of the costumes were damp.[56] But the music and choreography were bursting with a life-affirming joy. On stage, everyone was preparing to fight in the Great Patriotic War as the Kurds entered to the insistent, martial rhythms of Khachaturian's Sabre Dance. Nina stood in the wings. As the music moved unexpectedly to a lyrical yet passionate melody, she spread her arms. Offering her soul to the universe, she ran onstage.

EPILOGUE

Nina's star continued to rise, both as a dancer and as a choreographer.

In May 1943, she created the choreographic suite 'Russian Fairy Tales' to a libretto by Kostia. Following *Emelian Pugachev* and *Gayané*, the Kirov held one more premiere of a full-length production in Molotov, Rimsky-Korsakov's opera *The Night Before Christmas*, for which Nina conceived the dances. Invitations from other opera houses followed. In July 1943, the Sverdlovsk Opera staged her *Gayané*, and Nina was asked to choreograph the dances for a production of Emmerich Kálmán's operetta *The Circus Princess* at the Sverdlovsk Theatre of Musical Comedy. *Song of the Cranes*, her second full-length ballet, premiered at the Bashkir Opera House in Ufa on 9 May 1944, marking twenty-five years since Bashkiria had become an autonomous Soviet socialist republic. *Song of the Cranes* told a variation of an old Bashkir legend in which cranes – symbols of freedom and justice – help the Bashkirs defeat an evil enemy. In the ballet, which is about a bird-woman pursued by a hunter, the cranes help a couple in love find happiness. Staging it had been quite an operation: the Ufa dancers were taken to Molotov by steamship to work on the production. After long rehearsals, Nina returned with her dancers to Ufa to perform *Song of the Cranes*. It became the Ufa company's signature piece.[1]

In January 1944, Soviet forces broke through the German troops encircling Leningrad. Hitler's army was pushed away from the city. After almost 900 days, the siege was lifted. The cost had been enormous, claiming thirty-five times more civilian lives than the London Blitz, and four times more than the atomic bombing of Nagasaki and Hiroshima.[2] But the ravaged city slowly started returning to life. Exactly a week after the siege officially ended, Kisa Timofeeva, a music student and ardent balletomane, walked out of the Leningrad Conservatory, situated opposite the Kirov Theatre. Walking to the bus stop, she noticed people carrying firewood into the theatre. The door to the vestibule was open, and Kisa eagerly peeked inside to see the place so vividly connected to some of the happiest hours of her life. The Kirov's loyal fans were soon discussing rumours about the theatre's return in March or April.[3]

Nina and the Kirov returned to their native city in the summer of 1944. On 1 September, the theatre opened its doors to its audience. Once again, the company performed *Ivan Susanin*. Nina and Mikhail Mikhailov danced the opera's Krakowiak with their usual temperamental ardour. In December 1944, Nina returned to the Philharmonic with a new evening of dances.[4] In February 1945 she could finally show *Gayané* to the Kirov's Leningrad audience. But the end of the war brought the return of some of the male choreographers, and perhaps a reversion to the long-standing assumption that choreography was the preserve of men. Leonid Lavrovsky was appointed director of the Bolshoi Ballet in Moscow in 1944 and so never came back, but the talented Fedor Lopukhov was briefly reinstated as artistic director, having suffered ideological disgrace during the anti-formalism campaign of 1936.

Konstantin Sergeyev, who made his choreographic debut with Prokofiev's ballet *Cinderella* in 1946, was appointed principal choreographer in 1951; he was a jealous gatekeeper, giving his own work priority. Nina continued to receive significant new choreographic commissions – but not at the Kirov, where she was only asked to stage dances for the ballet *Don Quixote* and Prokofiev's opera *Betrothal at a Monastery*.

Yet there was no doubt that Nina had become a central fixture of Leningrad's ballet world. Natalya Gamba, daughter of the Kirov Opera soloist Tamara Smirnova and principal dancer Semen Kaplan, who excelled as Armen in *Gayané* in the 1940s and 1950s, could still remember Nina's special energy more than fifty years after the dancer had left the stage. Conversations she overheard at her childhood home singled out Anisimova as the Kirov's best, most irreplaceable performer of Spanish, gypsy and other character dances. Her dancing was not judged by its technique. Gamba remembers that when Anisimova appeared on stage, the audience 'were captivated, swept off their seats by an unbelievable energy emanating from the stage. What was happening on stage could not be measured by an understanding of stage temperament, this was already a phenomenon of a physiological order . . . the energetic features of her face, its meaningfulness and, of course, charisma made her face unforgettable. "The Plague Anisimova", you cannot put it better.'[5]

Nina's dancing embodied the magic of the theatre: hidden behind the steps and gestures was an internal strength that transmitted such a strong impulse, such a charge, 'that hundreds of people in the hall vibrated in unison'.[6] Shortly before leaving the stage in 1958, Nina still roused audiences to their feet: both Gamba and the Maly/Mikhailovsky Theatre principal dancer Anatoly Sidorov described how the audience went crazy over a brief number with castanets which Nina performed together with Robert Gerbek, another venerable dancer of steely character who had performed throughout the Leningrad siege. Nina was no longer as supple as she used to be, her figure was fuller, but she was still an unrivalled master of her castanets. Nowadays, dancers hold them like a prop, leaving their actual playing to a musician in the orchestra. That night, eyes blazing, Nina played them with a fire that would have raised the dead from their graves. The crowds leaped out of their seats once again. Even elegant Paris found her irresistible. In 1952, the first group of leading dancers from the Bolshoi and Kirov travelled across the Iron Curtain to show the West the best of Soviet ballet. When Nina and eight male dancers performed the Sabre Dance, the cool Parisians could not believe what had hit them and demanded an encore.[7]

Nina's personality was also larger than life offstage. With her shining, passionate eyes she continued to look at life with an interest in everything and everyone. Nina was not only a connoisseur of the fine arts and a talented painter, she was also a skilled craftswoman. She created fantastic earrings, bead necklaces and unusual clothes for herself, proudly parading in a skirt painted with algae, bubbles and octopi to depict life at the bottom of the sea. Visitors to Nina and Kostia's dacha in Komarova admired furniture that Nina had made with her own hands.[8]

Little wonder that Nina also acquired notoriety as, allegedly, the first woman behind the wheel in Leningrad, capable also of fixing her car. Whether or not she was indeed the city's first female motorist, her driving became the stuff of legend. Racing along Leningrad's avenues and streets, Nina had no intention of paying attention to any traffic rules. Stopped by a policeman, she shrugged her shoulders: 'Don't you see there is a woman behind the wheel?' She was well known to all the traffic patrols along Primorskoye Shosse, the highway leading to Komarova. Driving by Leningrad's Choreographic Institute in her Volga, Nina would lean out and shout up to the schoolboys looking out of the fifth-floor windows, asking them to run downstairs and check when she was supposed to have a class or rehearsal.[9]

Nina and Kostia had at last been reunited again. But back in Leningrad, their private life continued to be affected by the vagaries of Soviet ideological battles. Kostia was still writing about theatre and literature. He published a book on Voltaire in 1946, and another about the Bulgarian theatre in 1950. But despite brilliant recommendations by other academics, Kostia was never granted the title of doctor of philology, hampering his career progress.[10] In 1950, Pushkin House had to close its Western European literature section as a result of the regime's ideological war against 'cosmopolitanism'. Kostia lost his job. He was forced to move to Moscow to work at the Academy of Science's Institute for Slavic Studies.

Once again the couple were separated. Nina stayed with her theatre in Leningrad: the Kirov was the centre of her life. It was easy to travel between the two cities by night train, and they had no children to consider. Dedicated to their careers, perhaps neither of them minded too much about the division of their lives between the two cities. Kostia returned briefly to Leningrad's Pushkin House in 1955, before succumbing to a long illness on 2 November 1956.

Nina was left alone. Quitting the stage in 1958, she continued to choreograph. From 1963 until 1974 she taught choreography at the Leningrad Conservatory. Her service to Soviet ballet was recognised by numerous distinctions: in 1944, she was awarded the title of Honoured Artist of the Russian Soviet Federative Socialist Republic; in 1949, she received a Stalin prize for her role in Konstantin Sergeyev's new production of Glazunov's and Petipa's *Raymonda*; and in 1957, she was made a People's Artist of the Bashkir Autonomous Soviet Socialist Republic.

Nina's *Gayané* continued to live. The end of the war and the return to Leningrad had called for adjustments to Kostia's libretto – considered the ballet's weak spot – and to the staging, which had to be adapted to the Kirov's much larger proportions. On 20 February 1945, Leningrad audiences could see for themselves what the young choreographer had accomplished during the war. Two years later Nina staged the ballet in Yerevan, the capital of Armenia. Over time, Kostia's agitational libretto withered away and what remained were the life-affirming dances and Khachaturian's infectious music.

～

On the surface, Nina's story sounds like a dramatic socialist-realist tale about the evolution of an artist: seduced by the material comforts offered by a balletomane of suspect social origins and political convictions, a young dancer lost her way, was sent to the camps, and returned triumphantly, reforged and dedicated to upholding the ideology of the Soviet state. Nina had written in her last letter from Karlag that the camp had changed her, but not necessarily for the worse. Dreaming of staging her first ballet with her friend Zhora, she imagined how she would tell him off for his decadent aestheticism, urging him to create his theatrical productions not simply with his own artistic needs in mind but with the audience's.

But Nina had not been reformed as an artist by political re-education; her views had changed because, witnessing the daily horrors of the camps, she had seen human life distilled to its essence. No matter where she was – at the Kirov, at the Leningrad Philharmonic, Karlag, Molotov or the front – Nina was never dancing for Stalin, but for the human beings who were her audience.

Nina knew how lucky she was. She was living during a period of universal fear, when arbitrary arrest and Gulag sentences were part of everyday life.[11] She had seen what had happened to others; the extraordinary miracle that she had been able to resume her former life weighed more heavily on her than the twenty-one months of hell she had survived. Instead of withdrawing to a life of private bitterness, Nina had returned to centre stage with a bang. Her dances, and her dancing, were a tribute to the fragile joy of being alive.

The great character dancer Irina Gensler was once asked whether any members of the Kirov paid attention to the plot of *Gayané* when they were performing the ballet in the 1940s and 1950s. She laughed in response: they were used to plots like this from the movies and did not give them much attention. Instead, they revelled in performing Nina's life-affirming dances to Khachaturian's intensely danceable, joyful music.[12]

Nina's art was inspiring. On New Year's Eve 1945, Farida Nureyeva, a Tartar woman of peasant stock who was raising her four children in strained circumstances while her husband was away at the front, bought one ticket for *Song of the Cranes*. She managed to smuggle her children inside the theatre with her. The youngest, a small seven-year-old boy, was enchanted by what he saw: the crystal chandeliers, the luxurious interior, the velvet curtain. When the performance started, he felt that 'the gods came dancing'. Rudolf Nureyev would later remember this instant as the moment when he found his calling: 'I knew. That's it, that's my life, that will be my function. I wanted to be *everything* on stage.'[13] That small boy graduated from the Leningrad Choreographic Institute into the Kirov in 1958 and grew up to become one of the greatest male dancers of the twentieth century. On 16 June 1961, while on tour with the Kirov in Paris, Nureyev struck a major blow to the Soviet Union's international image: he defected to the West. His leap to freedom became one of the Cold War's most evocative symbols of protest against the Soviet repression of artistic and personal freedom.

Today, Nina's legacy continues. Her exuberant, radiant variations for *Gayané*'s leading characters are performed at competitions. Her alma mater in St Petersburg regularly teaches sequences from the ballet to educate the next generation of Russian dancers. In each performance, you can still sense the sensitive vivacity of its creator.

Nina died at the age of seventy on 23 September 1979. Six years later, the Soviet Union entered a new phase that would ultimately culminate in its dramatic collapse. Mikhail Gorbachev wanted to reform socialism to ensure the system's survival. Instead, *perestroika* – restructuring – marked the beginning of the end. The new policy of *glasnost* – increased transparency and freedom of expression – soon went well beyond Gorbachev's intentions. He had opened the floodgates: people began to speak publicly about the horrors of the past and to fill in the 'blank spots' of Soviet history. But, like many who had been illegally arrested and sent to the camps during the first thirty-six years of the Soviet regime, Nina had taken her story to the grave. With the passage of time, and the deaths of the few people who had known of her experiences, her story was lost. In many ways, her fate was not unusual: over 1,700,000 people were arrested across the Soviet Union on political charges during the Great Terror of 1937–8, of whom at least 725,000 were shot – an average of 1,000 per day.[14] During those two years, around 640,000 people were sent to the camps, 18,200 were exiled or deported and 10,000 more were punished in some other way.[15] In Leningrad alone, more than 40,000 people were killed during the sixteen months of the Great Terror, while thousands of others were sent to the camps.[16]

On 25 December 1991, the Soviet flag over the Kremlin was lowered and the Russian flag raised in its place. The Soviet Union had ceased to exist. Like the other former Union republics, Kazakhstan was now an independent state, facing its own unique challenges, which included a large arsenal of 'stranded' Soviet nuclear weapons and a potentially explosive mix of people: following a constant influx of prisoners and forced and voluntary settlers, ethnic Kazakhs comprised only about 40 per cent of the population. In fact, the multi-ethnic legacy of the Gulag in Kazakhstan led to an astonishing degree of tolerance: the Kazakhs had largely welcomed the prisoners arriving from all over the Soviet Union as fellow victims of the regime.

But there has never been a full, officially sanctioned admission of the crimes committed in the name of the Communist Party of the Soviet Union. The perpetrators were never brought to justice. The failure to have a fully fledged truth and reconciliation process engaging all levels of society would come to haunt Russia – and the world. Russia's greatest years of freedom were the Yeltsin years, but for many ordinary Russians, the democratic achievements of this period were overshadowed by their excesses: the rise of the oligarchs and the criminalisation of economic life. After President Yeltsin's resignation, former KGB officer Vladimir Putin became the head of a regime deeply rooted in the culture of the former Soviet security services.

Forced into exile after Russia's invasion of Ukraine in February 2022, Natalia Sindeyeva, founder of the independent television channel TV Rain (Dozhd), highlighted Russia's failure to fully confront and learn from its Soviet past as one of the root causes explaining the rise and empowerment of the Putin regime: 'We didn't get together as a country, as a society, to recognise the mistakes that were made . . . Markets did amazing things for the country's development and we didn't take the time to explain to people that if you move from communism to capitalism, it doesn't just mean you can start making money. There are values – private property, human life, freedom of speech, free elections . . . We didn't set those values. We didn't work out why they're important. It all went by in a flash.'[17]

On 28 February 2022, four days after Russia invaded Ukraine, Russia's Supreme Court rejected an appeal against its December 2021 decision to shut down Memorial, Russia's oldest human rights organisation, and its sister organisation,

Memorial Human Rights Centre. The timing of this decision was highly symbolic: founded in the 1980s to fight for the memory of victims of political repression in the Soviet Union, Memorial expanded its mission in 1992 to include monitoring contemporary human rights violations. For the last thirty years, Memorial and the Memorial Human Rights Centre have fought both for historical truth and for today's victims, notably during the Chechen wars. Not surprisingly, since 2014, the Memorial Human Rights Centre has been active in Eastern Ukraine.

Memorial's attorney Maria Eismont spoke at the last hearing of the appeal court: 'There are no words for the horror we are all living through ... It is revealing that the liquidation of the oldest human rights organisation is taking place at the same time as those events which the law forbids to call a war ... The darkness will undoubtedly disperse. The time of penitence will come, and when one will mourn all those who have died, people will ask: but how could this happen? Why did nobody warn us? But Memorial has been warning for all these thirty years.'

Alexander Cherkassov, Chairman of the Memorial Human Rights Centre, added: 'We must not be liquidated, but of course we are being liquidated. Is there something to reproach us for? Yes. We did not finish our work, we were unable to explain to our compatriots that the struggle for rights and freedom is a daily process. That striving for "greatness" can only lead to depressing shackles ... It is painful to realise that we have wasted thirty years of our lives, spinning around in these lessons from history that have not been learned, bloody lessons.'[18]

In October 2022, Memorial was awarded the Nobel Peace Prize, together with the Belarusian human rights advocate

Ales Bialiatski and the Ukrainian human rights organisation Centre for Civil Liberties. Despite its official 'liquidation,' Memorial has been continuing its work informally. Just a few hours after the announcement, a Russian court ordered the seizure of Memorial's Moscow office, commanding that it become state property. But Memorial responded that even the seizure of its office wouldn't end its work: 'Memorial – it's a network, it's people, it's a movement,' adding that 'it is not possible to forbid memory and freedom.'[19]

There are also other centres in Russia that are working to keep Russia's historical memory alive. Since 1991, Anatoly Razumov, the head of the 'Returned Names' centre (*Vozvrashchennye imena*) at St Petersburg's Russian National Library, has dedicated himself to recovering from the archives the documented names of those subjected to Soviet political repression in the city and its surrounding regions.[20] The result has been a multiple-volume publication – the *Leningrad Martyrology* – which is also available as an online database.[21] Razumov's work goes beyond recovering victims' names; when I first discussed Nina's case with him, he was still dedicating some of his time to securing official rehabilitation for particular individuals.

The centre is part of a wider network of similar organisations across Russia, Ukraine, Kazakhstan and Belarus, which have been working together since 2000 to establish an electronic database of victims of political repression.[22] Since 1989, thousands of books listing the names of the victims of Soviet repression have been published across Russia and former Soviet republics. On 14 April 2022, almost two months into Russia's war with Ukraine, Razumov shared the news that an encyclopedia had just been published that was dedicated to the victims of political repression in the city of Ekaterinburg between 1917 until the 1980s; it is the first book of remembrance published in 2022. Since then, the centre has regularly announced news about books or events commemorating the victims of Soviet political repression.

Behind every single name in the extensive databases is one individual's tragic history. Yet there is something particularly symbolic about telling the story of Stalin's repressions through the fate of a ballet dancer – after all, what kind of regime arrests its own cultural icons? Nina's story serves as a cautionary tale of what can happen to a society once the value of truth and the sanctity of individual human life have been lost. Against the odds, her story also symbolises a larger victory, that of art over politics. Beneath its superficial ideology, her work carried the torch of a cultural tradition that was older, and ultimately more enduring, than Bolshevism: her performances were acclaimed not for their ideological message, but for their extraordinary emotional intensity – her dancing celebrated life at a time when death was everywhere. Despite the regime's effort to gain total control over culture, thanks to artists like Nina, art proved elusive and continued to offer spiritual comfort and an alternative, humanist vision of dignity, beauty and joie de vivre to ordinary people living through the nightmarish experiences of Stalinism.

ACKNOWLEDGEMENTS

There are several people without whom this book would not have been possible. Anatoly Razumov, head of the centre 'Returned Names' (*Vozvrashchennye imena*) at St Petersburg's Russian National Library, recovered the record of Nina's case. Without his help, I could not have reconstructed her story. Philatelist David Skipton discovered Nina's letters from Karlag and presented them to me as a gift. His generosity enabled me to let Nina speak of her harrowing experiences in her own voice. From Kazakhstan, I would like to thank Nurlan Dulatbekov, a truly great man whose visionary and multifaceted work on Karlag is rooted in a firm belief that we cannot build our future without understanding our past. He created the project 'Karlag: Remembrance in the Name of the Future' at Karaganda's Bolashak Academy. My thanks to the project's staff for welcoming me during my visit to Karaganda. Nurlan Dulatbekov's and Ainash Mustoyapova's insights and generous responses to my endless questions and queries gave me a much broader perspective on Karlag than any written text could have done. A special thank you to Ainash for guiding me in Karaganda and Dolinka, and for helping me to source photos of Karlag for this book.

In St Petersburg I would like to thank the staff of Pushkin House (especially Olga Kuznetsova), the Central State Archive of Literature and Art (TsGALI) and the Library of the Union of Theatre Workers. I am grateful to Alexandra Shtarkman and Sergei Laletin from the St Petersburg State Museum of Theatre and Music and to Elena Lollo from the Mariinsky Theatre for sourcing photos for this book. Ekaterina Sirakanian generously helped me navigate the practical hurdles that arose when the Covid-19 pandemic made it impossible for me to travel to St Petersburg.

In Berlin, I would like to thank Wladislaw Hedeler for kindly sharing copies of documents preserved in Karlag's archive and the staff of the political archive of the German Foreign Office.

I am grateful to Maria Soulioutis for sorting through the Eugene A. Salome Papers at the Denver Public Library and to Marina Mikhailova for transcribing Kostia's almost undecipherable wartime letters for me. I'm indebted to Elizabeth Stern for her patient handling of my photocopy requests at TsGALI.

Throughout the course of my research, numerous academics and scholars generously shared their expertise, thoughts or contacts with me. My thanks go to Gábor Rittersporn, Simon Morrison, Daria Khitrova, Katharine Hodgson, Ludmila Stern, Olga Kuptsova, Elena Osokina, Erina Megowan and Pavel Gershenzon. Lynn Garafola gave me the precious opportunity to present my work in its very early stages at the Harriman Institute, Columbia University. Conversations with several people who met Nina provided invaluable insights: I am indebted to Natalia Gamba, daughter of Mariinsky principal dancer Semen Kaplan, the former Mariinsky ballerina Olga Moiseyeva, the former Mariinsky character dancer and Vaganova Academy character dance teacher Irina Gensler, and former Mikhailovsky Theatre principal dancer Anatoly Sidorova for sharing their memories of Nina and her times with me.

I am indebted to my agent, Jonathan Conway, for his belief in me and my project and for his inspiring and ongoing support. At Elliott & Thompson, I would like to thank Jennie Condell and Sarah Rigby for their early support. I owe a debt of gratitude to my editor, Olivia Bays, whose sensitive and astute editing kept Nina's story right on track, and to Pippa Crane as well as Linden Lawson. Many thanks to Priya Mistry for her powerful cover design.

I was lucky to be awarded an Antonia Fraser Grant by The Society of Authors, a work in progress award that helped greatly, enabling me in particular to conduct research in Kazakhstan. Lady Antonia Fraser's belief that Nina's story was worth telling was especially meaningful to me because her own work helped me discover my love for historical biographies while still a student.

A special thanks goes to my mother Bettina von Siemens, who has shared my love for the Mariinsky Ballet and St Petersburg for many years. Last but not least, I would like to thank my husband Ariel, my daughter Lina and my son Yariv. I know that my quasi-obsessive desire to reconstruct Nina's story has not always been easy to live with: I would like to apologise to my children for littering the flat with illustrated books about Stalinism and the Gulag. But I am deeply touched by the enthusiasm and empathy they developed for Nina's story throughout the years. Ariel has been my most steadfast supporter, my most loyal reader and my knight, accompanying me to Karaganda and Dolinka. Thank you.

A NOTE ON PROPER
NAMES AND
TRANSLATION

In my transliteration of Russian names to English, I have used a modified version of the Library of Congress (LOC) system in the text to reflect common English spelling of Russian names (Tchaikovsky, not Chaikovskii). I have changed the Russian 'ii' ending to 'y' in surnames (Trotsky, not Trotskii). To aid pronunciation, Sergeev becomes Sergeyev. I have dropped the Russian soft sign from personal and place names (Tat'iana becomes Tatiana and Vasil'evskii ostrov becomes Vasilyevsky Island). However, I have used strict LOC transliteration in source notes and in the bibliography to help readers wishing to locate the sources cited.

Unless noted, all translations are my own.

A NOTE ON THE
SOURCE MATERIAL

Piecing together Nina's and Kostia's story turned out to be an international operation. On that autumn day in St Petersburg, I left the archive determined to find out what had happened to the people whose names had been crossed out on the denunciation list. I first turned to Google – various searches in Russian yielded nothing, but an attempt to find something interesting in German led to a promising site: a webpage for collectors of Russian and Soviet stamps, which included a reference to an article about the letters that Nina Anisimova had sent from the Karlag labour camp. I immediately contacted the article's author and discovered that, instead of destroying the defiant letters Nina had written to him from the Gulag and from prison (according to Memorial, few letters from the camps survive because they were dangerous evidence of a citizen's contact with prisoners),[1] Kostia had carefully preserved them. After he and Nina died, and following the collapse of the Soviet Union, the letters had somehow found their way across the Atlantic and into the hands of the philatelist David Skipton in Wisconsin, an expert on Russian and Soviet mail censorship and surveillance, who generously gave them to me as a gift.

A plain envelope on which Kostia had written 'scraps from prison' contained three small notes measuring about six centimetres square, which Nina had managed to smuggle out of prison while she was still under investigation. Once the investigation of her case was over, she received permission to correspond with her family. Kostia meticulously numbered almost every letter, mostly in red pencil, sometimes adding the date he had received it; keeping track of Nina's letters was his only way of knowing whether she was still alive and healthy. In total, he received twenty-nine letters, of which only three appear to have been lost. Nina covered page after page in beautiful, clearly legible script, writing either in pencil or ink.

The mere existence of Nina's letters is highly unusual. What makes them unique, though, is that they go far beyond the question of bare survival. The right to correspond was above all a lifeline because it allowed prisoners to ask relatives for food and other necessities. Nina's letters are more than simply a prisoner's plea for help to survive – they are a record of the inner life of an artist imprisoned in a Soviet labour camp. Unfortunately, the letters Kostia sent to Nina in Karlag seem to have been lost, although she often refers to their content in her own letters.

Archives in St Petersburg contain the details of the case constructed against Nina by the NKVD, her fate in the Gulag, and the wartime correspondence between the couple, including the letters Kostia wrote to Nina from the besieged city of Leningrad. In total, there are fifty letters and postcards. There are also several letters from Nina's sister Valia from Leningrad.

In order to reconstruct Nina and Kostia's experiences as closely as possible, I have taken the narrative liberty of supplementing the facts of Nina's arrest and imprisonment with the testimonies of prisoners who were held in the same locations at that time. To do this, I have drawn extensively on databases and archives devoted to the testimonies of former political prisoners, namely the archives of Memorial in St Petersburg and Moscow and the online database of Moscow's Sakharov Centre. Additional sources about the Kirov Ballet's wartime evacuation include the theatre's own archive (which is held at the Central State Archive of Literature and Art in St Petersburg) and the memoirs of other dancers.

Nina Anisimova was sent to the Gulag on the fabricated charge of espionage as a result of her friendship with an employee of the German consulate in Leningrad, Dr Evgeny Salomé. Nazi Germany was, of course, engaged in genuine espionage activities in the Soviet Union at the time, so in order to disentangle fact from fiction, and to reconstruct the private and professional life of the alleged spymaster Salomé, I located the private papers of his widow in the manuscript collection of the Denver Public Library, and have also drawn extensively on the political archive of the German Foreign Office in Berlin.

Weaving together these different sources, I could finally tell Nina's story for the very first time.

NOTES

Epigraph

1. Quoted in Tomasz Kizny, *Gulag* (Hamburg: Hamburger Edition, 2004), p. 296.

Introduction

1. The post-Soviet *Russian Ballet Encyclopedia*, published in 1997, does not mention the fact that Anisimova had been a victim of political repression during the Stalin period. Similarly, there is no mention of repression in the biographical entry of another Kirov dancer and pedagogue, Ekaterina Heidenreich, founder of the famous ballet academy in Perm. Unlike that of Anisimova, however, Heidenreich's story was well known in the Soviet ballet world. As a former prisoner, Heidenreich was not allowed to leave the Perm region and return to Leningrad after the war. Stuck in Siberia, she went on to establish the Perm Ballet Academy. However, the encyclopedia does mention the repression of Mikhail Dudko, a former principal dancer of the Kirov Ballet. After his release from the Gulag, Dudko was only allowed to return to Leningrad at the very end of his life.

Chapter 1

1. TV interview, Aleksei Ratmansky, *Bilet v Bol'shoi*, RTR Planeta, June 2008, accessed on YouTube, 'Bolshoi Ballet – rehearsing *Flames of Paris* 1(2)', 4 July 2016.

2. Portrait of Nina Anisimova as Thérèse by B. Sharapov, reproduced in colour in *Russkii balet. Entsiklopediia* (Moscow: Bol'shaia Rossiiskaia Entsiklopediia and Soglasie, 1997), p. 23. Film footage of Anisimova in her dressing room and dancing, episode on Vasily Vainonen, TV programme *Absoliutnyi slukh*, 17 December 2014 (Rossia Kul'tura channel), available on YouTube, accessed 2 March 2016.

3. Irina Pushkina, 'N. A. Anisimova – tantsovshchitsa Leningradskikh teatrov', *Vydaiushchiesia mastera i vypusniki Peterburgskoi shkoly baleta 1738–2010. Sbornik statei. Chast' 2* (St Petersburg: Akademiia Russkogo baleta im. A. Ia. Vaganova, 2010), pp. 59–68 (p. 64).

4. Email exchange with Natalia Gamba, 26 March 2014; Marietta Frangopulo, *Nina Aleksandrovna Anisimova* (Leningrad: VTO, 1951), pp. 14–15.

5. G. S. Zhzhenov, *Sanochki: Rasskazy i povest'* (Moscow, 1997), available online at the Sakharov Centre, www.sakharov-center.ru/asfcd/auth/?t=page&num=4790, accessed 29 December 2015.

6. Oleg Khlevniuk, *The History of the Gulag: From Collectivization to the Great Terror* (New Haven and London: Yale University Press, 2004), pp. 145–6. For an excellent history of the Great Terror see Chapter 4, pp. 140–85.

7. Razumov, *Levashovskoe Memorial'noe Kladbishche* (St Petersburg: Russian National Library, Centre *Vozvrashchennye imena*, 2012), pp. 1–3.

8. Robert Conquest, *The Great Terror: A Reassessment* (London: Pimlico, 2008), p. 81.

9. Razumov, pp. 3–5; N. V. Petrov, K. V. Skorkin, *Kto rukovodil NKVD: 1934–1941*, available online at www.memo.ru/history/nkvd/kto/reg2.htm#_VPID_127, accessed 28 March 2016.

10. Razumov, p. 5; ibid., p. 3.

11. NKVD investigation file of Nina Anisimova, archive of the Centre *Vozvrashchennye imena*, editorial office of memorial books *Leningradskii martirolog*, Russian National Library, St Petersburg, l. 1.

12. O. A. Kuznetsova, E. V. Vinogradova, 'Istoricheskie sobytiia v posvednevnoi zhizni: po materialam iz archiva Niny Anisimovoi', *Vestnik Akademii Russkogo baleta im. A. Ia. Vaganovoi (Vestnik ARB)*, No. 5(34), 2014, pp. 9–24 (pp. 9–10).

13. Ibid., pp. 11, 15; Institut russkoi literatury rosiiskoi akademii nauk (Pushkin House), f. 859, op. 1, d. 75, ll. 1–2.

14. I. A. Pushkina, 'N. A. Anisimova: v nachale tvorcheskoi puti', *Vestnik ARB*, No. 2(20), 2008, pp. 180–6 (pp. 180, 182).

15. Kuznetsova, Vinogradova, p. 10; NKVD Nina Anisimova investigation file, l. 33.

16. Exchange based on experience of Georgy Zhzhenov, arrested in Leningrad during the night of 4–5 June 1938; Zhzhenov, *Sanochki*, p. 43, available at: www.sakharov-center.ru/asfcd/auth/?t=page&num=4790, accessed 29 December 2015.

17. NKVD Nina Anisimova investigation file, ll. 3–4; I do not know whether Nina was taken by car to prison or whether she had to walk, but transportation by car was more common. I also don't know the exact route she took, but this would have been the most direct way to the Shpalerka.

18. The description of Nina's arrival at prison is based on the memoirs of prisoners who were arrested around the same time. I do not know to what extent Nina's experience corresponded to these memories, but the procedure prisoners were subjected to upon arrival was standardised, even if methods of prisoner transportation could vary. Based on Nina Aleksandrovna Afanasova,

Zhiznennyi put' (St Petersburg, 2005), p. 100. Like many other such memoirs, available on the website of the Sakharov Centre: www.sakharov-center.ru/asfcd/auth/?t=page&num=1038, accessed 12 January 2013. Anne Applebaum also describes the standard procedures following arrest in *Gulag: A History of the Soviet Camps* (London: Penguin Books, 2004), pp. 135–8.

19. Afanasova, p. 100.

20. Natal'ia V. Lartseva, ed. E. Tulin, *Teatr rasstreliannyi* (Petrozavodsk: Petropress, 1998), p. 75, available online at the Sakharov Centre, www.sakharov-center.ru/asfcd/auth/?t=page&num=5946, accessed 2 October 2014.

21. Ia. I. Efrussi, *Kto na 'E'* (Moscow: Vosvrashchenie, 1996), p. 25, available online at the Sakharov Centre, www.sakharov-center.ru/asfcd/auth/?t=page&num=193, accessed 2 October 2014; Ol'ga Berggol'ts, *Ol'ga. Zapretnyi dnevnik. Dnevniki, pis'ma, proza, izbrannye stikhotvoreniia i poemy Ol'ga Berggol'ts* (St Petersburg: Azbuka-Klassika, 2010), p. 31.

22. Efrussi, p. 69, Afanasova, p. 101.

23. I have based my description of the cell and the prison routine on the memoirs of former prisoners held at the Shpalerka at the same time as Nina. Afanasova, pp. 101–3.

24. Ibid., p. 102; Mark Botvinnik, 'Kamera No. 25', in *Uroki gneva i liubvi: Sb. Vospominanii o godakh represii (1918 god–80-e gody)*, ed. T. V. Tigonen (St Petersburg, 1994), p. 67, available online at the Sakharov Centre, www.sakharov-center.ru/asfcd/auth/?t=page&num=7315, accessed 18 May 2015; Teodor Shumovskii, *Svet s vostoka* (St Petersburg: SPb. Un-ta, 2006), p. 76, available online at https://www.sakharov-center.ru/asfcd/auth/?t=page&num=10482, accessed 18 May 2015.

Chapter 2

1. Kuznetsova, Vinogradova, p. 17.

2. Pushkina, 'N. A. Anisimova: v nachale tvorcheskogo puti', p. 180.

3. Christina Ezrahi, *Swans of the Kremlin: Ballet and Power in Soviet Russia* (Pittsburgh: University of Pittsburgh Press, 2012), p. 25.

4. Kuznetsova, Vinogradova, p. 17.

5. Some sources give 1920 as the year in which Anisimova enrolled in the Leningrad Choreographic Institute, citing her archival school file: Pushkina, 'N. A. Anisimova: v nachale tvorcheskogo puti', p. 180. I am relying on the information given by Anisimova herself in her theatre work file (Tsentral'nyi gosudarstvennyi arkhiv literatury i iskusstva [TsGALI], f. 337, op. 2, d 14, l. 1). Anisimova's friend Marietta Frangopulo also gives 1919 as Anisimova's enrolment year in her monograph about the dancer: Frangopulo, *Nina Aleksandrovna Anisimova*, p. 5.

6. Pushkina, 'N. A. Anisimova: v nachale tvorcheskogo puti', p. 180.

7. Tat'iana Vecheslova, *Ia, balerina* (Leningrad: Iskusstvo, 1966), p. 25.

8. Memories of Anisimova's classmate Olga Iordan, quoted in Pushkina, 'N. A. Anisimova: v nachale tvorcheskogo puti', p. 181.

9. Vecheslova (Leningrad: VTO, 1951), pp. 14–15.

10. The best description of life at the Theatre School in the years leading up to the revolution and in the early post-revolutionary period available in English is given by Elizabeth Kendall in her book *Balanchine and the Lost Muse: Revolution and the Making of a Choreographer* (New York: Oxford University Press, 2013).

11. Anisimova quoted in Kuznetsova, Vinogradova, p. 18; Vecheslova, pp. 16–22.

12. N. A. Anisimova, 'Pervaia glava moei tvorcheskoi biografii', personal file, Library of the Soiuz teatral'nykh deiatelei rossiiskoi federatsii, St Petersburg (STD RF), pp. 1–2; Anisimova's memories also as quoted in Kuznetsova, Vinogradova, pp. 18, 19; memories of Anisimova's classmate Olga Iordan; Pushkina, 'N. A. Anisimova: v nachale tvorcheskogo puti', p. 181; Frangopulo, *Nina Aleksandrovna Anisimova*, p. 7.

13. A. B. Shiriaev, *Peterburgskii balet. Vospominaniia* (Leningrad: VTO, 1941), pp. 83–99.

14. Vecheslova, pp. 44–5.

15. Ibid., p. 45; Anisimova, 'Pervaia glava moei tvorcheskoi biografii', p. 1.

16. S. K., 'Talantlivaia Ak-baletnaia smena', *Rabochii i teatr*, 1926, No. 9(76); I. Sollertinskii, 'Talisman vypusknoi spektakl' Akad. Baletnogo uchilishcha' [newspaper details not given]; Iu. Brodersen, 'Svezhie sily v balete' [newspaper details not given]; reviews preserved in Anisimova's personal file, STD RF, pp. 17–20; Frangopulo, *Nina Aleksandrovna Anisimova*, pp. 6–7; Pushkina, 'N. A. Anisimova: v nachale tvorcheskogo puti', pp. 182–4; Kuznetsova, Vinogradova, p. 18.

17. Anisimova, 'Pervaia glava moei tvorcheskoi biografii', pp. 3–4; quote on p. 4.

18. Ibid., pp. 3–4.

19. Mikhail Mikhailov, *Zhizn' v balete* (Leningrad: Iskusstvo, 1966), pp. 238–9. For official prohibition to perform outside the theatre see K. Armashevskaia, N. Vainonen, *Baletmeister Vainonen* (Moscow: Iskusstvo, 1971), p. 36.

20. Anisimova, 'Pervaia glava moei tvorcheskoi biografii', pp. 4–5; Irina Pushkina, 'N. Anisimova na kontsertnykh ploshchadkakh Leningrada', *Vestnik ARB*, No. 27(1), 2012, pp. 363–4; Pushkina, 'N. A. Anisimova – tantsovshchitsa Leningradskikh teatrov', pp. 59–68 (pp. 60–1).

21. Anisimova, 'Pervaia glava moei tvorcheskoi biografii', pp. 6–7.

22. Ibid., p. 8; Frangopulo, pp. 9–15.

23. Anisimova, 'Pervaia glava moei tvorcheskoi biografii', pp. 8–10.

24. Ezrahi, *Swans of the Kremlin*, pp. 60–2.

25. Frangopulo, *Nina Aleksandrovna Anisimova*, p. 32.

26. Christina Ezrahi, 'Experiments in Character Dance: From Leningrad's "Estrada" to the Kirov Ballet', in *Russian Movement Culture of the 1920s and 1930s. A Symposium organized by Lynn Garafola and Catharine Theimer Nepomnyashchy, 12–13 February 2015*, ed. Lynn Garafola, Harriman Institute, Columbia University, pp. 59–62 (p. 61). Published online at https://harriman.columbia.edu/files/harriman/newsletter/Russian%20 Movement%20Culture%20Corrected%20July%202017pdf.pdf

27. Nina and Koren started working together on staging character dance numbers intended for Leningrad's rich concert scene in 1936. (Pushkina, 'N. Anisimova na kontsertnykh ploshchadakh Leningrada', pp. 363–8 (p. 365)).

Chapter 3

1. My description of Nina's call-up to interrogation is based on the experience of prisoners at the Shpalerka around the same time. Afanasova, p. 104; Efrussi, pp. 26–7, 37; Shumovskii, pp. 69–70.

2. Nikolai Alekseevich Zabolotsky, 'Istoriia moego zakliucheniia', in N. A. Zabolotskii, *Ogon', mertsaiushchii v sosude . . . : Stikhotvoreniia i poemy. Perevody. Pis'ma i stat'i. Zhizneopisaniia sovremennikov. Analiz tvorchestvo* (Moscow: Pedagogika Press, 1995), pp. 394–5, available online at the Sakharov Centre, http://www.sakharov-center.ru/asfcd/auth/, accessed 19 November 2014.

3. Khlevniuk, pp. 151 ff.

4. Although the NKVD's interrogation methods are well known, mainly thanks to memoirs written by former prisoners, it is impossible to reconstruct the specific experiences of the vast majority. In most cases, including Nina's, the only trace left of those nights at the Bolshoi Dom are official NKVD interrogation protocols, but they are unreliable. Protocols were not only routinely falsified: they provide no record of torture. The details of Nina's interrogation are lost, but, given the future progression of her case, it is likely that the protocols provide a fairly accurate record of the questions she was asked and the answers she gave.

5. Aleksandr Solzhenitsyn, *The Gulag Archipelago 1918–1956*, Vol. 1: *An Experiment in Literary Investigation* (New York: Harper Perennial Modern Classics, 2007), pp. 282–3.

6. Anna Timireva, 'O Volode Dmitrieve', in *'Milaia, obozhaemaia moia Anna Vasil'evna. . .'*, ed. T. F. Pavlova, F. F. Perchenok, I. K. Safonov (Moscow: Progress.Traditsiia. Rus. Put', 1996), cited online: https://elabuga.bezformata. com/listnews/vladimir-dmitriev-teatralnij-hudozhnik/5832373/, accessed 23 June 2021.

7. NKVD Nina Anisimova investigation file, interrogation 5 February 1938, ll. 10–14.

8. Denver Public Library, Box 3: curriculum vitae of Evgeny's son Eugene Salome; English translation of Swedish obituary upon Evgeny Salomé's death in Stockholm in 1963.

9. Auswärtiges Amt (AA), Politisches Archiv, R142620 (Generalkonsulat Leningrad, Persönliche Geldangelegenheiten, 1922–33), letter, Petersburg [*sic*], 14 October 1925.

10. Several notebooks filled with stories written by Tatiana Salome are held at the Denver Public Library, Western History/Genealogy, manuscript collection, Eugene A. Salome Papers (WH1492), Box 1. A few stories are explicitly marked as depicting real events. Most of the stories are set during the revolution or in the 1920s/early 1930s, in Soviet Russia or the Baltics. There is no way of knowing whether they are based on real events or fully imagined. The second-largest group is set in Nazi Germany during the Second World War. There are also some stories of American exile.

11. 'Okhochinskii Vladimir Konstantinovich', *Sotrudniki RNB – deiateli nauki i kul'tury. Biograficheskii slovar'*, t. *1–4*, available online at http://www.nlr.ru/nlr_history/persons/info.php?id=673, accessed 7 September 2015.

12. Eugene A. Salome Papers (WH1492), Box 1, notebooks. Green University of Colorado notebook, story 18, written down on 17 July 1971 (told in third person); Box 1, loose-leaf pages bound with white ribbon, story 23, 29 June 1971 (told initially in third person but finished in first person to recount detail of sheets).

13. Statement (*zaiavlenie*) sent by Konstantin Derzhavin to the Leningrad NKVD, 4 January 1939, received 5 January 1939. NKVD Nina Anisimova investigation file, pp. 30–45 (pp. 34–5). According to the dancer Rozanov, a witness at A. Levanenok's trial, Salomé was never backstage (transcript of trial included in Nina Anisimova's investigation file, p. 64). However, as it would not have been in Derzhavin's interest to overplay Salomé's access to the Kirov Theatre, he seems to be the more reliable source.

14. NKVD Nina Anisimova investigation file, interrogation, 5 February 1938, l. 12.

15. Ibid., l. 13.

16. Hans von Herwarth, *Zwischen Hitler und Stalin. Erlebte Zeitgeschichte 1931–1945* (Frankfurt: Ullstein Verlag, paperback edition, 1985), pp. 36–7, 43–4.

17. Julian and Margaret Bullard (eds), *Inside Stalin's Russia. The Diaries of Reader Bullard, 1930–1934* (Charlbury, Oxfordshire: Day Books, 2000), p. 82.

18. I am grateful to Elena Osokina at the University of South Carolina for clarifying that Salomé would not have been allowed to hold Soviet citizenship after acquiring German citizenship in 1918.

19. NKVD Nina Anisimova investigation file, interrogation, 5 February 1938, l. 13.

20. Solzhenitsyn, p. 117.

21. NKVD Nina Anisimova investigation file, interrogation, 5 February 1938, l. 13.

22. AA, Politisches Archiv, R142620 (Generalkonsulat Leningrad, Persönliche Geldangelegenheiten, 1922–33), order, Berlin, 18 March 1933; Reichsmark/ rouble Gosbank exchange rate for 1933: Matthias Heeke, *Reisen zu den Sowjets. Der ausländische Tourismus in Russland 1921–1941* (Münster: LIT Verlag Arbeiten zur Geschichte Osteuropas, 2003), p. 127.

23. Salomé initially received his salary in roubles. From 1 April 1927 until the end of his service, he was paid in Reichsmark. This information is based on the file 'Besoldungsakten betreffend Leningrad R 142620-1', political archive of the German Foreign Office (email correspondence with the political archive of the German Foreign Office, 27 March 2018). Soviet salaries: Mervyn Matthews, *Privilege in the Soviet Union* (Milton Park: Routledge Revivals, 2012), pp. 91–101; Elena Osokina, ed. Kate Transchel, *Our Daily Bread: Socialist Distribution and the Art of Survival in Stalin's Russia, 1927–1941* (Abingdon: Routledge, 2000), p. 225, fn. 47.

24. Webpage of Professor Elena Osokina, an expert on Torgsin https://sc.edu/ study/colleges_schools/artsandsciences/our-people/faculty-staff/osokina_ elena.php, accessed 20 March 2018.

25. Julie Hessler, *A Social History of Soviet Trade: Trade Policy, Retail Practice and Consumption, 1917–1953* (Princeton: Princeton University Press, 2004), p. 200.

26. von Herwarth, pp. 63–4.

27. Testimony given by Valery Rozanov, a Kirov Ballet dancer called up as a witness at the trial of Andrei Levanenok (protocol of trial included in Anisimova's file), NKVD Nina Anisimova investigation file, l. 64; denunciation note of the ballerina mentioned at the beginning of this book.

28. C. Evtuhov, D. Goldfrank, L. Hughes, R. Stites, *A History of Russia: Peoples, Legends, Events, Forces* (Boston: Houghton Mifflin Company, 2004), pp. 640, 696–9.

29. Khlevniuk, pp. 83, 87, 88.

30. Trial of Andrei Levanenok (protocol of trial included in Anisimova's file), NKVD Nina Anisimova investigation file, ll. 64, 65.

31. NKVD Nina Anisimova investigation file, interrogation, 5 February 1938, l. 13; denunciation note of the ballerina mentioned at the beginning of this book.

32. Letter by Konstantin Derzhavin to Leningrad NKVD, 4 January 1934, NKVD Nina Anisimova investigation file, l. 34.

33. AA, Politisches Archiv, Bestand P2 (männliche Angestellte, Teil 1), Personalakte Salomé; Eugene A. Salome Papers (WH1492), Box 2, resumé of

Eugene Salome junior; Box 4, obituary of Evgeny Salomé; Box 3, letter by
Mrs von Matthiesen, 16 June 1966; Box 1, green notebook, personal memoir
'Moi dolg synu'; Box 5, letters by Evgeny Salomé to his son.

34. NKVD Nina Anisimova investigation file, interrogation, 5 February 1938,
ll. 11, 12; letter by Konstantin Derzhavin to the NKVD, 4 January 1939,
p. 12 (l. 41 in the investigation file).

35. Wikipedia entry for Hotel Astoria, https://en.wikipedia.org/wiki/Hotel_
Astoria_(Saint_Petersburg), accessed 1 May 2018.

36. Bullard, pp. 87, 101; NKVD Nina Anisimova investigation file, interrogation, 5 February 1938, pp. 11, 12; Naum Sindalovskii, 'Nemetskie
stranitsy russkoi istorii v Peterburgskom gorodskom folklore', *Neva*,
2017 (2), available online: https://magazines.gorky.media/wp-content/
uploads/2017/03/09_SINDALOVSKIJ.pdf, accessed 23 June 2021.

37. Hiroaki Kuromiya, Andrzej Pepłoński, 'The Great Terror: Polish Japanese
Connections', *Cahiers du monde russe*, No. 50(2–3), 2009, pp. 647–70 (647–9).

38. Solzhenitsyn, p. 121.

39. Conquest, p. 271.

40. Gábor T. Rittersporn, *Anguish, Anger, and Folkways in Soviet Russia* (Pittsburgh: University of Pittsburgh Press, 2014), p. 39.

41. Stephen Kotkin, *Stalin*, Vol. 2: *Waiting for Hitler, 1928–1941* (London: Allen
Lane, 2017), p. 429.

42. J. Arch Getty, Oleg V. Naumov, *The Road to Terror: Stalin and the Self-
Destruction of the Bolsheviks, 1932–1939* (New Haven and London: Yale
University Press, updated and abridged edition 2010), p. 59.

43. Evtuhov et al., pp. 668–9.

44. Kotkin, Vol. 2, pp. 478–9 (*New York Times* quote on p. 479); Geoffrey Hosking, *The First Socialist Society: A History of the Soviet Union from Within* (Cambridge, Mass.: Harvard University Press; second, enlarged edition, 1992),
pp. 188–9; Conquest, pp. 341–3.

45. Karl Schlögel, *Das Sowjetische Jahrhundert. Archäologie einer untergegangenen
Welt* (Munich: C. H. Beck, 2017), pp. 744–5.

46. Conquest, p. 167.

47. Ibid., p. 182; Hosking, *The First Socialist Society*, p. 194; Evtuhov et al., p. 673.

48. Evtuhov et al., p. 673.

49. Rittersporn, p. 47.

50. Kotkin, Vol. 2, p. 453.

51. Khlevniuk, pp. 144–5.

52. Kuromiya, Pepłoński, in particular pp. 653, 660, 665, 666.

53. Ibid., pp. 656, 658; Rittersporn, p. 42. Rittersporn's source is Nadezhda S. Plotnikova's PhD dissertation for the Academy of the Federal Service of Security of the Russian Federation, Moscow, 2002, 'Organy OGPU-NKVD-NKGB SSR v bor'be so spetssluzhbami Germanii, 1933–1941 gg'.

54. AA, Politisches Archiv, Personalakte Rudolf Sommer 014565, letter by von Baumbach to Herr Bohle, secretary of state at the Foreign Office, 1 April 1938.

55. AA, Politisches Archiv, R104371 (Deutsche diplomatische und konsularische Vertretungen in Russland, 1936–1941), letter from the German embassy in Moscow to Berlin, 27 May 1937; excerpt from a letter by Ambassador Schulenburg to Herr Schliep, 30 August 1937; telegram, Berlin, 29 September 1937.

56. AA, Politisches Archiv, Aktenband R104371, telegram from Berlin to German embassy in Moscow, 14 October 1937.

57. Ibid., telegram from Moscow to Berlin, 15 January 1938.

58. Ibid., Berlin, 2 March 1938.

59. Ibid., 'Deutsche diplomatische und konsularische Vertretungen in Russland', telegram sent by Ambassador Schulenburg from Moscow to Berlin, 13 October 1937; AA, Politisches Archiv, Personalakte Rudolf Sommer 014565, letter from von Baumbach to Herr Bohle, secretary of state at the Foreign Office, 1 April 1938; *Leningradskii martirolog*, searchable online at http://visz.nlr.ru; information about Sommer's driver: letter from Sommer to the German embassy in Moscow, Berlin, 7 December 1937, AA, Politisches Archiv, Aktenband R104371.

60. *Leningradskii martirolog*, searchable online http://visz.nlr.ru; information about Sommer's driver: letter from Sommer to the German embassy in Moscow, Berlin, 7 December 1937, AA, Politisches Archiv, Aktenband R104371. I could not establish the fate of the consulate's remaining local employees, if there were any.

61. NKVD Nina Anisimova investigation file, p. 14; Solzhenitsyn, p. 112.

Chapter 4

1. Afanasova, pp. 102–3, Shumovskii, p. 66.

2. Afanasova, p. 102; Efrussi, p. 26.

3. Conquest, p. 263.

4. Afanasova, pp. 102–3.

5. Nina Anisimova, notes from prison to her family, author's private collection.

6. Efrussi, p. 30; Afanasova, p. 103.

7. Afanasova, pp. 102–3.

8. Natal'ia Gromova, *Ol'ga Berggol'ts: Smerti ne bylo i net* (Moscow: AST 2017), available online at https://etazhi-lit.ru/publishing/prose/656-tyuremnye-strasti-olgi-berggolc.html, accessed 11 October 2018.

9. Solzhenitsyn, p. 142; Conquest, pp. 123–4.

10. Afanasova, pp. 104–5.

11. Solzhenitsyn, pp. 181, 182.

12. Afanasova, p. 104; Zabolotsky, p. 395; Liubarskaya, p. 159.

13. Attribution by Shalamov: Applebaum, p. 156.

14. Afanasova, p. 103.

15. Ibid.

16. Botvinnik, pp. 67–74.

17. Boris Sokolov, 'Kamera No. 9', in Lartseva, pp. 84–6 (p. 84).

18. Botvinnik, pp. 75–84 (p. 82).

19. The online database compiled by the organisation *Vozvrashchennye imena* in St Petersburg focuses on arrests that ended in a death sentence. On occasion, the database includes cases where arrests resulted in exile or a term in a labour camp, but this data is incomplete.

20. Khlevniuk, pp. 152–3.

21. Review of the case in 1958: 'Opredelenie No. 1573 – i-58 Voennyi tribunal Leningradskogo voennogo okruga', involving the cases of Lev Vitels, Dmitry Gotovtsev and Ivan Ulanov, Russian National Library, St Petersburg, Centre *Vozvrashchennye imena*.

22. Lartseva, p. 84.

23. Liubarskaia, p. 157.

24. Inna Klause, *Der Klang des Gulag. Musik und Musiker in den sowjetischen Zwangsarbeiterlagern der 1920er- bis 1950er-Jahre* (Göttingen: V & R Unipress, 2014), pp. 577–80.

25. Male prisoners had no opportunity to shave (Efrussi, p. 41). Levanenok had been arrested on 26 October 1937. By the time of his confrontation with Nina, he had been in prison for five months. We don't know what Levanenok looked like, but several sources describe male prisoners of that period as having long beards, long fingernails and a strange grey skin colour. Compare, for example, Boris Sokolov, 'Dva aresta: iz vozpominanii', *Neva* (2001, No. 4), p. 143, available at https://www.sakharov-center.ru/asfcd/auth/?t=page&num=10446, accessed 26 November 2016. Bullard, p. 184.

26. NKVD Nina Anisimova investigation file, l. 19. Protocol of confrontation between Nina Anisimova and Andrei Levanenok, ll. 19–23.

27. Conquest, p. 123.

28. Ivan Alikhanov, '*Dnei minuvshikh anekdoty ...*' (Moscow: Agraf, 2004), Chapter 1: 'Oblomki genealogicheskogo dreva',

available online at http://www.e-reading.club/bookreader.php/1028160/ Alihanov_-_Dney_minuvshih_anekdoty.html, accessed 30 August 2020.

29. Liubov B. Shaporina, *Dnevnik. Tom 1* (Moscow: Novoe Literaturnoe Obozrenie, 2011), p. 220.

30. Ibid., pp. 214–15.

31. Ibid., p. 215.

32. Ibid., p. 221.

33. Ibid., p. 222.

Chapter 5

1. *Fundamental'naia elektronnaia biblioteka Russkaia Literatura i Folklor*, http://feb-web.ru/feb/person/person/feb/derzhavin.htm

   Sotrudniki RNB – deiateli nauki i kul'tury, Biograficheskii slovar', t. 1–4, http://www.nlr.ru/nlr_history/persons/info.php?id=42

   Russian Wikipedia entry on Nikolai Derzhavin, https://ru.wikipedia. org, all accessed on 21 September 2019.

2. Ol'ga Kuptsova, '. . . "Vsegda pomnil vas i vse, o chem my s vami govorili . . ." O pis'makh K. N. Derzhavina V. E. Meyerkhol'dy', in *Meierkhol'dovskii sbornik: Vypusk 2: Meierkhol'd i drugie: dokumenty i materially*, ed. O. M. Fel'dman (Moscow: Gos. in-t iskusstvoznania, 1992), pp. 567–611; p. 574, fn. 13; p. 574, fn. 13; the course took place 21 June–23 August 1918.

3. Konstantin Rudnitsky, *Russian and Soviet Theatre: Tradition and the Avant-Garde* (London: Thames & Hudson, paperback, 2000), pp. 44, 68–9; Richard Stites, *Revolutionary Dreams: Utopian Vision and Experimental Life in the Russian Revolution* (Oxford: Oxford University Press, 1989), p. 41; for the avant-garde theorist Viktor Shklovsky's description of the avant-garde's attitude towards the Bolshevik Revolution see Serena Vitale, trans. Jamie Richards, *Shklovsky. Witness to an Era*. Interviews by Serena Vitale (Champaign, Ill: Dalkey Archive Press, 2012), pp. 124–5.

4. Katerina Clark, *Petersburg, Crucible of Cultural Revolution* (Cambridge, Mass.: Harvard University Press, 1995), p. 115; David Zolotnitskii, *Zori teatral'nogo Oktiabria* (Leningrad: Iskusstvo, 1976), p. 63.

5. Mary McAuley, *Bread and Justice: State and Society in Petrograd 1917–1922* (Oxford: Oxford University Press, 1991), pp. 263, 264.

6. A. L. Gripich, 'Uchitel' stseny' in *Vstrechi s Meierkhol'dom: Sbornik vospominanii* (Moscow: VTO, 1967), p. 145.

7. Orlando Figes, *A People's Tragedy: The Russian Revolution, 1891–1924* (London: Pimlico, 1997), pp. 484, 491, 494.

8. Marc Slonim, *Russian Theatre. From the Empire to the Soviets* (New York: Collier Books, 1962), p. 229; Yuri Annenkov, *Dnevnik moikh vstrech. Tsikl tragedii* (Moscow: Klub 36'6, 2019), p. 100.

9. Annenkov, p. 102; for sarcastic comment see N. D. Volkov, *Teatral'nye vechera* (Moscow: Iskusstvo, 1966), p. 31; Annenkov, p. 104. The description of the spectacle is based on Annenkov, pp. 98–106, N. Petrov, *50 i 500: 50 let tvorcheskoi deiatel'nosti i 500 postanovok* (Moscow: VTO, 1960) pp. 194–5; Volkov, pp. 27–31. I would like to thank Daria Khitrova of Harvard University for sharing this material with me. Rudnitsky, pp. 44, 68–9; Stites, *Revolutionary Dreams*, pp. 93–7.

10. Kuptsova writes that Kostia was beginning to draw close to the students of the Petrograd Choreographic Institute as early as 1918: Kuptsova, fn. 2, p. 590; Letter K. Derzhavin to Vs. Meyerhold, 13 June 1921, Kuptsova, pp. 587–9.

11. Kuptsova, p. 570; for information on Derzhavin's work for the cinema see http://m.kino-teatr.ru/kino/screenwriter/sov/46070/works/

12. Letter 12A, Karlag, 28 December 1938. Anisimova's letters from prison and Karlag are in the author's private possession.

13. Konstantin Derzhavin, petition to the Leningrad NKVD, 4 January 1939, NKVD Nina Anisimova investigation file, l. 30.

14. Ibid., l. 31.

15. Conquest, p. 263.

16. NKVD Nina Anisimova investigation file, ll. 24–7.

17. 'Protokol sudebnogo zasedaniia voennogo tribunala LVO', 21 May 1938, NKVD Nina Anisimova investigation file, ll. 62–5; excerpts of investigation file/Andrei Levanenok: Archive of the Centre *Vozvrashchennye imena*, editorial office of the memorial books *Leningradskii martirolog*.

18. Efrussi, p. 46.

19. Anna Akhmatova, *Akhmatova: Poems*, ed. Peter Washington, trans. D. M. Thomas (London: Everyman's Library, 2006), p. 183.

20. Afanasova, p. 106.

21. Ibid., p. 107.

22. NKVD Nina Anisimova investigation file, ll. 24–8; *zaiavlenie* written by Konstantin Derzhavin to the Leningrad NKVD, 4 January 1939, NKVD Nina Anisimova investigation file, l. 31.

23. Entry for 'osoboe soveshshanie pri OGPU-NKVD SSSR' in *Bol'shaia rossiiskaia entsiklopediia – elektronnaia versia*, https://bigenc.ru/military_science/text/2681196; Vladimir Filioppovich Nekrasov (ed.), *MVD Rossii. Entsiklopediia* (Moscow: Olma-Pres: 2002), entry for 'vnesudebnye repressii', pp. 66–7; Wikipedia.ru entries for 'osoboe soveshchanie pri NKVD SSSR', https://ru.wikipedia.org/wiki/Особое_совещание_при_НКВД_СССР, accessed 7 March 2019.

24. Solzhenitsyn, p. 284.

25. Letter No. 1 by Nina Anisimova to her family, 11 September 1938.

26. For descriptions of waiting to be called up, walking down the long corridors and the meeting room see memoirs of Nina Afanasova, pp. 117–18; for photos of Leningrad's women's prison taken probably around 1912 see http://www.citywalls.ru/house8493.html

27. Letter No. 2, 19 September 1938. Nina Afanasova writes in her memoirs that meetings had to be short, but nonetheless gave enormous moral support. Afanasova, p. 118.

28. Letter No. 2.

29. Ibid.

30. Ibid.

31. Ibid.

32. Ibid.

33. Afanasova, pp. 117, 119; photos of cells available online at http://www.citywalls.ru/house8493.html

34. Letter No. 3, undated.

35. Ibid.

36. Ibid.

37. Letter No. 4, undated.

38. Ibid.

39. Meinhard Stark, *Frauen im Gulag. Alltag und Überleben 1936 bis 1956* (Augsburg: Weltbild, 2006), pp. 51, 88.

40. Letter No. 4.

41. Ibid.

42. Georgii Zhzhenov, 'Ia pozlal tebe chernuiu rozu...', *Sanochki: Rasskazy i povesti* (Moscow: 1997), pp. 61–2; available online: https://www.sakharov-center.ru/asfcd/auth/?t=page&num=4792, accessed 8 April 2019.

43. Zhzhenov, 'Ia pozlal tebe chernuiu rozu...', pp. 61–2.

44. Liudmila Granovskaya, 'Arest', *Neva*, No. 9, 1991, pp. 193–8, quote on p. 195, available online at https://www.sakharov-center.ru/asfcd/auth/?t=book&num=152. Granovskaya was convicted as the wife of an enemy of the people. Her drive from the Kresty to the train station took place in early 1938, probably in April 1938.

45. Applebaum, p. 161.

46. Afanasova, p. 121.

47. Applebaum, pp. 162–3; Stark, pp. 53–5. Own observation at the museum-memorial complex of victims of political repression built on the site of ALZHIR outside Nur-Sultan in Kazakhstan.

48. Applebaum, pp. 162–3 (including prisoner quotes); Stark, p. 59.

49. Applebaum, pp. 162–3.

50. For transport to Potma see Granovskaya, p. 195; transport to Karaganda, Afanasova, p. 121.

51. Stark, pp. 56–61.

52. Stephen Kotkin, *Stalin*, Vol. 1: *Paradoxes of Power, 1878–1928* (New York: Penguin Books, 2014), p. 281.

53. Stark, p. 73.

54. Afanasova, p. 121.

55. Letter No. 5, 27 September 1938.

56. Stark, pp. 63–9.

57. Letter No. 5.

58. David M. Skipton, 'Dancing in the Karlag', *The British Journal of Russian Philately*, 96/97, 2007, pp. 97–109. A pdf of the article including images of the adversity envelope and note was kindly provided to me by the article's author.

Chapter 6

1. The descriptions of the camp and of its procedures are taken from memoirs written by camp survivors in Karlag around the same time as Nina Anisimova. While we cannot know the exact circumstances of Anisimova's arrival, the conditions tended to be similar and the procedures standardised. Wladislaw Hedeler, Meinhard Stark, *Das Grab in der Steppe. Leben im Gulag: Die Geschichte eines Sowjetischen 'Besserungsarbeitslagers' 1930–1959* (Paderborn: Ferdinand Schöningh, 2008), pp. 214, 218. Daniil Fibikh, *Dnevniki i vospominaniia* (Moscow: Izdatel'stvo 'Pervoe sentiabria', 2010), p. 391 f., Georgii Levin, ... *V ego minuty rokovye*, p. 170, available on www.sakharov-center.ru, *Vozpominaniia o GULAGe i ikh avtory* (accessed 26 March 2014). Hedeler and Stark translate Karabas as 'Black Stone', but several prisoner memoirs state the name was derived from the Kazakh word *karabash*, meaning 'black head'; Fibikh, p. 392; Nina Afanasova, *Zhiznennyi put'*, p. 122.

2. Geoffrey Hosking, *Russia: People & Empire, 1552–1917* (London: Fontana, 1997), pp. 3–18, 38–9; John Channon, with Robert Hudson, *The Penguin Historical Atlas of Russia* (London: Penguin Books, 1995), pp. 42–3, 54, 74–5; Evtuhov et al., pp. 125–6, p. 400.

3. Evtuhov et. al., pp. 572–3, 646–8, 656–62; Hosking, *The First Socialist Society*, pp. 112–13, 242–4; Kotkin, *Stalin. Vol. I*, pp. 372–6.

4. Kotkin, *Stalin. Vol. II*, pp. 9–11, p. 76; pp. 127–9; p. 941, fn. pp. 468, 470.

5. Khlevniuk, pp. 9, 10; for numbers see Applebaum, p. 4, for general history pp. 66, 67.

6. V. V. Kozina, 'Rol' repressivnoi politiki sovetskogo gosudarstva v osushchestvlenii modernizatsii tsentral'nogo Kazakhstana v 30-e gody XX veka', in *'Pamiat' vo imia budushchego'. Sbornik materialov mezhdunarodnoi*

nauchno-prakticheskoi konferentsii, posviashchennoi Dniu pamiati zhertv polit-icheskoi repressii (Karaganda: Bolashak-Baspa, 2011), pp. 83–6; Steven A. Barnes, *Death and Redemption: The Gulag and the Shaping of Soviet Society* (Princeton: Princeton University Press, 2011), pp. 30–1.

7. E. Chilikova, 'K voprosu istorii sozdaniia Karlaga: sotsial'nye deportatsii (po dokumentam i knizhnomu archiva prezidenta respubliki Kazakhstana)', in *Sbornik materialov*, pp. 11–15 (p. 14).

8. Numbers given for the population of the territory assigned to Karlag diverge: I am using an average value based on several sources. Nurlan Dulatbekov, *Karlag* (Karaganda, Kazakhstan: Karagandinskii universitet 'Bolashak', 2012), p. 221; Nurlan Dulatbekov, *Karlag: Creativity in Captivity* (Karaganda: University 'Bolashak', 2009), p. 12; K. T. Temirgalieva, 'Istoriia Karlaga', in *Sbornik materialov mezhdunarodnoi nauchno-prakticheskoi kon-ferentsii, posviashchennoi Dniu pamiati zhertv politicheskoi repressii*, pp. 131–3 (p. 131–2); S. D. Shaimukhanova, ibid., pp. 127–30 (p. 130); Hedeler, Stark, p. 33.

9. Hedeler, Stark, pp. 16, 61.

10. Nurlan Dulatbekov in conversation with the author. Also: 'O chem pisali gazety Karlaga?' Portal 'Istoriia Kazakhstana', https://e-history/kz/ru/pub-lications/view/3456, accessed 16 May 2019; Dulatbekov, *Karlag: Creativity in Captivity*, pp. 12–13; Barnes, p. 31.

11. Dulatbekov, *Karlag* (2012), pp. 211, 219, 247; Barnes, p. 31.

12. Stark, pp. 87–8.

13. Hedeler, Stark, pp. 214–5; Fibikh, p. 392.

14. Hedeler, Stark, p. 223; Margarete Buber-Neumann, *Als Gefangene bei Stalin und Hitler* (Munich: Verlag der Zwölf, 1949), p. 70.

15. Fibikh, p. 392; Afanasova, p. 123; Hedeler, Stark, pp. 216, 220–1.

16. Hedeler, Stark, pp. 218, 225; Buber-Neumann, p. 67.

17. For *zemlianka* description see Buber-Neumann, p. 67; Hedeler, Stark, p. 220.

18. Fibikh, p. 394.

19. Hedeler, Stark, p. 218.

20. Ibid., pp. 176, 403; Stark, pp. 448–9.

21. Letter No. 8, undated.

22. Stark, p. 60.

23. Letter No. 8.

24. Letter No. 9, 30 October 1938.

25. Ibid.

26. Ibid.

27. Fibikh, p. 393; Hedeler, Stark, pp. 216–21; Afanasova, p. 123.

28. Afanasova, p. 123; Buber-Neumann, pp. 70 ff.

29. Buber-Neumann, pp. 70–2; Hedeler, Stark, pp. 221 ff.

30. Afanasova, p. 123; Buber-Neumann, p. 72; Levin, . . . *V ego minuty rokovye*, p. 170.

31. Buber-Neumann, p. 72 ff.; Fibikh, p. 392; Galina Semenova, 'Nakazanie bez prestupleniia', in *Karlag: Vechnaia bol' surovykh vremen (vospominaniia)*, Vol. 3 (Karaganda, Kazakhstan: Karagandinskii universitet 'Bolashak', 2010), p. 310.

32. Letter No. 10 from Nina Anisimova to Konstantin Derzhavin, 14 November 1938. The letter is in the possession of David Skipton, who made a scanned copy of the letter available to me by email, 1 June 2014. Skipton published the envelope and part of the first page of the letter on 'The Rossica Society Virtual Gallery' as part of the virtual exhibit 'Zek. The Soviet Slave-Labour Empire and its Successors, 1917–2000', available at http://www.rossica.org/RVG/myPh3/album/Zek/Frame-4, accessed 18 June 2019.

33. Letter No. 10, 14 November 1938.

34. Afanasova, p. 124; Buber-Neumann, pp. 68–9.

35. Letter No. 10.

36. Postcard No. 11, 25 November 1938.

37. Letter No. 12B, 30 December 1938.

38. I am grateful to Ainash Mustoyapova, lecturer at Karaganda State University named after E. A. Buketov, to point out to me that only somebody in Moscow would have had the power to give the order to pull Nina off the transport.

39. Letter No. 12A, 28 December 1938.

40. Kostia would refer to this episode in a letter to Nina in 1941. Pushkin House, f. 859, op. 1, d. 17, l. 3.

41. David Skipton, the Russian mail and censorship expert who kindly provided Nina's correspondence to me, believes that the delay was probably due to camp censorship. Email communication, 1 June 2014. Skipton came across Anisimova's Gulag letters in the late 1990s and published an article that put me on their trail: 'Dancing in the Karlag', *British Journal of Philately*, issue 96/97, 2007, pp. 97–109.

42. Letter No. 12B. Written at the same time to different sets of family members, the content of letters 12A and 12B overlaps.

43. Letter No. 12A.

44. Tat'iana Okunevskaia, *Tat'ianin den'* (Moscow: Vagrius, 1998), p. 342, available online: https://www.sakharov-center.ru/asfcd/auth/?t=book&num=987

45. Letter No. 12A.

46. Varlam Shalamov, trans. John Glad, *Kolyma Tales* (London: Penguin Books, 1994), p. 32.

47. Letter No. 12A.

48. Ibid.

49. Hedeler, Stark, p. 223.

50. Hedeler, Stark, pp. 223–4.

51. Letter 12B.

52. Ibid.

53. Ibid.

54. Ibid.

Chapter 7

1. Kostia's *zaiavlenie*: NKVD Nina Anisimova investigation file, ll. 30–45. The full text of Kostia's *zaiavlenie* was published by the Vaganova Academy's academic journal *Vestnik ARB*, No. 4 (51), 2017, pp. 155–68, available online at https://vaganov.elpub.ru/jour/article/view/455/447

2. Ludmila Stern, *Western Intellectuals and the Soviet Union, 1920–40: From Red Square to the Left Bank* (London: BASEES/Routledge Series on Russian and East European Studies Book 31, 2007), Kindle edition, pp. 86–7.

3. Theodore Dreiser, *Dreiser's Russian Diary*, ed. by Thomas P. Riggio, James L. W. West, III (Philadelphia: University of Pennsylvania Press, 1996), pp. 141–3.

4. I am grateful to Professor Ludmila Stern from UNSW Sydney for this information.

5. Quoted in Boris L'vov-Anokhin, *Sergei Koren'* (Moscow: Iskusstvo, 1988), p. 31.

6. Online database *Leningradskii martirolog*; 'Stalinskie rasstrelnye spiski', webpage of the human rights organisation Memorial. Source of list mentioning Grinfel'd: Arkhiv presidenta RF, op. 23, d. 414, list 339: Leningradskii oblast', 2-ia kategoriia (this meant the individuals on this list were meant to be sent to the Gulag; 1st category meant execution). Grinfel'd is the second name mentioned on this specific list comprising seven people: http://stalin.memor.ru/spiski/pgo6339.htm. I. V. Vaganova, 'Na izlome sudby: 1937 god v zhizni A. Ia. Vaganovoi', *Vestnik ARB*, No. 5 (58), 2018, pp. 18–24 (for the date of Grinfel'd's arrest see p. 19, fn 4). Additional information on Grinfel'd: '1938 god v kino': http://www.rudata.ru/wiki/1938_год_в_кино, entry for 3 February 1938. Both pages accessed 26 May 2015.

7. 'Smelee vydvigat' sposobnuiu molodezh', *Za sovetskoe iskusstvo*, 3 October 1937, p. 4.

8. Vaganova, p. 23.

9. 'Doklad L. M. Lavrovskogo, khudozhestvennogo rukovoditelia baletnoi truppy teatra opery i baleta im. Kirova, o perspektivakh raboty teatra na 1938 god', 2 February 1938, STD RF, in card index: biblioteka LO VTO, 316-c; l. 11.

10. The transcripts of the meetings were discussed and photographic images of their pages shown in the TV programme *Absoliutnyi slukh* on the Rossiya K channel. http://tvkultura.ru/video/show/brand_id/20892/episode_id/314606/video_id/314606/viewtype/picture, accessed 17 February 2014.

11. Vaganova, pp. 21, 23; Tsentral'nyi gosudarstevennyi arkhiv istoriko-politicheskikh dokumentov (TsGAIPD), f. 2245, op. 1, ed. khr. 38, ll. 101–14.

12. Biulleten' Vsesoiuznogo Komiteta po delam iskusstv pri SNK Soiuza SSR, No. 12 (Moscow: Iskusstvo, 1937), p. 40; Biulleten' Vsesoiuznogo Komiteta po delam iskusstv pri SNK Soiuza SSR, No. 5-6 (Moscow: Iskusstvo, 1938), p. 23.

13. Center *Vozvrashchennye imena*, Redaktsiia Knigi pamiati 'Leningradskii martirolog', investigation file of Andrei Levanenok, l. 6; for information about Mikhailov's arrest and execution see *Leningradskii martirolog, Vol. 11*.

14. Kostia's *zaiavlenie*: NKVD Nina Anisimova's investigation file, ll. 30–45; written confirmation that it was received by the NKVD on 5 January 1939, l. 67.

Chapter 8

1. Letter No. 13, 14 January 1939.

2. Hedeler, Stark, p. 324.

3. For information on the food situation see Hedeler, Stark, pp. 316, 322, 324–7; Stark, pp. 241–4.

4. Hedeler, Stark, p. 329.

5. Ibid., pp. 253–4; 316; 338–41.

6. Ibid., pp. 331–2; Stark, p. 244.

7. Hedeler, Stark, pp. 239–43.

8. Letter No. 13.

9. Karl Schlögel, *Terror und Traum. Moskau 1937* (Frankfurt am Main: Fischer Taschenbuch Verlag, 2011), pp. 394–9.

10. For the estimated number of deaths and annual releases see Barnes, pp. 1, 10.

11. Applebaum, p. 222.

12. I would like to thank Wladislaw Hedeler for generously sharing copies of documents preserved in Karlag's archive.

13. Aimar Ventsel, Baurzhan Zhangutin, Dinara Khamidul-lina, 'Social Meaning of Culture in a Stalinist Prison Camp', pp. 13–14, http://www.folklore.ee/folklore/vol56/ventsel.pdf

14. Kizny, p. 259.

15. Applebaum, p. 220.

16. G. I. Levin, 'Artisty v GULAGe', http://www.ruthenia.ru/folktee/CYBERSTOL/GULAG/Levin.html

17. Letter No. 14, undated.

18. Mikhailov, p. 258.

19. Information given by a tour guide at the Karlag Museum in Dolinka, 12 July 2019.

20. http://gulaghistory.org/archive/files/l_79b1dae2d9.90.pdf

21. Richard Stites, *Serfdom, Society, and the Arts in Imperial Russia: The Pleasure and the Power* (New Haven: Yale University Press, 2005), p. 27.

22. This argument is commonly made by people studying the culture of the region. Compare for example E. P. Gavrilova, *Memorial Karagandy, KarLAG, kul'tura, khudozhniki* (Karaganda: Arko, 2003), pp. 44–5.

23. Anatoly Karpinchuk, *Vospominaniia o prebyvanii v Karlage*, Memorial/Moscow, collection of memoirs, f. 2, op. 1, ed. kh. 72, ll. 3, 11–12.

24. Ibid., ll. 19–20.

25. Letter No. 14.

26. Ibid.

27. Hedeler, Stark, p. 257.

28. Karpinchuk, l. 4.

29. Ibid., ll. 17–18.

30. Okunevskaia, p. 355.

31. Applebaum, pp. 329–37.

32. Ibid. pp. 264–5; Hedeler, Stark p. 299; Buber-Neumann, p. 96.

33. Buber-Neumann, pp. 83–5; Hedeler, Stark, pp. 189, 234–5, 237–8; Applebaum, p. 190; prisoner double bunk beds exhibited in Karlag Museum in Dolinka; technical barracks, letter No. 15, 17 February 1939; technical food ration, letter No. 18, dated 6 May 1939.

34. Letter No. 14.

35. http://gulaghistory.org/archive/files/l_bd113194e3.86.pdf

36. Elena Ter-Asaturova, *Vospominaniiam ugasnut' ne dano. Vospominaniia Ter-Asaturova Eleny Konstantinovny* (Karaganda: Bolashak-Baspa, 2014), p. 211; Lidiia Sooster, 'Khudozhnik Iulo Sooster', in *Teatr GULAGa*, ed. M. M. Korallova (Moscow: Memorial, 1995), p. 3; V. Mogil'nitski, 'Muzy Karlaga', *Temirtauskii rabochii*, 9 March 2016 (No. 10), p. 15; G. I. Levin, ... *V ego minuty rokovye* [*rokovyie* elsewhere]; Karpinchuk, ll. 3, 15; E. Kuznetsova, 'SG-555 v "prisutstvii okrushchikh lits"', in Kuznetsova, *Karlag:*

po obe storony 'koliuchki' (Surgut: Defis, 2001), p. 199, available online at https://www.sakharov-center.ru/asfcd/auth/?num=5661&t=page, accessed 21 April 2020.

37. Letter No. 15, 17 and 20 February 1939.

38. Ibid.

39. Hedeler, Stark, pp. 371–4.

40. Ter-Asaturova, pp. 192–3.

41. Letter No. 15.

42. Ibid.

43. Iadviga Verezhinskaya, *Vospominaniia. 1992 g., S.-Peterburg*, Memorial/Moscow, collection of memoirs, f. 2, op. 1, d. 33, l. 51.

44. Letter No. 15.

45. Letter No. 16, undated.

46. Sharifa Ustinova, *Moi ispoved': Vospominaniia*, Memorial/Moscow, collection of memoirs, f. 2, op. 1, d. 120, ll. 63–4; Hedeler, Stark, p. 404.

47. Buber-Neumann, p. 96; Afanasova, p. 122.

48. V. V. Sterligov, 'Vospominanie o Petre Ivanoviche Sokolove', in S. M. Turutina, Evgeny F. Kovtun, M. M. Grigor'eva, *Avantgard, ostanovlennyi na begu* (Leningrad: Avrora, 1989), p. 26.

49. Ibid., p. 24.

50. Gavrilova, pp. 58–61; https://ru.wikipedia.org/wiki/Ермолаева,_Вера_Михайловна

51. Irina Kulle, *Teni na suglinke*, Memorial/Moscow, collection of memoirs, f. 2, op. 3, d. 28, l. 23.

52. Karpinchuk describes what was customary in the 1940s. It is likely that not much had changed since Nina's time.

53. Ustinova, ll. 58–9.

54. Some of the drawings and sketches of Irina Borkhman, including her landscape painted with pig's blood, are kept in the archive of Memorial/Moscow. They are also reproduced in Gavrilova, pp. 68–70.

55. Maria Goldberg, *Rasskaz a tom, chto bylo i chto ne povtoritsia*, dated 1962/63, Memorial/Moscow, collection of memoirs, f. 2, op. 1, d. 47, l. 47.

56. Karpinchuk, l. 1.

57. Ibid., ll. 15-16.

58. Letter No. 17, undated.

59. Ibid.

60. Barnes, p. 71.

61. Letter No. 17.

62. Ibid.

63. Ibid.

64. Letter No. 18, 6 May 1939.

65. Ibid.

66. Anna Kniper, *Milaia, obozhaemaia moia Anna Vasil'evna*, compiled by T. F. Pavlova, F. F. Perchenok, I. K. Safonov (Moscow: Progress, Traditsiia, Rus. Put'', 1996), pp. 299–300, available online at etextlib.ru/Book/Details/38958, accessed 26 February 2019.

67. Ter-Asaturova, p. 208.

68. Letter No. 18.

69. I am grateful to Ainash Mustoyapova for drawing my attention to this story. 'Kurt – dragotsennyi kamen', *Limonad* (student magazine, Bolashak, Karaganda University), No. 5(146), 27 May 2014, p. 22. The article is also available online at https://e-history.kz/ru/publications/view/1139

70. Letter No. 18.

Chapter 9

1. NKVD Nina Anisimova investigation file, l. 48.

2. http://old.memo.ru/history/nkvd/kto/index.htm

3. http://old.memo.ru/history/nkvd/kto/biogr/gb288.htm

4. Khlevniuk, pp. 186–7 and biographical appendix.

5. Ibid., pp. 186–93.

6. NKVD Nina Anisimova investigation file, ll. 50–1.

7. Ibid., ll. 52–3.

8. NKVD Nina Anisimova investigation file, l. 61.

9. Vecheslova, pp. 30–3.

10. http://www.ria1914.info/index.php/Вечеслов_Захарий_Михайлович

11. Information available on the search database of *Vozvrashchennye imena* available at http://visz.nlr.ru/person, accessed 27 May 2020.

12. NKVD Nina Anisimova investigation file, l. 61.

13. Ibid., l. 59.

14. Ibid., ll. 56–7.

15. Ibid., l. 55.

16. Ibid., ll. 67–8.

17. Letter No. 20; Nina's letter is dated in Kostia's hand 20 September 1939. His own letter, followed by notes from Nina's mother and Valia is dated 11 September 1939.

18. Letter No. 21, undated; letter No. 22, undated; letter No. 24, 7 October 1939.

19. Letter No. 23, 1 October 1939.

20. Letter No. 24, 7 October 1939.

21. Letter No. 27, undated.

22. NKVD Nina Anisimova investigation file, l. 70.

23. Ibid., l. 69.

24. Ibid., l. 72.

25. Ibid., ll. 69, 73.

26. TsGALI, f. 337, op. 2, d. 14; *anketnyi* list mentioning arrest, l. 5; the form is not dated, but it gives the years 1928–38 for her employment at the Kirov, and therefore must have been the form filled in upon her return to the Kirov after her release. Notarised copy of NKVD certificate, l. 35, second to last page of the file.

27. *Leningradskie teatry* (Leningrad: Iskusstvo), No. 65, 21–5 December 1939, No. 1, 1–5 January 1940, listings for performances at the Kirov Theatre.

28. Natal'ia Sheremetevskaia, *Dlinnye teni (O vremeni, o tantse, o sebe). Zapiski istorika balet i baletnogo kritika* (Moscow: Redaktsii zhurnala 'Baleta', 2007), p. 104.

29. Marietta Frangopulo, 'Na vechere kharakternogo tantsa v Filarmonii', *Za sovetskoe iskusstvo*, 23 February 1940, No. 5.

30. Introductory remarks to Marietta Frangopulo, 'V dni voiny', *Vestnik ARB*, No. 3(38), 2015, p. 11. Available online: https://vaganov.elpub.ru/jour/article/view/79/75, accessed 16 June 2020.

31. Berggolts, p. 30.

32. Berggolts, p. 31.

33. I am grateful to Professor Gábor Rittersporn for sharing his archival notes taken on Medalinskaya's appeal: GARF (State Archive of the Russian Federation, Moscow), f. 5446, op. 81a, d. 353, ll. 10–15. Confirmation of Oppengeim's and Sidorovskaya's cases: online search database of *Vozvrashchennye imena* (http://visz.nlr.ru/person). Oppengeim was held in prison from 23 February 1938 until 5 March 1938; Sidorovskaya from 20 June 1938 until 17 December 1938. Their cases were closed and they were released from prison.

34. https://www.thedailybeast.com/when-stalin-met-lady-macbeth, accessed on 1 June 2020.

35. http://ptj.spb.ru/archive/10/all-10/dyadya-ko/, accessed 1 June 2020.

36. I. Ginzburg, Boris Leo, A. Flit, *Leningradskii balet v druzheskikh sharzhakh* (Leningrad: Izdanie tsentral'noi kassy, 1940), p. 21.

37. STD RF, St Petersburg, personal file Nina Anisimova, l. 158.

38. V. Pastukhov, 'Kontsert ansamblia Leningradskogo teatra opery i baleta v Dzintari', *Trudovaia gazeta*, No. 31; typed copy of article in STD RF,

personal file Nina Anisimova, l. 44; information on brigade: TsGALI, f. 238, op. 2, d. 3813, 'Otchet Len. Oblastnoi voenno-shefskoi komissi Soiuza Rabotnikov Iskusstva, 1.1.–31.12.1940', l. 10.

39. V. Metal'nikov, 'Iskusstvo kharakternogo tantsa', *Iskusstvo i zhizn'*, 1941, No. 1, pp. 43–4; typed copy of this article, and excerpts from other reviews, in STD RF, personal file Nina Anisimova RF ll. 46–51.

40. N. Anisimova, 'Eshche raz o kharakternom tantse', *Za sovetskoe iskusstvo*, 27 March 1940, No. 3, typed copy in STD RF, personal file Nina Anisimova, ll. 42–3.

41. http://www.khachaturian.am/rus/works/ballets_1.htm; *Aram Khachaturian. Stat'i i vospominaniia* (Moscow: Sovetskii kompozitor, 1980), p. 131.

42. N. Anisimova, 'Solnechnyi spektakl' and E. Radin, 'Nakanune novogo goda', *Za sovetskoe iskusstvo*, 31 December 1940, p. 3.

43. TsGALI, f. 337, op. 1, d. 199, ll. 4, 9 ; ll. 26, 28, 38, 45, 46, 68, 76.

44. I would like to thank Professor Simon Morrison for generously sharing his archival notes on *Happiness*: RGALI (Russian State Archive of Literature and Art, Moscow), f. 652, op. 6, ed. khr. 214, ll. 2–3, ll. 15–21. List of persons: *A. Khachaturian. Noto-bibliograficheskii spravochnik*, compiled by D. M. Person (Moscow: Sovetskii kompozitor, 1979), pp. 15–16.

45. Letter No. 18, 6 May 1939.

46. TsGALI, f. 337, op. 1, d. 199, ll. 52-67.

47. N. Anisimova, 'K postanovke balet "Schast'e"', *Za sovetskoe iskusstvo*, 15 March 1941, p. 1.

48. TsGALI, f. 337, op. 1, d. 199, ll. 38, 40, 49–50 ; 'Podgotovka baleta "Schast'e"', *Za sovetskoe iskusstvo*, 5 April 1941, p. 1, http://www.khachaturian.am/rus/works/ballets_1.htm, accessed 10 June 2020.

49. TsGALI, f. 337, op. 1, d. 199, ll. 84-4 ob.

50. Ibid., ll. 85–5 ob.

51. Ibid., ll. 96 ob., 100, 107.

52. Ibid., ll. 115–15 ob.

53. Ibid., ll. 119 ob.–120 ob.

54. Ibid., ll. 123–23 ob.

55. Ibid., ll. 124–24 ob.

56. Ibid., l. 128.

Chapter 10

1. Anna Reid, *Leningrad: Tragedy of a City Under Siege, 1941–44* (London: Bloomsbury, 2011, paperback edition, 2012), pp. 14, 18–20, 39; Evtuhov et al., p. 702.

2. 'Obsluzhivanie mobilizatsionnykh punktov', *Za sovetskoe iskusstvo*, 28 June 1941, p. 3.

3. Ivan Nechaev, Natalia Sakhnovskaia, Olga Iordan, *Tantsuia pod obstrelami. Dnevniki artistov Kirovskogo teatra 1941-1944 gg. iz osazhdennogo Leningrada* (Vyborg: Voennyi muzei Karel'skogo peresheika, 2019), p. 106.

4. https://www.mariinsky.ru/about/exhibitions/war/summer_1941/, accessed on 28 June 2020.

5. Nechaev et al., p. 107.

6. 'Pravila povedeniia rabotnikov teatra po ugrozhaemomu polozheniiu, vozduzhnoi trevoge, khimicheskoi trevoge i po otboiu trevoge', *Za sovetskoe iskusstvo*, 28 June 1941, p. 4.

7. Nechaev et al., pp. 21, 107; Marietta Frangopulo, 'V dni voiny', *Vestnik ARB*, No. 3(38), 2015, pp. 12–28 (p. 12).

8. STD RF, personal file Nina Anisimova, pp. 189–91.

9. Frangopulo, 'V dni voiny', *Vestnik ARB*, No. 3 , p. 12; Nechaev et al., pp. 21, 107; Vecheslova, p. 140.

10. Reid, pp. 44–5, 50.

11. https://www.mariinsky.ru/about/exhibitions/war/summer_1941/, accessed on 28 June 2020; Vecheslova, p. 140; Nechaev et al., p. 22.

12. Evtuhov et al., p. 707; https://en.wikipedia.org/wiki/World_War_II_casualties#Total_deaths_by_country, accessed 30 June 2020.

13. Erina Megowan, unpublished PhD dissertation, 'For Fatherland, for Culture: State, Intelligentsia and Evacuated Culture in Russia's Regions, 1941–1945', Georgetown University, 15 July 2015, pp. 1–4, 38–53, 302. Available online at https://repository.library.georgetown.edu/bitstream/handle/10822/1042895/Megowan_georgetown_0076D_13461.pdf?sequence=1&isAllowed=y, accessed on 30 June 2020.

14. Reid, pp. 356–61.

15. Vecheslova, p. 140; https://www.mariinsky.ru/about/exhibitions/war/summer_1941/

16. Reid, pp. 92, 104, 108; Larisa Abyzova, *Igor' Bel'skii. Simfoniia zhizni* (St Petersburg: Akademiia russkogo baleta im. A. Ia. Vaganovoi, 2000), p. 30.

17. Pushkin House, f. 859, d. 1, op. 17, ll. 43–5.

18. Ibid., l. 39.

19. Larisa Abyzova, *Istoriia khoreograpbicheskogo iskusstvo. Otechestvennyi balet XX – nachala XXI veka* (St Petersburg: Kompozitor, 2012), p. 118; Megowan, pp. 74–5, 169; Vecheslova, p. 142.

20. Megowan, pp. 200–2.

21. Vecheslova, p. 142.

22. Abyzova, *Igor' Bel'skii*, p. 31.

23. STD RF, personal file Natal'ia Dudinskaia, transcript of 'Tvorcheskaia vstrecha Leningradskogo baleta s laureatom Stalinskoi premii N. M. Dudinskoi i zazl. artistami F. I. Balabinoi i K. M. Sergeevym', 13 August 1943, l. 2.

24. https://www.mariinsky.ru/about/exhibitions/war/kirovsky_in_molotov/; Frangopulo, 'V dni voiny', *Vestnik ARB*, No. 3, p. 13; Vecheslova, pp. 145–6.

25. Abyzova, *Igor' Bel'skii*, p. 44; https://www.youtube.com/watch?v=C4NYrCx3E7E&t=35s.

26. Vecheslova, p. 146.

27. Shaporina, *Dnevnik. Tom I* (Moscow: Novoe Literaturnoe Obozrenie, 2017), Kindle edition, diary entry for 4 September 1941, location 7692.

28. Pushkin House, f. 859, op. 1, d. 17, ll. 39–41. Letter dated 3 August 1941, but it is clear from the context that the letter was written on 3 September 1941.

29. Megowan, p. 82.

30. Pushkin House, f. 859, op. 1, d. 17, ll. 46–7.

31. Shaporina, *Dnevnik. Tom I*, Kindle edition, diary entry for 9 September 1941, location 7733–5.

32. Reid, p. 109.

33. Ibid., p. 144; https://www.mariinsky.ru/about/exhibitions/war/teatralnaya/

34. Pushkin House, f. 859, op. 1, d. 77, l. 1.

35. Shaporina, *Dnevnik. Tom I*, Kindle edition, diary entry for 22 September 1941, location 8026.

36. Reid, pp. 151–2.

37. Pushkin House, f. 859, op. 1, d. 17, l. 1.

38. Evtuhov et al., p. 697; Reid, pp. 20–1.

39. Reid, pp. 128–36.

40. Pushkin House, f. 859, op. 1, d. 17, l. 3.

41. Ibid.

42. Ibid.

43. Ibid., d. 21, l. 1.

44. Ibid., d. 17, l. 4.

45. Ibid., l. 4.

46. Reid, p. 174.

47. Pushkin House, f. 859, op. 1, d. 77, l. 2.

48. Ibid.

49. Cynthia Simmons and Nina Perlina, *Writing the Siege of Leningrad: Women's Diaries, Memoirs, and Documentary Prose* (Pittsburgh: University of Pittsburgh Press, 2002), p. 47.

50. Reid, pp. 182–3.

51. Shaporina, *Dnevnik, Tom 1*, Kindle edition, diary entry for 26 October 1941, location 8683–702.

52. Pushkin House, f. 859, op. 1, d. 77, ll. 2–3.

53. Ibid., l. 3.

54. Reid, pp. 180–2.

55. Pushkin House, f. 859, op. 1, d. 17, l. 9.

56. Ibid.

57. Ibid., d. 77, l. 4.

58. Ibid., d. 17, l. 9; Ibid., d. 77, l. 3.

59. Ibid., l. 4.

60. Ibid., d. 17, letter dated 1 November 1941. The archival page number is written unclearly, it should be 11.

61. Reid, p. 168.

Chapter 11

1. 'Khronika', *Za sovetskoe iskusstvo*, 21 January 1942, p. 4.

2. Pushkin House, f. 859, op. 1, d. 21, l. 3.

3. Ibid., l. 11.

4. Ibid., ll. 3–4.

5. Ibid., l. 4.

6. Frangopulo, 'V dni voiny', *Vestnik ARB*, No. 3, 2015, p. 18.

7. Pushkin House, f. 859, op. 1, d. 21, l. 3.

8. Ibid., l. 5.

9. Ibid.

10. Ibid., ll. 6–7.

11. STD RF, personal file Natal'ia Dudinskaia, 'Tvorcheskaia vstrecha Leningradskogo baleta s laureatom Stalinskoi premii N. M. Dudinskoi i zazl. artistami F. I. Balabinoi i K. M. Sergeevym', 13 August 1943, ll. 2, 4; Abyzova, *Igor' Bel'skii*, pp. 41, 47.

12. Pushkin House, f. 859, op. 1, d. 17, l. 20.

13. Ibid., ll. 20–1.

14. Ibid., l. 21.

15. Ibid., d. 21, ll. 8–9.

16. Ibid., l. 9.

17. Ibid., l. 10.

18. Ibid., l. 11.

19. Ibid., l. 10.

20. Ibid., l. 15.

21. Ibid., d. 17, ll. 24–5.

22. Ibid.

23. Ibid., d. 21, ll. 14, 16–9, 22.

24. Ibid., l. 23.

25. Ibid.

26. Ibid.

27. Ibid., l. 24.

28. Ibid.

29. Ibid., l. 25.

30. Ibid., l. 26.

31. Ibid., l. 28.

32. Ibid., ll. 32–3.

33. Frangopulo, *Nina Aleksandrovna Anisimova*, pp. 39–40; Vecheslova, pp. 154–5.

34. Evtuhov et al., pp. 712–3.

35. Russian National Library, St Petersburg, manuscript department, f. 1477, op. 1, ed. khr. 394, ll. 1–2.

36. Konstantin Derzhavin, libretto for *Gayané*, Molotov 1942, TsGALI, f. 337, op. 1, d. 199, ll. 193–205.

37. TsGALI, f. 337, op. 1, d. 199, ll. 144–5, 146 ob., 149, 157, 161.

38. *Aram Khachaturian. Stat'i i vospominaniia*, pp. 131–2.

39. Vecheslova, pp. 144–5.

40. TsGALI, f. 337, op. 1, d. 199, l. 143.

41. 'Balet. Baletmeistera. Opera', *Aram Khachaturian. Stranitsy zhizni i tvorchestva. Iz besed s G. M. Shneersonom* (Moscow: Sovetskii kompozitor, 1982), p. 128; Ezrahi, *Swans of the Kremlin*, p. 205.

42. TsGALI, f. 337, op. 1, d. 199, ll. 132–4 ob. (quote on l. 134).

43. Ibid., ll. 136–8; N. Anisimova, 'O rabote nad baletom Gayane', *Za sovetskoe iskusstvo*, 20 October 1942.

44. TsGALI, f. 337, op. 1, d. 199, ll. 144 ob.–145.

45. Ibid., l. 146.

46. Ibid., l. 148.

47. Ibid., l. 147.

48. Ibid., ll. 153–4.

49. Ibid., ll. 160, 156–7, 159–61.

50. Ibid., l. 164.

51. Anisimova, 'O rabote nad baletom Gayane'.

52. *Aram Khachaturian. Stat'i i vospominaniia*, pp. 132–3.

53. https://en.wikipedia.org/wiki/Sabre_Dance#cite_note-ungmusic-10

54. *Aram Khachaturian. Stat'i i vospominaniia*, p. 132.

55. TsGALI, f. 337, op. 1, d. 199, ll. 173–92.

56. The description of the fire and premiere are based on Frangopulo, 'V dni voiny', *Vestnik ARB*, No. 4(39), 2015, pp. 24–6; https://www.mariinsky. ru/about/exhibitions/war/kirovsky_in_molotov/; Abyzova, *Igor' Bel'skii*, pp. 43–4; STD RF, personal file Natal'ia Dudinskaya, 'Tvorcheskaia vstrecha Leningradskogo baleta s laureatom Stalinskoi premii N. M. Dudinskoi i zazl. artistami F. I. Balabinoi i K. M. Sergeevym', 13 August 1943, l. 3.

Epilogue

1. Zhilenko, 'Zhemchuzhina natsional'noi khoreografii'; Nina Zhilenko, 'I novykh "zhuravlia" vzmetnulas' staia....: K 95-letiiu so dnia rozhdeniia izv. tanstovshchitsy Niny Anisimovu', *Respublika Bashkortostan*, available online at http://forum.balletfriends.ru/viewtopic.php?p=7889&highlight=%C0% F8%F2%EE%ED, accessed 21 August 2020.

2. Reid, p. 1.

3. Russian National Library, St Petersburg, manuscript department, f. 1477, op. 2, ed. khr. 324; letter by I. Timofeeva to Natalia Dudinskaya, 4 February 1944.

4. Professor V. Shcherbachev, 'Ivan Susanin na otkrytii Teatra opery i baleta imeni S. M. Kirova', *Leningradskaia Pravda*, 2 September 1944, No. 210, STD RF, personal file Nina Anisimova, l. 100; programme for 'Evening of Dances/Nina Anisimova', STD RF, personal file Nina Anisimova, ll. 101–2.

5. Private email communication by Natalia Gamba, 26 March 2014.

6. Ibid.

7. Nina Zhilenko, 'Zhemchuzhina natsional'noi khoreografii', p. 3, available online at https://kulturarb.ru/images/HW/PDF/jurpesn.pdf, accessed 21 August 2020.

8. Ibid.; telephone interview with Anatoly Sidorov, 23 September 2014.

9. Zhilenko, 'Zhemchuzhina natsional'noi khoreografii', p. 3; private email communication with Natalia Gamba, 20 and 26 March 2014; telephone interview with Anatoly Sidorov, 23 September 2014.

10. Soviet academic titles do not correspond to their English linguistic equivalent: the Russian equivalent to an academic doctor title in the Anglo-Saxon world would be candidate of science. The title of doctor of science is one degree higher.

11. I would like to thank Ainash Mustoyapova for engaging with me on this topic over a cup of coffee in Karaganda.

12. Personal interview with Irina Gensler, St Petersburg, 30 November 2014.

13. Julie Kavanagh, *Rudolf Nureyev: The Life* (London: Fig Tree, 2007), p. 15.

14. Memorial, 'Zhertvy politicheskogo terrora v SSSR' (versiia ot 24.12.2015), http://lists.memo.ru/index.htm, accessed 9 March 2016.

15. Khlevniuk, p. 290.

16. Razumov, p. 3.

17. Max Seddon, 'Russia's unlikely revolutionary', *Financial Times*, Life & Arts, 14 April 2022, p. 2.

18. https://memohrc.org/ru/news_old/pc-memorial-likvidirovan-reshenie-vstupilo-v-silu; accessed on 27 April 2022.

19. https://www.dw.com/en/russia-seizes-office-of-nobel-peace-prize-winner-memorial/a-63375519, accessed on 24 October 2022.

20. http://rus.postimees.ee/700992/anatoliy-razumov-izuchaet-vse-dokumenty-pogibshih-v-gody-stalinskikh-repressiy

21. http://visz.nlr.ru/person

22. https://visz.nlr.ru/pages/centr-vozvraschennye-imena; accessed on 29 April 2022.

A note on the source material

1. Irina Ostrovskaya, 'A Note from Memorial', in Orlando Figes, *Just Send Me Word: A True Story of Love and Survival in the Gulag* (London: Penguin Books, 2013), p. 297.

SELECTED
BIBLIOGRAPHY

Archives

Central State Archive of Historical Political Documents, St Petersburg (TsGAIPD SPb)

Central State Archive of Literature and Art, St Petersburg (TsGALI)

Denver Public Library, Western History/Genealogy, manuscript collection

Institute of Russian Literature, Russian Academy of Sciences, St Petersburg (IRL RAN, 'Pushkin House')

Library of the Union of Theatre Workers of the Russian Federation (STD RF), St Petersburg (personal files Nina Anisimova, Natalia Dudinskaya)

Nina Anisimova's letters from prison and Karlag: author's private collection

Political Archive, German Foreign Office (AA, Politisches Archiv), Berlin

Russian National Library, St Petersburg, Archive of the Centre *Vozvrashchennye imena*, editorial office of the memorial books *Leningradskii martirolog* (searchable online http://visz.nlr.ru)

Russian National Library, St Petersburg, manuscript department

Collection of Gulag memoirs, Memorial/Moscow

Goldberg, Maria. 'Rasskaz a tom, chto bylo i chto ne povtoritsia', f. 2, op. 1, d. 47

Karpinchuk, Anatoly. 'Vospominaniia o prebyvanii v Karlage', f. 2, op. 1, ed. kh. 72

Kulle, Irina. 'Teni na suglinke', f. 2, op. 3, d. 28

Ustinova, Sharifa. 'Moi ispoved': Vospominaniia', f. 2, op. 1, d. 120

Verezhinskaya, Iadviga. 'Vospominaniia. 1992 g., S.-Peterburg', f. 2, op. 1, d. 33

Zakharov Centre, online Gulag memoirs

The following memoirs are available on https://www.sakharov-center.ru/asfcd/auth/

Afanasova, Nina. *Zhiznennyi put'* (St Petersburg: 2005)

Botvinnik, Mark. 'Kamera No. 25', in *Uroki gneva i liubvi: Sb. Vospominanii o godakh represii (1918 god–80-e gody)*, ed. T. V. Tigonen (St Petersburg: 1994)

Efrussi, Ia. I. *Kto na 'E'* (Moscow: Vosvrashchenie, 1996)

Granovskaia, Liudmila. 'Arest', *Neva*, No. 9, 1991

Kuznetsova, Elena. *Karlag: po obe storony 'koliuchki'* (Surgut: Defis, 2001)

Kuznetsova, Elena. 'SG-555 v 'prisutstvii okrushchikh lits', in Kuznetsova, *Karlag: po obe storony 'koliuchki'* (Surgut: Defis, 2001)

Lartseva, Natalia V., ed. E. Tulin. *Teatr rasstrel'iannyi* (Petrozavodsk: Petropress, 1998)

Levin, Georgii. '. . . V ego minuty rokovye', in E. Kuznetsova, *Karlag: po obe storony 'koliuchki'*, pp. 169–89.

Liubarskaia, A. I., commentary by A. Razumov. 'Za tiurmenoi stenoi', *Neva*, No. 5, 1998

Okunevskaia, Tatiana. *Tat'ianin den'* (Moscow: Vagrius, 1998)

Shumovskii, Teodor. *Svet s vostoka* (St Petersburg: SPb. Un-ta, 2006)

Sokolov, Boris. 'Dva aresta: iz vozpominanii', *Neva*, No. 4, 2001

Sooster, Lidiia. 'Khudozhnik Iulo Sooster', in *Teatr GULAGa*, ed. M. M. Korallova (Moscow: Memorial, 1995)

Zabolotskii, Nikolai. 'Istoriia moego zakliucheniia', in N. A. Zabolotskii, *Ogon', mertsaiushchii v sosude. . .: Stikhotvoreniia i poemy. Perevody. Pis'ma i stat'i. Zhizneopisaniia sovremennikov. Analiz tvorchestva* (Moscow: Pedagogika-Press, 1995)

Zhzhenov, G. S. *Sanochki: Rasskazy i povest'* (Moscow: 1997)

Books

Abyzova, Larisa. *Igor' Bel'skii. Simfoniia zhizni* (St Petersburg: Akademiia russkogo baleta im. A. Ia. Vaganovoi, 2000)

Abyzova, Larisa. *Istoriia khoreographicheskogo iskusstvo. Otechestvennyi balet XX – nachala XXI veka* (St Petersburg: Kompositor, 2012)

Akhmatova, Anna. *Akhmatova: Poems*, ed. Peter Washington, trans. D. M. Thomas (London: Everyman's Library, 2006)

Annenkov, Yuri. *Dnevnik moikh vstrech. Tsikl tragedii* (Moscow: Klub 36'6, 2019)

Applebaum, Anne. *Gulag: A History of the Soviet Camps* (London: Penguin Books, 2004)

Armashevskaia, K., Vainonen, N. *Baletmeister Vainonen* (Moscow: Iskusstvo, 1971)

Barnes, Steven A. *Death and Redemption: The Gulag and the Shaping of Soviet Society* (Princeton: Princeton University Press, 2011)

Berggol'ts, Ol'ga. *Ol'ga. Zapretnyi dnevnik. Dnevniki, pis'ma, proza, izbrannye stikhotvoreniia i poemy Ol'ga Berggol'ts* (St Petersburg: Azbuka-Klassika, 2010)

Brummel, Paul. *Kazakhstan* (Chalfont St Peter, Bucks: Bradt Travel Guides, third edition, 2018)

Buber-Neumann, Margarete. *Als Gefangene bei Stalin und Hitler* (Munich: Verlag der Zwölf, 1949)

Julian and Margaret Bullard (eds). *Inside Stalin's Russia. The Diaries of Reader Bullard, 1930–1934* (Charlbury, Oxon: Day Books, 2000)

Channon, John, with Robert Hudson. *The Penguin Historical Atlas of Russia* (London: Penguin Books, 1995)

Clark, Katerina. *Petersburg, Crucible of Cultural Revolution* (Cambridge, Mass.: Harvard University Press, 1995)

Conquest, Robert. *The Great Terror: A Reassessment* (London: Pimlico, 2008)

Dreiser, Theodore. *Dreiser's Russian Diary*, ed. Thomas P. Riggio, James L. W. West III (Philadelphia: University of Pennsylvania Press, 1996)

Dulatbekov, Nurlan. *Karlag: Creativity in Captivity* (Karaganda: University 'Bolashak', 2009)

Dulatbekov, Nurlan. *Karlag* (Karaganda: Karagandinskii universitet 'Bolashak', 2012)

Evtuhov, C., Goldfrank, D., Hughes, L., Stites, R. *A History of Russia: Peoples, Legends, Events, Forces* (Boston: Houghton Mifflin Company, 2004)

Ezrahi, Christina. *Swans of the Kremlin: Ballet and Power in Soviet Russia* (Pittsburgh: University of Pittsburgh Press, 2012)

Fibikh, Daniil. *Dnevniki i vospominaniia* (Moscow: Izdatel'stvo 'Pervoe sentiabria', 2010)

Figes, Orlando. *A People's Tragedy: The Russian Revolution, 1891–1924* (London: Pimlico, 1997)

Figes, Orlando. *Just Send Me Word: A True Story of Love and Survival in the Gulag* (London: Penguin Books, 2013)

Fitzpatrick, Sheila. *The Cultural Front: Power and Culture in Revolutionary Russia* (Ithaca, NY: Cornell University Press, 1992)

Frangopulo, Marietta. *Nina Aleksandrovna Anisimova* (Leningrad: VTO, 1951)

Frankopan, Peter. *The Silk Roads: A New History of the World* (London: Bloomsbury, 2015)

Gaevsky, Vadim, Gershenzon, Pavel. *Razgovory o russkom balete: Kommentarii k noveishei istorii* (Moscow: Novoe izdatel'stvo, 2010)

Gavrilova, E. P. *Memorial Karagandy, KarLAG, kul'tura, khudozhniki* (Karaganda: Arko, 2003)

Getty, J. Arch, Naumov, Oleg V. *The Road to Terror: Stalin and the Self-Destruction of the Bolsheviks, 1932–1939* (New Haven and London: Yale University Press, updated and abridged edition, 2010)

Ginzburg, I., Leo, Boris, Flit, A. *Leningradskii balet v druzheskikh sharzhakh* (Leningrad: Izdanie tsentral'noi kassy, 1940)

Hedeler, Wladislaw, Stark, Meinhard. *Das Grab in der Steppe. Leben im Gulag: Die Geschichte eines Sowjetischen 'Besserungsarbeitslagers' 1930–1959* (Paderborn: Ferdinand Schöningh, 2008)

Heeke, Matthias. *Reisen zu den Sowjets. Der ausländische Tourismus in Russland 1921–1941* (Münster LIT Verlag Arbeiten zur Geschichte Osteuropas, 2003)

von Herwarth, Hans. *Zwischen Hitler und Stalin. Erlebte Zeitgeschichte 1931–1945* (Frankfurt: Ullstein Verlag, paperback edition, 1985)

Hessler, Julie. *A Social History of Soviet Trade: Trade Policy, Retail Practice and Consumption, 1917–1953* (Princeton: Princeton University Press, 2004)

Hosking, Geoffrey. *The First Socialist Society: A History of the Soviet Union from Within* (Cambridge, Mass.: Harvard University Press; second, enlarged edition, 1992)

Hosking, Geoffrey. *Russia: People & Empire. 1552–1917* (London: Fontana, 1997)

Karlag: Vechnaia bol' surovykh vremen (vospominaniia), Vol. 3 (Karaganda: Karagandinskii universitet 'Bolashak', 2010)

Kavanagh, Julie. *Rudolf Nureyev: The Life* (London: Fig Tree, 2007)

Kendall, Elizabeth. *Balanchine and the Lost Muse: Revolution and the Making of a Choreographer* (New York: Oxford University Press, 2013)

Aram Khachaturian. Stat'i i vospominaniia (Moscow: Sovetskii kompozitor, 1980)

Aram Khachaturian. Stranitsy zhizni i tvorchestva. Iz besed s G. M. Shneersonom (Moscow: Sovetskii kompozitor, 1982)

Khlevniuk, Oleg. *The History of the Gulag: From Collectivization to the Great Terror* (New Haven and London: Yale University Press, 2004)

Kizny, Tomasz. *Gulag* (Hamburg: Hamburger Edition, 2004)

Klause, Inna. *Der Klang des Gulag. Musik und Musiker in den sowjetischen Zwangsarbeiterlagern der 1920er- bis 1950er- Jahre* (Göttingen: V & R Unipress, 2014)

Kotkin, Stephen. *Stalin*, Vol. 1: *Paradoxes of Power, 1878–1928* (New York: Penguin Books, 2014)

Kotkin, Stephen. *Stalin*, Vol. 2: *Waiting for Hitler, 1928–1941* (London: Allen Lane, 2017)

Lartseva, Natalia V., ed. E. Tulin. *Teatr rasstreliannyi* (Petrozavodsk: Petropress, 1998)

Lipper, Elinor. *Eleven Years in Soviet Prison Camps* (Washington, D. C.: Henry Regnery Company, 1951), Kindle edition

L'vov-Anokhin, Boris. *Sergei Koren'* (Moscow: Iskusstvo, 1988)

Matthews, Mervyn. *Privilege in the Soviet Union* (Milton Park, Abingdon-on-Thames: Routledge Revivals, 2012)

McAuley, Mary. *Bread and Justice: State and Society in Petrograd 1917–1922* (Oxford: Oxford University Press, 1991)

Megowan, Erina. Unpublished PhD dissertation, 'For Fatherland, for Culture: State, Intelligentsia and Evacuated Culture in Russia's Regions, 1941–1945', Georgetown University, 15 July 2015, available online at https://repository.library.georgetown.edu/bitstream/handle/10822/1042895/Megowan_georgetown_0076D_13461.pdf?sequence=1&isAllowed=y

Mikhailov, Mikhail. *Zhizn' v balete* (Leningrad: Iskusstvo, 1966)

Nechaev, Ivan, Sakhnovskaia, Natal'ia, Iordan, Ol'ga. *Tantsuia pod obstrelami. Dnevniki artistov Kirovskogo teatra 1941–1944 gg. iz osazhdennogo Leningrada* (Vyborg: Voennyi muzei Karel'skogo peresheika, 2019)

Nekrasov, Vladimir Filioppovich (ed.). *MVD Rossii. Entsiklopediia* (Moscow: Olma-Pres: 2002)

Osokina, Elena, ed. Kate Transchel. *Our Daily Bread: Socialist Distribution and the Art of Survival in Stalin's Russia, 1927–1941* (Abingdon: Routledge, 2000)

Pamiat' v imia budushchego: Sbornik materialov mezhdunarodnoi nauchno-prakticheskoi konferentsii, posviashchennoi Dniu pamiati zhertv politicheskoi repressii (Karaganda: Bolashak-Baspa, 2011)

Petrov, Nikolai. *50 i 500: 50 let tvorcheskoi deiatel'nosti i 500 postanovok* (Moscow: VTO, 1960)

Razumov, Anatolii. *Levashovskoe Memorial'noe Kladbishche* (St Petersburg: Russian National Library, Centre *Vozvrashchennye imena*, 2012)

Reid, Anna. *Leningrad: Tragedy of a City Under Siege, 1941–44* (London: Bloomsbury, 2011; paperback edition, 2012)

Rittersporn, Gábor T. *Anguish, Anger, and Folkways in Soviet Russia* (Pittsburgh: University of Pittsburgh Press, 2014)

Robbins, Christopher. *In Search of Kazakhstan: The Land that Disappeared* (London: Profile Books, 2008)

Rudnitsky, Konstantin. *Russian and Soviet Theatre: Tradition and Avant-Garde* (London: Thames & Hudson, paperback, 2000)

Russkii balet. Entsiklopediia (Moscow: Bol'shaia Rossiiskaia Entsiklopediia and Soglasie, 1997)

Schlögel, Karl. *Terror und Traum. Moskau 1937* (Frankfurt am Main: Fischer Taschenbuch Verlag, 2011)

Schlögel, Karl. *Das Sowjetische Jahrhundert. Archäologie einer untergegangenen Welt* (Munich: C. H. Beck, 2017)

Sebag Montefiori, Simon. *Stalin: The Court of the Red Tsar* (London: Phoenix, 2004)

Service, Robert. *Stalin: A Biography* (London: Macmillan, 2004)

Shalamov, Varlam, trans. John Glad. *Kolyma Tales* (London: Penguin Books, 1994)

Shaporina, Liubov'. *Dnevnik. Tom 1* (Moscow: Novoe Literaturnoe Obozrenie, 2011)

Shaporina, Liubov'. *Dnevnik. Tom 1* (Moscow: Novoe Literaturnoe Obozrenie, 2017), Kindle edition

Sheremetevskaia, Natal'ia. *Dlinnye teni (O vremeni, o tantse, o sebe). Zapiski istorika balet i baletnogo kritika* (Moscow: Redaktsii zhurnala 'Baleta', 2007)

Shiriaev, A. B. *Peterburgskii balet. Vospominaniia* (Leningrad: VTO, 1941)

Simmons, Cynthia and Perlina, Nina. *Writing the Siege of Leningrad: Women's Diaries, Memoirs, and Documentary Prose* (Pittsburgh: University of Pittsburgh Press, 2002)

Sindalovskii, Naum. *Istoriia Peterburga v predeniiakh i legendakh* (St Petersburg: Norint, 1997)

Slonim, Marc. *Russian Theatre. From the Empire to the Soviets* (New York: Collier Books, 1962)

Solzhenitsyn, Aleksandr. *The Gulag Archipelago 1918–1956*, Vol. 1: *An Experiment in Literary Investigation* (New York: Harper Perennial Modern Classics, 2007)

Stark, Meinhard. *Frauen im Gulag. Alltag und Überleben 1936 bis 1956* (Augsburg: Weltbild, 2006)

Stern, Ludmila. *Western Intellectuals and the Soviet Union, 1920–40: From Red Square to the Left Bank* (London: BASEES/Routledge Series on Russian and East European Studies Book 31, 2007), Kindle edition

Stites, Richard. *Revolutionary Dreams: Utopian Vision and Experimental Life in the Russian Revolution* (Oxford: Oxford University Press, 1989)

Stites, Richard. *Serfdom, Society, and the Arts in Imperial Russia: The Pleasure and the Power* (New Haven and London: Yale University Press, 2005)

Ter-Asaturova, Elena. *Vospominaniiam ugasnut' ne dano. Vospominaniia Ter-Asaturova Eleny Konstantinovny* (Karaganda: Bolashak-Baspa, 2014)

Tigonen, T. V. (ed.). *Uroki gneva i liubvi: Sb. Vospominanii o godakh repressii (1918 god –80-e gody)* (St Petersburg: 1994)

Turutina, S. M., Kovtun, Evgenii F., Grigor'eva, M. M. *Avantgard, ostanovlennyi na begu* (Leningrad: Avrora, 1989)

Vecheslova, Tat'iana. *Ia, balerina* (Leningrad: Iskusstvo, 1966)

Vitale, Serena, trans. Jamie Richards. *Shklovsky. Witness to an Era. Interviews by Serena Vitale* (Champaign, Ill.: Dalkey Archive Press, 2012)

Volkov, N. D. *Teatral'nye vechera* (Moscow: Iskusstvo, 1966)

Zolotnitskii, David. *Zori teatral'nogo Oktiabria* (Leningrad: Iskusstvo, 1976)

Articles, chapters in books

Frangopulo, Marietta. 'V dni voiny', *Vestnik Akademii Russkogo baleta im. A. Ia Vaganovoi* (*Vestnik ARB*), No. 1 (38), 2015

Frangopulo, M. 'V dni voiny', *Vestnik ARB*, No. 4 (39), 2015

Gripich, A. L. 'Uchitel' stseny', in *Vstrechi s Meierkhol'dom: Sbornik vospominanii* (Moscow: VTO, 1967)

Kuptsova, Ol'ga, '. . . "Vsegda pomnil vas i vse, o chem my s vami govorili . . ." O pis'makh K. N. Derzhavina V. E. Meyerkhol'dy', in *Meierkhol'dovskii sbornik: Vypusk 2: Meierkhol'd i drugie: dokumenty i materially*, ed. O. M. Fel'dman (Moscow: Gos. in-t iskusstvoznania, 1992)

Kuromiya, Hiroaki, Pepłoński, Andrzej. 'The Great Terror: Polish Japanese Connections', *Cahiers du monde russe*, 50/2–3, 2009, pp. 647–70

Kuznetsova, O. A., Vinogradova, E. V. 'Istoricheskie sobytiia v posvednevnoi zhizni: po materialam iz archiva Niny Anisimovoi', *Vestnik ARB*, No. 5 (34), 2014, pp. 9–24

Pushkina, Irina. 'N. A. Anisimova: v nachale tvorcheskoi puti', *Vestnik ARB*, No. 2 (20) 2008, pp. 180–6

Pushkina, Irina. 'N. A. Anisimova – tantsovshchitsa Leningradskikh teatrov', *Vydaiushchiesia mastera i vypusniki Peterburgskoi shkoly baleta 1738–2010. Sbornik statei. Chast' 2* (St Petersburg: Akademiia Russkogo baleta imeni A. Ia. Vaganova, 2010)

Pushkina, Irina. 'N. Anisimova na kontsertnykh ploshchadkakh Leningrada', *Vestnik ARB*, No. 27 (1), 2012

Skipton, David M. 'Dancing in the Karlag', *The British Journal of Russian Philately* (issue 96/97, 2007), pp. 97–109

Vaganova, I. V. 'Na izlome sudby: 1937 god v zhizni A. Ia. Vaganovoi', *Vestnik ARB*, No. 5 (58), 2018, pp. 18–24

Ventsel, Aimar, Zhangutin, Baurzhan, Khamidullina, Dinara. 'Social meaning of culture in a Stalinist prison camp', pp. 13–14, http://www.folklore.ee/folklore/vol56/ventsel.pdf

Newspapers, journals
Za sovetskoe iskusstvo, in-house newspaper of the Kirov Theatre
Vestnik Akademii Russkogo baleta im. A. Ia. Vaganovoi https://vaganov.elpub.ru/jour/issue/archive

Videos
Scan the QR codes for performances choreographed by Nina Anisimova.

Sabre Dance
(performed by Nina) and
other excerpts from *Gayané*

Song of the Cranes
(filmed for the cinema
in 1959)

Index

A

A Life for the Tsar (M. Glinka) 244

Adoptee, The 87

Afanasova, Nina 66–70, 141

air raids on Leningrad 280–1, 286

Akhmatova, Anna 99

Akmolinsk division 186, 226

Alexandrinsky Theatre 17, 224

Alexandrov, Alexander 'Serge'
        87–8

All-Russian Theatrical Society
        171

All-Union Society of Cultural
        Relations with Foreign
        Countries (VOKS) 161

Alma-Ata Theatre 272

Andalusian Wedding 31, 91–2, 146,
        152, 169, 222, 237

Anisimov, Alexander 8, 176–7

Anisimova (née Alekseyeva), Maria
        8–9, 36, 62–4, 83, 85, 101–2,
        106–8, 111–12, 123–4, 134,
        144–6, 190, 212–14, 239,
        276, 292, 298, 303

Anisimova, Nina
        in *Andalusian Wedding* 31, 91,
                146, 169, 237
        Andrei Levanenok
                confrontation 75–80
        arrest 9–10
        case indictment (April 1938)
                95–7

case reviewed by NKVD
        229–38, 240–2

in *The Cavalry Halt* 24

character dance 21–4, 26–7, 32,
        159, 162–3, 238, 250–2

character witnesses 233–8

choreographs Kirov's
        production of *The Night
        Before Christmas* 325

choreographs 'Russian Fairy
        Tales' 325

choreographs *The Circus
        Princess* 325

choreography and direction
        31–2, 92, 103, 146–7, 172,
        225–8, 240, 251–2, 253,
        259–62, 293–4, 296, 298–9,
        301–3, 305–7, 310–14,
        317–18, 319, 325, 330

in *Colas Breugnon* 210

dancing with Joseph
        Kschessinsky 27–8

death of 332

denunciation xv, 6, 174

Dolinka's Central Club 195–6,
        199–200, 204, 207–8,
        210–11, 216–17, 222–3

driving 328–9

evacuation of Kirov Theatre
        270–3, 276

family background 8–9,
        176–7

Anisimova, Nina (continued)
in *The Flames of Paris* 1–3, 13,
28, 37, 91, 92, 169
folk/national dances 162,
244–5, 250, 260
graduation piece from *Talisman*
23
health issues 83, 208
honours and awards 249,
330
in Karabas camp 125, 132–7,
140–7
in Karlag, Dolinka camp
148–53, 185, 190, 195–6,
199–200, 205–6, 207–14,
217–18
international workers' day
production 302–3, 305–6
interrogation 33–4, 36–8, 40,
43, 49, 58–9, 64, 75–80,
232
labour camp sentence 100–2,
103–4, 109–10, 112–13
letters from Karabas camp
134–7, 140–8
letters from Karlag, Dolinka
camp 150–3, 185, 190,
195–6, 199–200, 207–14,
220–8, 254, 330–1
letters from Perm 284–5, 289,
292, 296–8, 301–6
letters from prison 101–15,
239–40
letters from transit prisons
122–4
letters from Valia 281, 286–7,
289
letters/telegrams received from
Kostia 272–3, 279–80,
282–6, 289, 293–5, 299
Maly Theatre 25

Mariinsky Theatre 23, 24,
27
mastery of castanets 196, 251,
328
in *Partisan Days* 32, 169
performs for Red Army 250,
265
in Perm 276–7, 279–80, 291–4,
296–7, 301–7
pet dog, Stepa 64, 106, 111,
113–15, 123, 136–7, 214,
281, 284–5, 286, 287, 296
Petrograd Choreographic
Institute 15, 17, 18–24,
233–4, 329
post-release performances
244–6
production of *Happiness/Gayané*
253–62, 267, 293, 309–15,
320, 324, 326–7, 330, 332
recalled from train at Karabas
144
receives parcels and letters at
Dolinka 144–8, 212–13,
220, 221–3, 237
Red Army 24th anniversary
production 293–4, 296,
298–9
release from prison 242–4
retirement 327–8
the Sabre Dance from *Gayané*
319, 320, 324, 328
sealed room 10, 103, 107,
109
secret notes to family 63–4
Shpalerka prison 10–14, 61–6,
83, 98, 231–2, 238–9 (*see also*
above interrogation)
Spanish dances 13, 23, 27, 29,
91, 195, 211, 244–5, 251,
277

summer breaks in Detskoe Selo
233–4
theatrical costumes 102, 104,
108, 123, 153, 196, 199–200,
211, 222
theatrical material requests
from Dolinka 199–200,
210–11, 223–4
ties to German consulate and
Evgeny Salomé 7, 38, 40,
43, 48–9, 58–9, 74, 77, 95–7,
100, 157–8, 163–4, 166–8,
171, 174–5, 177–9, 232,
235–6
women's prison, Leningrad 98,
101–3, 108–9
see also Derzhavin, Konstantin
'Kostia'
Anisimova, Valentina 'Valia' 8–9,
36, 62, 106, 107, 111,
113–14, 123, 135, 136,
144, 212, 239, 270, 272–3,
281–2, 285–90, 291–4,
297–8, 302
Annenkov, Yuri 89
anti-formalism campaign 30–1
Arkhangelsk region 202
Artamanov, Junior Lieutenant
G. B. 183, 229–30, 232,
235–6, 238
assassinations 47, 52, 57–8, 79,
96, 215
Aurora, cruiser 89, 90
avant-garde artists, Soviet 86–91,
160, 215
Azbukin, Vasily 266

B

Baikov, Alexander 240–3
Balabina, Feya 40, 278, 308

balanda 115, 122, 186
ballet in imperial St. Petersburg
18–20
balletomans 18
Barbusse, Henri 161
Bartered Bride, The (B. Smetana)
210
Baumbach, Lieutenant-
Commander Norbert von
56, 58
Bayadère, La (M. Petipa) 18, 23
Bekefi, Alfred 22
Belarus 336
Beliakov, Alexander 281
Berggolts, Olga 66, 247
Beria, Lavrenty 230–1, 240–3
Betrothal at a Monastery
(S. Prokofiev) 327
Bialiatski, Ales 336
Billboard charts, US 320
Blok, Alexander 116
Blok, Lyubov 116
Bolsheviks/Bolshevism 16–17, 24,
30, 36, 39, 46, 85–9, 120,
126, 162–3, 192, 218
Bolshoi Ballet, Moscow 326,
328
Bolshoi Dom 4–5
Bolshoi Theatre, Moscow 30, 73,
171, 194, 209, 211, 214,
215, 252
Boris Godunov (A. Pushkin) 208
Borkhman, Irina 219
Bright Stream, The
(D. Shostakovich) 30
Brodersen, Yuri 23
Buber-Neumann, Margarete 141,
205
Bubnov, Andrei 169
Bukharin, Mikhail 52
Bukhstein, Veniamin 164

C

camouflage production, Leningrad
265
Carmen (G. Bizet) 227
cattle wagons 117–19
Cavalry Halt, The 24
cellmate solidarity 67–70
Central Club, Dolinka 195–6,
197–200, 204, 207–8, 211,
215–17, 219, 222–3
Centre for Civil Liberties 336
Chabukiani, Vakhtang 37, 40, 153,
174, 244, 299–300
character dance 21–4, 26–9, 32,
159, 162–3, 238, 250–2, 331
Cheka 9, 121
Cherkassov, Alexander 335
Chizhevsky, Alexander 201
Choreographic Institute,
Petrograd 15–17, 18,
18–20, 233–4
Chudakova, Marietta 80
Churbai-Nurinskoe District,
Karlag 207
Cinderella (S. Prokofiev) 327
Circus Princess, The (E. Kálmán)
325
civil war, Russian 17, 38, 86–7,
235
coal resources 129
Colas Breugnon (D. Kabalevsky)
210
cold conditions 19, 135, 150, 288,
289
collection cells, prison 115
collectivisation 49, 51, 127, 130
communism 27, 30, 35, 41, 191
see also Bolsheviks/Bolshevism;
Great Terror; labour camps;
NKVD; Red Army; Stalin,
Joseph

confrontation interrogations
75–80
Coppélia (A. Saint-Léon) 23
Council for Evacuation 267–8,
274
Countess Maritza (E. Kálmán)
225
cultural activities in prison 70
cultural-educational departments
(KVChs), labour camp
193–5, 211
Curious Incident, The (C. Goldoni)
211, 224

D

Davies, Joseph 52–3
de-kulakisation 127, 130
Decembrists 69
defence industry, Ural military
274–5
dekady festivals 252–3
denunciations xiii–xvi, 6, 47, 103,
174
Der Sprung über den Schatten
(E. Krenek) 26
Derzhavin, Konstantin 'Kostia' 36,
64, 85, 86–95, 145–7, 160,
329
argues against Nina as a social
danger 176–83
evacuated from Leningrad 291
highlights Nina's artistic value
to NKVD 159, 161–3,
168–71
in Kazan 291–6, 300
Kirov's production of
Happiness/Gayané 253–4,
256, 261–2, 312–13
Kirov's 'Russian Fairy Tales'
325

letters from Nina 101–2,
    104–11, 114–15, 122, 134–7,
    140, 143–8, 150–3, 185, 190,
    195–6, 199–200, 207–14,
    220–4, 272–3, 279–80,
    282–6, 289, 296–8, 301–6
letters from Valia 293–4,
    297–8, 302
letters, parcels and telegrams
    sent to Nina 144–8, 214,
    220, 221–3, 239, 272–3,
    279–80, 282–6, 288–90,
    294–5, 299
petition to Alexander Baikov
    240–2
protests Nina's innocence
    93–5, 100, 155–83, 165–6
stays in the city, siege of
    Leningrad 270, 272–3,
    279–86, 288–90
visits Nina in prison 104–5, 111
Derzhavin, Nikolai 85, 241–2, 272
Directorate of Arts Affairs,
    Leningrad 170
Dmitriev, Vladimir 'Volodia'
    26, 28, 31, 36, 80, 87, 91,
    212–13, 214, 227, 237, 291
Dog in the Manger, The (L. de Vega)
    211, 223
Dolinka camp and settlement 130,
    148–53, 197–201, 205–6,
    215
    Central Club 195–6, 197–200,
    204, 207–8, 210–11, 215–17,
    219, 222–3
Dolukhanova, Elizaveta 36, 80–1
Don Quixote 18, 327
Dorfman, Lidya 317–18
drambalet 28
Dreiser, Theodore 161
Dubinin, Vladimir 215

Dudinskaya, Natalia 37, 40, 43,
    97–8, 166, 173–4, 277, 324
Duranty, Walter 52–3

E
Edanova, Anna 186
Efimovich, Mikhail 297
Eismont, Maria 335
Ekaterinburg 121, 274, 337
    see also Sverdlovsk
Emelian Pugachev (M. Koval) 309,
    324
Ermolaeva, Vera 215
Esmeralda 92, 146
espionage 51, 53–5
    accusations of 51–3, 72–4,
    97–8, 157, 173, 174, 229
    foreign operations 55–8
Eugene Onegin (P. Tchaikovsky) 71
evacuations programmes, Second
    World War 266–8, 270–6
executions 5–6, 51–3, 71–2, 80–3,
    98, 121, 164, 169, 170, 171,
    174, 217, 230–1, 248, 333

F
farming, collective 126–7
fascism *see* Nazi Germany
Fedorova, Nadezhda 152
Feldt, Pavel 314–15, 323–4
Finland 50, 56, 249
First World War 49
Five Year Plan (1928) 126–7
Flames of Paris, The (V. Vainonen)
    1–3, 13, 28–9, 31, 37, 91, 92,
    169, 291
folk dance 22, 24, 30, 162, 250
Frangopulo, Marietta 245–6
Frolova, Zinaida 19

G

Galebsky, Roman 79–80, 96, 232
Gamba, Natalya 327
Gantman, Saul 93, 94, 156
Gayané/Happiness
    (A. Khachaturian) 253–62,
    293, 309–16, 319–24, 326–7,
    330–2
Gensler, Irina 331
Gerbek, Robert 328
German consulate closures 56–8
German general consulate,
    Leningrad xv, 7, 38–9,
    41–2, 44, 48–9, 57, 77, 96,
    157, 163, 181, 235, 238
German High Command 54
German intelligence service 43,
    50, 52, 54–6
German Navy 56
Germany *see* Hitler, Adolf; Nazi
    Germany
Gestapo 205
Glass of Water, The (E. Scribe)
    211
Goglidze, Sergei 229–30
gold reserves 128
Goldoni, Carlo 211, 224
Gorbachev, Mikhail 332–3
Gran, Viktor 235
Great Britain 52
Great Terror xiii–xvi, 4–7, 34–5,
    50, 54–5, 65, 72, 81–3, 99,
    101, 118, 134, 161, 172,
    230–1, 248, 297, 333
Grigorovich, Yuri 278
Grinfeld, Natan 164
Grossman, Vasily 266
Gulag 125, 129, 130, 191–4, 198,
    204, 218–19, 267, 275, 333
    see also labour camps
Gypsies, The (A. Pushkin) 208

H

Halder, Franz 283
Happiness/Gayané
    (A. Khachaturian) 253–62,
    293, 309–16, 319–24, 326–7,
    330–2
Heart of the Mountain
    (V. Chabukiani) 258, 323
Hitler, Adolf 42, 46, 191, 249, 266,
    282–3, 318–19, 326
Hörmann, Arthur 200
housing shortage, Leningrad 93,
    103
hunger and rationing 19, 51, 127,
    278, 281, 283, 286–8, 290,
    293–4, 303–4

I

Imperial Army 8, 36, 38, 79, 235
industrialisation, plans for rapid
    42, 44, 51, 126–8
Institute of Literature of the
    Academy of Sciences 270,
    272, 279, 289, 295
Instructor's Courses in the
    Training in the Craft of
    Stage Productions 86–7
international workers' day 223,
    302–3, 305–6
interrogations 33–8, 40, 43, 49,
    57–8, 64–7, 71, 75–80,
    232–8
Iordan, Olga 40, 150, 264, 266, 297
Isenberg, Tatiana 39, 48
Isenberg, Vladimir 39, 48
Ivan Susanin (M. Glinka) 13, 244,
    264, 267, 276, 326
Ivanovna, Maria 85
Izraelit, Assistant Procurator 94,
    157

J

Japan 49–51, 54–6, 56, 72

K

Kalatozov, Mikhail 93
Kalinin, Mikhail 249
Kamenev, Lev 160–1
Kameneva, Olga 160–1
Karabas prison 125, 132–9
Karaganda region 129–30, 197
Kargopollag camp 202
Karlag (Karagandinsky corrective
    labour camp) 117, 129–31,
    139, 185–9, 194–5, 205–6,
    226
  cultural activities 194–202,
    206, 208, 211, 215–20,
    222–4
Karpinchuk, Anatoly 197, 200,
    206–7, 219
Kazakh Soviet Socialist Republic
    126–7, 130
Kazakhstan/Kazakhs 124, 125–30,
    135, 141, 151, 204, 226, 227,
    333–4, 336
Kerensky, Alexander 90
Khachaturian, Aram 252, 253,
    256, 257, 261, 293, 310–14,
    319–20
Khaikin, Boris 37
Kharkov Opera 211
Kirov, cruiser 56
Kirov, Sergei 47, 52, 79, 96, 196,
    215, 235
Kirov Theatre of Opera and Ballet,
    Leningrad xv–xvi, 1, 12,
    29, 31, 46, 47–9, 71, 75, 92,
    103, 137, 142–3, 155, 164–5,
    171–3, 233, 243–9, 252,
    253–62, 326–8, 332

  evacuated to Perm 270–8, 279,
    293–4, 296–324
  fire at the Molotov Opera
    321–3
  response to German invasion of
    Soviet Russia 264–7
  staff arrests 70–3
  theatre building bombed 281
  Za sovetskoe iskusstvo 165,
    245–6, 252, 253, 319
Kniper, Anna 37, 211, 224, 225
Kokhanenko, Captain 7
Kolchak, General 37, 126, 235
Kolesnikov, M. 36, 96
Kolodkin, Lieutenant Anatoly 35,
    36
komandirovka 279–80, 289
komandirovki 197
Koner, Pauline 245
Konstantinogradsky Street transit
    prison 116–17
Kontorovich, Maria 297, 300–1
Kontorovich, Mikhail 106
Koren, Sergei 'Serezha' 13, 32, 37,
    137, 152, 153, 170, 196, 214,
    233, 235–6, 244, 245, 246,
    250–1, 253, 265
Kostrovitskaya, Vera 287
Krestinsky, Nikolai 52
Kresty prison, Leningrad 98,
    115–16
Kschessinskaya, Mathilda 27
Kschessinsky, Joseph 27–8
kulaks 51, 127, 129–30
Kulle, Irina 217
Kulle, Robert 217
Kurgan transit prison 124
Kuznetsova, Galina 173, 174
KVCh (labour camp cultural-
    educational departments)
    193–5, 211

L

labour camps 5, 62, 66, 100–2,
    103, 109–10, 112–13, 205–6,
    333
  administrator-managers
    inspection 139
  communist ideology 191–3
  creation of 127–31
  criminal prisoners 122, 132,
    134, 138–9, 193, 203–4
  cultural brigades 194–207,
    210–11, 215–20, 222–4
  cultural-educational
    departments (KVCh)
    193–5, 211
  disease and ill-health 209
  food and water 119–23, 134,
    135, 139, 185–8, 203–5
  guards 132–3, 138–9, 206–7
  hygiene and sanitation 132–3,
    141, 188–9
  Karabas camp 125, 132–42
  medical examinations 139, 149
  prisoner hierarchy 203–4
  Sverdlovsk transit prison
    120–2
  theft 122, 132, 138–9
  transportation to 116–20,
    131–2
  visits from family 220–1
  weather conditions 135, 141–2,
    150–1, 204, 214–15
lagpunkty 197
Latvia 50
Laurenzia (V. Chabukiani) 244
Lavrovsky, Leonid 29, 171, 251–2,
    260–1, 299, 301, 326
Leeb, Wilhelm von 283
Lenin, Vladimir 52, 90
Leningrad Choreographic Institute
    31, 146, 329, 332

Leningrad Martyrology
    (A. Razumov) 336
Leningrad Military District 97–8,
    157
Leontiev, Leonid 246, 260
Ler, Marianna 225
Levanenok, Andrei 46–7, 75–80,
    96–8, 159, 166, 168, 173–6,
    181, 229, 232, 238
Lidval, Fyodor 49
Likhosherstova, Varvara 17
Linin, Otto 221
Little Hump-backed Horse, The 27
Litvin, Mikhail 6, 230
Liubarskaya, Alexandra 73
living space shortage, Leningrad
    93, 103
Lohengrin (R. Wagner) 264
Lopukhov, Andrei 293, 297
Lopukhov, Fedor 27, 30–1, 257,
    326
Lunacharsky, Anatoly 16

M

Magadan camps 39, 198
malaria 208, 209
Maly Theatre, Leningrad 25–6,
    30, 40, 70, 210, 248
Mankovsky, Yuri 322
Marchenko, Comrade 97
Mariinsky Theatre, St Petersburg
    18–20, 23, 24, 27–9, 31,
    196, 308
  see also Kirov Theatre of Opera
    and Ballet, Leningrad
Marr, Nikolai 86
marriages, Soviet unofficial 64
Marxism 64
Medalinskaya, Tamara 179, 248
Memorial 334–6

Mérimée, Prosper 31, 146
Meyer-Heydenhagen, Maximilian
    57
Meyerhold, Vsevolod 86–7, 91,
    160–1, 224, 248
Mikhailov, Andrei 46, 97–8, 166,
    173–4, 232, 248
Mikhailov, Mikhail 293, 297,
    326
Mikhailovsky Theatre, Leningrad
    25, 37, 328
    see also Maly Theatre, Leningrad
Miklos, Baron 15
Mikoyan, Anastas 252
Mistress of the Inn, The (C. Goldoni)
    211
Molotov see Perm
Molotov Opera 275–6, 285–6,
    321–3
Molotov–Ribbentrop
    non-aggression pact 264
Molotov, Vyacheslav 263, 270
Mordvinov, Boris 194
Morse code 69–70
Moseyev, Georgy 'Zhora' 222,
    227, 233, 237–8, 331
Mungalova, Olga 266
Mutnykh, Vladimir 171
My Crime (L. Verneuil & G. Berr)
    211

N

Nansen, Fridtjof 161
Narkompros 86, 161
Nazi Germany 46–7, 50, 74, 97,
    249, 263, 266, 269, 282–3,
    309, 318–19, 326
Nelepp, Georgy 265
New Economic Policy (NEP) 27
New York Times 52–3

Nicholas II, Tsar 27, 121
Night Before Christmas, The
    (N. Rimsky-Korsakov) 325
NKVD xiv, 4–6
    Elizaveta Dolukhanova's arrest
        80–1
    end of the Great Terror 230–1
    and Evgeny Salomé 7, 42–6
    interrogations 35, 39, 57, 66–7,
        74–80
    Kirov Theatre and Ballet
        employees 72–3, 173–4,
        179
    Kostia Derzhavin's appeals
        93–5, 155–83, 229
    Nina's arrest 7–10, 93
    Nina's sealed room 10, 103,
        107, 109
    order no. 00447 54
    review of Nina's case 229–38,
        240–2
    Special Council 96–7, 100–2,
        155–6, 158, 238, 240–3, 248
    stool pigeons 70
    see also Great Terror; labour
        camps; Salomé, Evgeny;
        Shpalerka prison
nomadic tribes 125–6, 130
non-aggression pact, Germany and
    Russia 249, 264
Novosibirsk, German consulate 57
Nureyeva, Farida 331–2
Nureyev, Rudolf 332
Nutcracker, The (P. Tchaikovsky)
    18, 214

O

October Revolution (1917) 1–2, 8,
    32, 38, 73, 85–7, 89–90, 126
Odessa, German consulate 57

oil fields, Azerbaijan 318
Okhochinsky, Vladimir 39
Okunevskaya, Tatiana 145, 202
Oloveinikova, Ekaterina 219
Operation Barbarossa 263–4, 282
Operation Case Blue 318–19
Oppengeim, Tatiana 70
Osipovna, Evdokia 17
Ovanesian, Gevork 252–4

P

Palagina, Nina 307–8
Paquita (E. Deldevez) 23
Partisan Days (V. Vainonen) 32,
    169, 172, 258
Pasternak, Boris 307
Pavlova, Anna 19
Pazovsky, Ari 274, 301
People's Comedy Theatre 87–8
Pereshkolnik, Nina 201
Perm 270, 272–80, 291, 296, 300,
    311
Perm Ballet 322
Petipa, Marius 18, 22, 24
Philharmonic, Leningrad 26, 49,
    92, 235, 326
Piotrovsky, Adrian 29, 30, 171
Pique Dame (P. Tchaikovsky)
    200
Poland 49–51, 55, 56, 57, 249
polar expedition, Soviet 190–1
Politburo 5, 51, 127–8, 230
Popov, Gavriil 280
Popov-Raisky, Viktorin 70
Potemkin, Vladimir 57–8
Pozern, Boris 94, 156–7
Pravda 30–1, 53
Preobrazhenskaya, Olga 17
Profitable Position, A (A. Ostrovsky)
    216

propaganda xiii, 29, 30, 51, 53,
    127, 193, 196, 247, 268
Provisional Government 90
Puppet Theatre, Leningrad 81
Pushkin, Alexander 170, 200, 208
Pushkin Theatre, Moscow 37,
    73, 92
Pushkiniana 170
Putin, Vladimir 334
Pyatakov, Georgy 51

Q

quarantine zone, Karabas prison
    132–7

R

Radek, Karl 51
Radin, Evgeny 257–9, 298, 301,
    316–17, 319, 321–2
Radlov, Sergei 28–9, 37, 87–8, 92
Rafail, Mikhail 160
Raguzin, Evgeny 47
Raikh, Zinaida 248
railways, Siberian 55–6
Raisky, Viktorin 70
Rakovsky, Christian 52
Rashchevskaia, N. 225
Ravensbrück concentration camp
    205
Raymonda (A. Glazunov) 27, 172,
    330
Razumov, Anatoly 336
Red Army 9, 17, 54, 95, 176–7,
    249, 268
    24th anniversary celebrations
    293–4, 296, 298–9
Red Guards 90
revolutionary theatre 86–91
Romanov, Grand Duke Andrei 28

Romeo and Juliet (S. Prokofiev) 29, 171

Rose-Marie (R. Friml & H. Stothart) 225

Rozovsky, Naum 95, 157

'Russian Fairy Tales' dance suite 325

Russian National Library, St Petersburg's 336

Russian Revolution 15–17

Rykov, Alexei 51

S

Salomé, Evgeny xv, 7, 38–48, 58–9, 70, 77, 78, 95–8, 100, 158, 163–4, 166–8, 171, 174–5, 177–9, 181–3, 232, 235–6, 248

Salomé, Gustav 38

Samosud, Samuil 25

Sats, Natalia 82

Schulenburg, Count 57–8

Second World War 98, 128, 249, 267–70

    see also evacuations; Hitler, Adolph; Kirov Theatre of Opera and Ballet, Leningrad; Nazi Germany; siege of Leningrad; Stalingrad, battle for

Semenova, Marina 234

serf theatres 198

Sergeyev, Konstantin 40, 277–8, 308, 324, 327, 330

Shakhty trial (1928) 27

Shalamov, Varlam 69, 146

Shapiro, Ruvim 164

Shaporin, Yuri 81

Shaporina, Lyubov 81–3, 278–80, 282, 287–8

Shavrov, Boris 315

Sheremetevskaya, Natalia 244–5

Shiryaev, Alexander 22–3

Shkodenko, Antonina 233, 236–7

Shmulevich, Comrade 96, 100, 157–8, 181–3

Shostakovich, Dmitry 30, 269–70, 307

show trials (1936–38) 51–3, 160

Shpalerka prison 5, 10–14, 33–8, 61–70, 83, 98

    cellmate solidarity 67–70

    communication with the outside 62–4

    cultural activities 70

    food 61

    heat in cells 65, 98

    hygiene 65

    money 62

    prisoners' Morse code 69

    sleep deprivation 66–9

    starosta 14, 65

    stool pigeons 70

Sidorov, Anatoly 328

siege of Leningrad 98, 269–70, 278–90, 326

Sindeyeva, Natalia 334

sleep deprivation as torture 66–9

Sleeping Beauty, The (I. Vsevolozhsky) 18

Smolny Institute for Noble Girls 17

socialist realism 28–9, 30

Sokolov, Boris 71

Sokolov, Petr 215

Solovyov, Vladimir 31, 92

Solzhenitsyn, Aleksander 43, 50, 59, 66, 68

Sommer, Rudolf 48–9, 56–8, 95, 97, 232

Song of the Cranes (L. Stepanov) 332
Sorge, Richard 263
Source, La (A. Saint-Léon) 23
Soviet and Weimar Germany relations 46–7
Soviet Information Bureau 266
Soviet Navy 56
Soviet Union, fall of the 333
Spanish dances 23, 29, 91, 195, 211, 251
  Swan Lake 13, 27, 244, 277
'Spanish Suite' 92, 251
Spartacus (A. Khachaturian) 312
Special Council, NKVD 96–7, 100–2, 155–6, 158, 238, 240–3, 248
Special Far Eastern Army 54
Spendiaryan Theatre of Opera and Ballet 253
Stalin, Joseph
  and Adolph Hitler 249
  appreciation of ballet 1
  assassination of Sergei Kirov 47
  collective farming 126–7
  as Commissar of Nationalities 32
  German invasion of Soviet Union 263, 264
  obsession with spies 55
  plans for rapid industrialisation 44, 126–8
  supporting results of the Great Terror 231
Stalingrad, battle for 318–19
Stalin, Joseph
  see also Great Terror
Stanislavsky, Konstantin 2
starosta 14, 65
steppe landscape 215

Sterligov, Vladimir 215–16
Stolypin, Pyotr 117
Stolypin wagons 117–19
stool pigeons 70
storming of the Winter Palace (1917) 89
Strub, Lotte 189
submarine fleet, Soviet 56
Summer Garden, Leningrad 26
Supreme Court 334
Supreme Soviet 240–1
Sverdlovsk 120–2, 122, 124, 274, 325
Sverdlovsk Opera 325
Sverdlovsk Theatre of Musical Comedy 325
Sverdlovsk transit prison 120–2
Swan Lake (P. Tchaikovsky) 13, 18, 27, 209, 244, 264, 267, 276–7
Symphony No. 7 (D. Shostakovich) 269–70

T
Taglioni, Marie 18
Talisman (M. Petipa) 23
Taras Bulba (V. Solovyov-Sedoi) 252, 257–8
Tchaikovsky, Peter 200, 227
technical barracks, Dolinka camp 205, 208
Ter-Asaturova, Elena 209, 225
Theatre School *see* Choreographic Institute, Petrograd
theatre staff disappearances, Kirov 71–4, 172–4, 179
  see also Anisimova, Nina; Levanenok, Andrei
theatrical productions, Gulag 194–7

Time magazine 269
Timofeeva, Kisa 326
Torgsin stores 44
torture 35, 39, 66–9, 80
troikas 34–5, 94, 101
Trotsky, Leon 51, 54, 128, 160
Trotskyite-rightist bloc 52
Tsilshtein, Emmanuil 170
Tukhachevsky, Marshal 54
Turkestan 126
TV Rain (Dozhd) 334

U
Ukraine 334, 335, 336
Ulanova, Galina 37, 40, 43, 265, 302, 305
Ustinova, Sharifa 213, 217

V
Vaganova Academy of Russian Ballet 16
Vaganova, Agrippina 21–2, 29, 47, 116, 172–3, 246, 305
Vainonen, Vasily 26, 28, 31–2, 37, 142, 172, 214, 258
valenki 151, 205, 212
Vecheslova, Tatiana 37, 40, 43, 233–5, 244, 246, 262, 275–6, 278, 305–6, 311–12, 324
Verbo, Alla 200, 201
Verses about a Beautiful Lady (A. Blok) 116
Vitels, Lev 71
Vladivostok, German consulate 57
von Herwarth, Hans 41–2, 44
Vorkuta camp 194
Voroshilov, Kliment 50

Vozvrashchennye imena ('Returned Names' centre) 98, 336
Vyshinsky, Andrei 51, 94

W
Walther, Karl 48–9, 58, 95, 181, 232
war tribunal, Leningrad Military District 97–8
White Russian forces 17, 88, 126, 176, 235
Winter Palace, Leningrad October Revolution re-enactment 88–90
Winter War (1939) 249
women's prison, Leningrad 99–102, 108–9

Y
Yagoda, Genrikh 52, 231
Yakobson, Leonid 312
Yaroslavsky, Yemelyan 324
Yeltsin, Boris 334
Yermak, icebreaker 191
Yezhov, Nikolai 6, 50, 230–1
Yuryev, Yuri 224
Yusupova, Countess Zinaida 233

Z
Za sovetskoe iskusstvo 165, 245–6, 252, 253, 319
Zabolotsky, Nikolai 68
Zakovsky, Leonid 5, 94, 156–7
Zhdanov, Andrei 57–8, 72
Zhzhenov, Georgy 115–16
Zinoviev, Grigory 88
Zubkovsky, Nikolai 266, 324

ABOUT THE AUTHOR

Christina Ezrahi is an award-winning historian of Soviet cultural politics and Russian ballet. She has studied at University College London, Princeton and Oxford, and worked for the United Nations in Moscow. Her first book, *Swans of the Kremlin: Ballet and Power in Soviet Russia*, was awarded the 2017 prize for Best Dance Book published in France. Christina appears in the media as an expert on the relationship between Russian politics and ballet and has recently acted as historical advisor to Ralph Fiennes on a film about Rudolf Nureyev. Born in Munich, Christina lives in Berlin, and is a fellow of the Royal Historical Society. She is also a trained classical dancer.